WHEN WE WERE THEM

Reclaiming the African American Connection to Biblical Israel

ANTONIO M. PALMER

WHEN WE WERE THEM
Reclaiming African American Connection with the Biblical Israel

Published by
Kingdom Publishing, LLC
1350 Blair Drive, Odenton, MD 21113, USA

Printed in the United States of America (USA)

ISBN: 978-1-967006-05-2 Paperback
ISBN: 978-1-967006-07-6 Hardback

TABLE OF CONTENTS

APPENDICES

Statement of Faith and Disclaimer

I, the author, profess faith in YHWH, the God of Abraham, Isaac, and Jacob as revealed in the Hebrew Bible. I affirm that God manifested Himself in Yeshua the Messiah, "reconciling the world unto Himself" (2 Corinthians 5:19), and that "in the Messiah dwelt the fullness of the Godhead bodily" (Colossians 2:9). I believe Yeshua is God's only begotten son, born of the virgin Mary, conceived by the Holy Ghost, was crucified, buried, and rose from the dead after three full days and nights as documented in Scripture.

TERMINOLOGY NOTE

While acknowledging various pronunciations of the divine name YHWH (including Yahawah, Yahuah, Yehowah), I primarily use "Yahweh" throughout this work for consistency and reader familiarity. Similarly, I may alternate between "Yeshua" and "Jesus" when referring to the Messiah, recognizing both as valid designations of the same historical and spiritual figure.

SCHOLARLY POSITION

This work represents independent scholarship and historical research. While I respect and acknowledge the diverse perspectives within communities teaching about Hebrew heritage among African Americans, I maintain no formal affiliation with any Black Hebrew Israelite organization or camp. My research stands on its own merits rather than representing any particular denominational position.

PURPOSE STATEMENT

This book is presented as a historical investigation, not as religious proselytization. Its primary objective is to examine and document the historical connections between African Americans and biblical Israel through scholarly analysis of available evidence. Readers are encouraged to evaluate the presented research according to their own scholarly and spiritual discernment.

"The river of history runs deeper than the eye can see. For African Americans, the currents that connect our present to ancient Israel are not merely academic curiosities, but living waters of identity, spiritual inheritance, and prophetic purpose."

Vincent L. Wimbush, *African Americans and the Bible: Sacred Texts and Social Structures* (New York: Continuum International Publishing Group, 2000), 45.

INTRODUCTION

"Until the Lion tells the story, the hunter will always be the hero."[1]

THE FORGOTTEN KINGDOM

Perhaps the most extraordinary continent on the face of the earth is Africa, where human life originated, a rich and glorious land. To this day, nations scramble to have a footing in Africa and leverage its abundant resources. One million carats of diamonds are recovered annually between Angola, Botswana, the Democratic Republic of the Congo, Namibia, and the Republic of South Africa. In 2021, the North African country of Algeria had the largest gold holding, with over 174 metric tons, followed by South Africa, which had 125 metric tons of gold. Other precious African metals and gemstones are tanzanite, opal, rubies, emeralds, topaz, sapphire, and dozens more.

Africa's majestic animal kingdom tells a story of unparalleled natural splendor. In its natural safaris, you can hear Africa's excellent wildlife symphony as the king of the jungle roars in harmony with the trumpeting sound of elephants coupled with the percussing gallop of gazelles gracefully gliding across the dusty wilderness. Giraffes walk dignified in sunsets, while Cheetahs, leopards, Zebras, Rhinos, Hippos, and wildebeests add to the august aesthetics of the Serengeti of Tanzania.

Yet the animal kingdom must bow in reverence to the kingdoms of Africa built by human hands. Kingdoms of this world pale in comparison to the tremendous dynastic kingdoms birthed on African soil. Other world rulers studied, emulated, and copied the architecture

---

1 African proverb, widely attributed to various African cultures but specific origin uncertain.

of Nubia and Egypt's strongholds, palaces, and pyramids. Monarchs and hierarchies drooled over the massive libraries of Timbuktu.

Throughout the years, Africa had the most prominent kings and queens. From Ramesses II (the Great) and Amenhotep III (the Magnificent) of Egypt, to Menelik II, Tirhakah and Haile Selassie of Ethiopia, to the Kandake (Candace) who ruled both Egypt and Ethiopia, Makeda the Queen of Sheba, and Queen Nandi of the Zulu nation.

Modern history books failed to proclaim the splendor and wealth amassed by the great king of Mali, Mansa Musa. He had so much wealth that historians described him as the wealthiest man in history. On his famous 4,000-mile pilgrimage to Mecca, he was accompanied by thousands of richly dressed servants and supporters. In Cairo, Egypt, the Emperor gave out so much gold that he generated a brief decline in its value.

I honor all the great kings and queens of Africa, that land widely referred to in ancient times as Alkebulan, the mother of mankind or the garden of Eden, or in the Bible as the land of Ham. But this book narrates another dark-skinned ethnic group that lost its once vibrant, glorious kingdom and eventually became buried in the graveyard of false narratives. This thriving kingdom hailing from the African tectonic plate was so glorious that it left the queen of the South breathless. It was from this kingdom that men witnessed patterns and prototypes of the splendor of heaven.

THE BURIED TRUTH

In this book, we shall exhume this kingdom's buried history—the history of an ethnic group that was scattered from its original residence as far east as Papa New Guinea and as far west as the Americas.

Many of their migrations were forced. They had to endure the degradation of pogroms and massacres when they settled among people who eventually became infuriated by their presence. They faced inquisitions when Iberian monarchs opposed their belief system, killing many while shipping others off to the West African coastlands of Guinea and São Tomé Island. Some dispersed used trade routes and settled in West African hinterlands, which European cartographers labeled

"Negroland." This ethnic group was among those taken in the diaspora to the New World.

Their history was quieted by the narrative created by their conquerors and subdued by colonials who soon evangelized them with their twisted Constantinian gospel, that same gospel that kept them oppressed for hundreds of years.

This book is to remind our people who were labeled African American, Afro-American, Negro, Black, and Colored that we have a rich history that was borrowed, buried and butchered. The above labels are not names of ethnic groups but merely a tactical way of grouping every descendant of enslaved people into one category, ensuring that they never be simply called an American. Before these labels were placed upon us, what ethnic group did our ancestors belong to? Who were we before the Transatlantic Slave Trade?

IDENTITY IS KEY

Identity is so important. It provides a sense of individuality and uniqueness, contributing to one's self-esteem and self-worth. It also allows individuals to be recognized and differentiated from others and can play a role in personal and societal relationships and interactions. Additionally, identity can be tied to cultural and social groups, providing a sense of belonging and connection to others with similar experiences, values, and beliefs.

Our conquerors knew that taking away the names and identities of a people group would successfully allow them to be controlled. Therefore, we were stripped of everything that would give us an inclination of who we really are – our names, our languages, our God, our land, and a disconnection from our ancestors. Our distinct identity, which made us unique and different, suffered a significant blow that knocked us down for the count and unconscious from the vibrant yesteryears we once championed.

> *"A people without the knowledge of their past history, origin and culture is like a tree without roots."*[2]

---

2 Marcus Garvey, *Philosophy and Opinions of Marcus Garvey*, ed. Amy Jacques-Garvey (New York: Atheneum, 1992), 5.

Identity is powerful. We are often told about our Hamitic ancestry, and often from a derogatory perspective. Whenever people refer to Ham, the son of Noah, who saw his father's nakedness, they refer to him as the one who was cursed. They say that his descendants were cursed alongside him. This is far from the truth, and I will prove it in this book.

Little is known or shared about our S[h]emitic bloodline. This book will capture our S[h]emitic ancestry and deal with the misnomer of the curse of Ham. Like Yeshua and the Hebrews, African Americans have a mixed bloodline, primarily from Shem and Ham. However, the origin of their bloodline is S[h]emitic. I will prove that S[h]emitic people would be classified as Black in today's societal construct. This will also challenge current identities about us and other ethnicities.

TELLING THE TRUTH ABOUT US

As South African singer Miriam Makeba, affectionately known as Mama Africa, once said:

> *"The conqueror writes history, they came, they conquered, and they write. You don't expect the people who came to invade us, to tell the truth about us."*[3]

The truth about us is our quest. Much of today's history was written with a twisted narrative from our conquerors. These conquerors are whom the Bible calls Gentiles. They have ruled the world for more than two millennials. Their domination dates back to the Greek and Roman empires and the European nations that subdued the African and American continents.

The Gentiles pillaged, conquered, colonized, oppressed, and then wrote most of history as we know it today to fit their narrative. A prime example is how archeologists, through technology, try to reimage the Egyptian Sphynx's face by narrowing its nose and lips. Michelangelo and other European artists' paintings of Bible characters such as Jesus, Mary, the apostles, and the patriarchs to look European are more proof of history being obscured by the conqueror.

3 Miriam Makeba, interview by Banning Eyre, Afropop Worldwide, National Public Radio, October 2006.

I believe that no matter how deep truth is buried, the conqueror cannot wipe it totally out. Truth leaves traces of its existence for the diligent researcher to find when it's hidden. Thus, I put on my imaginary cargo pants and safari hat to dig deep into yesterday's jungle, hoping to recapture the truth about us.

When We Were Them is a book challenging the present conqueror's narrative about us. Would you believe me if I told you that those who performed miracles, slew giants, healed diseases, and walked on water were blood relatives of many African Americans? Would you be convinced that some of the greatest civilizations and kingdoms were built by people who look like you? Do you agree that there is something distinctively unique about Black America? This book is my opportunity to prove our great heritage and the linkage between African Americans and ancient Israel—God's chosen people.

The world is under the notion that this unique people group no longer exists, the tribes of Israel are lost, the Christian church replaced Israel, or that those who now occupy Palestine are the people that Yah chose. We will benchmark the Romans 11 prophecy that foretells Israel's negligence, Gentile rule, and Israel's salvation. This book is based on Yah's end-time intention to save His "natural branches," i.e., bloodline Israel.

We will use a different canvas, and a new painting will unfold with every brush stroke. This time, it is not the conqueror or the colonizer painting the picture. It is not the hunter but the lion telling the story.

"Historical truth isn't determined by who has the most powerful voice, but by what evidence actually remains when honestly examined."

Section 1

GOD'S CHOSEN PEOPLE

The Hebrew Bible's concept of chosen-ness never implies racial superiority, but rather describes a particular historical relationship established through covenant, marked by ethical responsibility and anchored in the narrative of redemption from Egypt."

Levenson, Jon D. *The Death and Resurrection of the Beloved Son: The Transformation of Child Sacrifice in Judaism and Christianity.* New Haven: Yale University Press, 1993.

Chapter 1

God's Chosen People

"For you are a holy people to the Lord your God; the Lord your God has chosen you to be a people for His own possession out of all the peoples who are on the face of the earth."[1]

THE DIVINE SELECTION

What I'm about to share with you are hidden jewels extracted from one of the world's most treasured resources—the Holy Bible. The Bible is not only a spiritual text but a repository of historical narratives spanning millennia. It contains the most detailed and valid historical account of a particular ethnic group, their relationship with their God, YHWH or Yahweh, and their interactions with other nations and peoples. Although this book's purpose is not necessarily religious, I cannot escape discussing the Elohim (God) of the Bible, for the people I'm discussing are known as "God's chosen people," and I posit that we, African Americans, were them.

The most extraordinary honor on Earth is to be considered God's chosen people. The book of Genesis, authored by the prophet Moses, details how a nation became handpicked by God to be His select ethnic group. Moses narrates the creation story, the formation of mankind, humanity's God-prepared dwelling (Eden), and tragically, humanity's disobedience to God resulting in the Fall.

After Adam and Eve's fall in the Garden of Eden, human pride and depravity increased on Earth over centuries. Humanity lived contrary to and independent from the will and pleasure of Yahweh. Wickedness

---

1 Deuteronomy 7:6 and 14:2 (New American Standard Bible).

and corruption grew so pervasive that it broke Yahweh's heart to the point where He regretted creating the human race. As Genesis 6:5-6 states, "The Lord saw how great the wickedness of the human race had become on the earth, and that every inclination of the thoughts of the human heart was only evil all the time. The Lord regretted that he had made human beings on the earth, and his heart was deeply troubled."[2] Yahweh used a great deluge to cleanse the earth of wickedness and begin anew with Noah and his family.

THE LINEAGE OF SELECTION

After the flood, Noah and his sons—Ham, Shem, and Japheth—repopulated the earth. Chapter 10 of Genesis, often called the Table of Nations, details each son's family tree.[3] However, in Genesis 11, following the incident at Babel where God confused humanity's language and caused them to disperse and settle in different regions, the author provides more detailed information specifically about Shem's posterity. This focus is crucial because it reveals God's process of selecting a people on earth to represent Him.

Moses traces the genealogy from Shem to Arphaxad (born two years after the flood), extending to Terah and his sons Abram (later renamed Abraham by God), Nahor, and Haran. Terah takes Abram, Sarai, and his grandson Lot toward Canaan but settles in Haran, where he dies. Abram remains in Haran with his barren wife and a nephew who has lost both father and grandfather.

According to Joshua 24:2, "Joshua said to all the people, 'This is what the Lord, the God of Israel, says: Long ago your ancestors, including Terah the father of Abraham and Nahor, lived beyond the Euphrates River and worshiped other gods.'"[4] This passage reveals that Abram—who later became known as the father of faith—was initially an idol worshiper. His wife, Sarai, now in her mid-60s (with Abram in his mid-

---

2 Genesis 6:5-6 (New International Version).

3 Walter Brueggemann, *Genesis: Interpretation: A Bible Commentary for Teaching and Preaching* (Louisville: Westminster John Knox Press, 2010), 97-105.

4 Joshua 24:2 (New International Version).

70s), was barren. In ancient Mesopotamia, having children, particularly sons, was paramount to carrying on family legacy and inheritance and was considered a divine blessing. Archaeological evidence from Ur, Abram's birthplace, suggests the couple likely worshiped fertility deities such as Marduk or Enki, hoping to persuade these gods to make Sarai fruitful.[5]

Despite their religious background and Sarai's barrenness, the 75-year-old Abram encounters Yahweh, the Creator of heaven and earth. Genesis 12 documents Yahweh specifically choosing this idol worshiper from the line of Shem:

> "Now the Lord said to Abram, 'Go forth from your country, and from your relatives and from your father's house, to the land which I will show you; and I will make you a great nation, and I will bless you, and make your name great; and so you shall be a blessing; and I will bless those who bless you, and the one who curses you I will curse. And in you all the families of the earth will be blessed.'"[6]

DIVINE INSTRUCTIONS

Yahweh personally selected Abram without committee or council—it was a sovereign decision. As evidenced in the scripture above, Yahweh's choice came with specific instructions. God directed Abram to:

1. Leave his country and relatives
2. Go to the land which Yahweh would show him

Had Abram failed to follow these instructions, his election might have been forfeited. Fortunately, he obeyed. Abram left his kinfolk in Haran and journeyed to the land where Yahweh guided him. Consider that Abram didn't see anyone; he merely heard a new voice, however audibly. Biblical scholar Walter Brueggemann notes that this call narrative represents "one of the most dramatic moments of discontinuity in

---

5 Leonard Woolley, *Ur of the Chaldees: A Record of Seven Years of Excavation* (London: Ernest Benn Limited, 1929), 123-135.
6 Genesis 12:1-3 (New American Standard Bible).

biblical faith."[7] The voice Abram heard was undoubtedly distinctive from any he had encountered before—the voice of a divine being.

We can reasonably assume many friends and relatives thought Abram was losing his sanity. Some likely advised him to remain in the security of his homeland. Nevertheless, he obeyed Yahweh's voice and began his journey to Canaan. Thus began his walk of faith, initiating Yahweh's plan for a chosen ethnic group.

THE CHOSEN LINEAGE

After approximately 25 years, when Abraham (formerly Abram) was about 99 years old and Sarah (formerly Sarai) was 89, God miraculously enabled Sarah's "dead womb" to conceive a child. They named this miraculous child Isaac, meaning "laughter"—an apt name considering Sarah's response to God's promise of a son in her old age. Isaac and his wife Rebekah faced a similar situation of barrenness but eventually had twins—Esau and Jacob. Jacob, whom Yahweh renamed Israel, secured both the birthright and blessing from his father Isaac.

According to scripture, Abraham had sons through two other women—his concubine Hagar (Ishmael) and his second wife Keturah (after Sarah's death). God blessed these sons with kings, princes, and material wealth. However, God did not select them to carry out His divine plan on the earth. Similarly, Esau forfeited whatever God had planned for him. Esau's disdain and neglect of divine purpose and his hereditary connection to Abraham and Isaac were so severe that God himself declared, "Jacob I loved, but Esau I hated."[8] Consider how Esau devalued his birthright, exchanging it for a mere bowl of lentil soup!

Thus, Abraham's chosen lineage continued through his son Isaac and grandson Jacob (Israel). Eventually, Israel fathered twelve sons—Reuben, Simeon, Levi, Judah, Issachar, Zebulun, Dan, Naphtali, Gad, Asher, Joseph, and Benjamin. From these sons emerged the twelve tribes of Israel, which ultimately formed the nation of Israel. This nation became

---

7 Walter Brueggemann, *Theology of the Old Testament: Testimony, Dispute, Advocacy* (Minneapolis: Fortress Press, 1997), 145.

8 Romans 9:13 (New American Standard Bible), referring to Malachi 1:2-3.

Yahweh's chosen ethnic group to bear the honor of being "God's chosen people."

WHY DID GOD CHOOSE ISRAEL?

Theologian John MacArthur suggests, "God chose him [Abraham] because He wanted to choose him. And when God spoke to him, he listened; when God promised, he trusted; when God commanded, he obeyed."[9] Simply put, only God Himself knows why He specifically chose Abraham. Perhaps in His infinite wisdom—His omniscience and foreknowledge—He knew Abraham would listen, trust, and obey Him.

While we may only speculate about God's direct selection of Abraham, we can discern His purposes through His conversations with Abraham. The Lord committed Himself to fulfill specific promises to Abraham:

1. Showing him a land (which He would give to Abraham and his descendants)
2. Making him (through his descendants) become a great nation
3. Blessing him
4. Making his name great
5. Making him into a blessing
6. Blessing those who bless him and cursing those who curse him
7. Blessing all the families of the earth through his seed

These promises required divine intervention as they exceeded human capability. Consider that Abraham and Sarah were physically incapable of having children. Essentially, everything God promised Abraham centered around him having a son. Without offspring, one cannot become a great nation. Without a nation, there is no need for a land like Canaan. And the capacity to bless all families of the earth would come through the Messiah, who would descend from Abraham's lineage.

God chose Abraham knowing it was humanly impossible for him to have a child, thus demonstrating that His election of a people was solely

---

9 John MacArthur, *The MacArthur Bible Commentary* (Nashville: Thomas Nelson, 2005), 33.

a divine act. Abraham's yielding to God allowed Him to bring forth a chosen people through a "dead womb"—literally from nothing. As Paul later observed in Romans 4:17, Abraham believed in "the God who gives life to the dead and calls into being things that were not."[10] If Yahweh could bring forth a son through the dead womb of a 90-year-old woman, could he not bring forth a son through the womb of an untouched virgin? Indeed, He specializes in the impossible!

Without God's decision to choose Abram, there would be no nation of Israel. Abram would have died childless, without legacy. The fulfillment of these promises rested solely on God's infinite wisdom and power.

GOD'S ETERNAL COVENANT

Prior to enabling Sarah to conceive, Yahweh appeared to Abraham and informed him that He would establish an everlasting covenant with him and his descendants:

> "I will establish My covenant between Me and you and your descendants after you throughout their generations for an *everlasting* covenant, to be God to you and your descendants after you."[11]

This conversation was necessary because descendants were imminent. What Yahweh promised Abraham, He intended for his descendants to understand, participate in, and enjoy. The covenant would remind them that they were the living fulfillment of God's promise to Abraham and that He would always be their God, and they would always be His people.

This eternal covenant challenges the concept of "Replacement Theology," which erroneously teaches that the Church has become the "true spiritual Israel" and somehow replaced natural Israel. Biblical scholar Michael L. Brown argues, "The New Testament does not teach that the Church replaces Israel. Rather, it teaches that the Church participates in the promises made to Israel."[12] God promised that Israel

---

10 Romans 4:17 (New International Version).

11 Genesis 17:7 (New American Standard Bible).

12 Michael L. Brown, *Our Hands Are Stained with Blood: The Tragic Story of the Church and the Jewish People* (Shippensburg, PA: Destiny Image

would always be His chosen people. Even after centuries of enslavement in Egypt, God delivered them because He "remembered His covenant with Abraham, Isaac, and Jacob."

> "And God heard their groaning, and God remembered his covenant with Abraham, with Isaac, and with Jacob."[13]

The Lord will never forget His covenant with Israel. He made an eternal commitment to which He bound Himself. Not only did He remember His covenant with Abraham and his descendants, but He reminded them that He indeed chose them for a divine purpose:

> "'Now if you obey me fully and keep my covenant, then out of all nations you will be my treasured possession. Although the whole earth is mine, you will be for me a kingdom of priests and a holy nation.' These are the words you shall speak to the Israelites."[14]

ISRAEL'S PURPOSE REVEALED

The above scripture reveals God's purpose in choosing Israel. Through their obedience to Yahweh and keeping of the covenant, they would be His treasured possession. God chose them from among all nations to become "a kingdom of priests and a holy nation."

What does it mean to be "a kingdom of priests and a holy nation"?

First, we must understand a priest's role. A priest mediates between God and humanity to facilitate reconciliation. For example, the Levites were selected from among Israel's tribes to approach God on behalf of the entire nation for atonement. They were God's representatives, acting on His behalf when confirming whether God accepted sacrifices and forgave sins. Similarly, Yahweh intended the entire nation of Israel to function as a priesthood to the rest of the world—His representatives on Earth. Their relationship with God was to be exemplary, "like a city upon a hill" illuminated for all to see. God's call to Abraham initiated a supernatural strategy to reconcile the world to Himself.

Publishers, 1992), 89.

13 Exodus 2:24 (English Standard Version).

14 Exodus 19:5-6 (New International Version).

Israel was also to be a holy nation. "Holy" means to be set apart. They were to be set apart exclusively for Yahweh's purposes. His desire was for them to be distinctively different in culture and custom. Israel's laws, religion, education, economics, and social structures were unlike any other nation. Everything they did was to bring honor and glory to Yahweh. They centered their way of living around obedience to God, typically following the Law (Torah) and the prophets.

The uniqueness of their relationship depended upon their responsibility to represent God to the entire world. God did not necessarily "favor" them for their self-importance. Although they benefited from their covenant relationship with Yahweh, they were not His only concern. He had the entire world in mind! When He stated, "Although the whole earth is mine," He implied His concern for everyone. Furthermore, when He promised Abraham, "In you, ALL THE FAMILIES OF THE EARTH shall be blessed," He demonstrated His universal purpose.

It's noteworthy that God never called Abraham, Isaac, Jacob, and their descendants His "favorite people," but rather His "chosen people." This distinction is crucial. As theologian Christopher Wright explains, "Election is not favoritism that arbitrarily benefits Israel; rather, it is a summons to universal service on behalf of all nations."[15] Israel was chosen not for privilege but for responsibility—to be the conduit through which God would reveal Himself to the world and ultimately bring forth the Messiah.

---

15 Christopher J.H. Wright, *The Mission of God: Unlocking the Bible's Grand Narrative* (Downers Grove: IVP Academic, 2006), 256.

Chapter 2

No Other Gods

"For thou shalt worship no other god: for the LORD, whose name is Jealous, is a jealous God."[1]

THE DIVINE COVENANT

The great mandate given to Israel to represent Yahweh required an intimate, personal relationship with Him. A comprehensive reading of the Old and New Testament scriptures reveals Yahweh as a passionate God who deeply loves Israel. He espoused Himself to them through a covenant that delineated agreements and expectations for both parties to uphold and honor. Biblical scholar Frank Moore Cross describes this relationship as a "kinship-bond," noting that "the covenant formula in the Bible of 'I shall be your God and you shall be my people' follows precisely the legal formula of ancient Near Eastern adoption documents."[2] Yahweh promised unwavering faithfulness and eternal commitment to Israel while desiring their exclusive devotion in return. He was adamant that they worship no other gods besides Him.

When asked which commandment was the greatest, Yeshua replied, "Thou shalt love the Lord thy God with all thy heart, and with all thy soul, and with all thy mind. This is the first and great commandment."[3] The primary cultural attribute of God's chosen people was to have wholehearted love toward Yahweh. This cultural attribute would ideally shape their entire way of life, making them distinctly different from

1 Exodus 34:14 (King James Version).

2 Frank Moore Cross, *From Epic to Canon: History and Literature in Ancient Israel* (Baltimore: Johns Hopkins University Press, 1998), 11.

3 Matthew 22:37-38 (King James Version).

surrounding nations. For Israel to function as "a kingdom of priests and a holy nation," they needed to maintain wholehearted, exclusive devotion to Yahweh.

DIVINE FAITHFULNESS

Yahweh undoubtedly upheld His part of the covenant. He demonstrated love, compassion, forgiveness, patience, and faithfulness. He protected Israel and provided abundantly for them. In one of his most renowned psalms, King David poetically describes Yahweh's care: "The Lord is my shepherd I shall not lack... my cup runs over... surely goodness and mercy shall follow me all the days of my life."[4] Later in life, this great king reflected on Yahweh's faithfulness: "I have been young, and now I am old, but I have never seen a righteous person abandoned or his descendants begging for food."[5] Yahweh took exceptional care of His chosen people, leaving them no justifiable reason not to fully commit to Him and represent Him well to the world. Through Israel's witness, surrounding nations should have recognized Yahweh as the only true and living God by observing the profound love relationship He maintained with Israel.

Evidence of Yahweh's faithfulness spans all generations. When He liberated Israel from Egyptian bondage, He did so with spectacular demonstrations of power. With Moses as their deliverer, Yahweh performed ten significant miracles. Egyptologist James K. Hoffmeier observes that "each plague was a direct challenge to specific Egyptian deities, demonstrating Yahweh's supremacy over Egypt's pantheon."[6] For example, the first plague, turning the Nile to blood, directly challenged Hapi, the Nile god and bringer of fertility, while the plague of darkness challenged Ra, the sun god. Through these demonstrations, Yahweh proved to Israel that He was supreme among all gods, eliminating any rationale for worshiping others. Furthermore, as He guided them

---

4 Psalm 23 (New American Standard Bible).

5 Psalm 37:25 (New American Standard Bible).

6 James K. Hoffmeier, *Israel in Egypt: The Evidence for the Authenticity of the Exodus Tradition* (Oxford: Oxford University Press, 1997), 146.

through the perilous wilderness, He performed additional miracles, consistently protecting and providing for them.

ISRAEL BECOMES A NATION

Israel entered Egypt with merely seventy people but emerged as a nation of approximately two million.[7] God thus fulfilled His promise to Abraham of making him into a great nation. From one miraculous seed came a nation prepared to possess the promised land and become that holy nation for the world to witness—a nation representing the eternal God, the Creator, the great I AM.

With Joshua leading, God's chosen ethnic group crossed the Jordan River. Yahweh supernaturally caused the waters to "heap up" (Joshua 3:16), creating a clear path for the Israelites, just as He had done for Moses at the Sea of Reeds (Yam Suph).[8] Archaeological evidence from Jericho suggests a catastrophic event consistent with the biblical narrative. Archaeologist Bryant G. Wood notes, "The evidence reveals that the walls of Jericho did indeed fall as described in the biblical account. What is more, they fell outward, allowing the Israelites easy access into the city."[9] News of Yahweh's mighty deeds spread throughout Canaan. Rahab, a resident of Jericho, allied herself with Hebrew spies, confessing:

> "I know that the LORD has given you the land, and that the terror of you has fallen on us, and that all the inhabitants of the land have melted away before you. For we have heard how the LORD dried up the water of the Red Sea before you when

---

7 Based on Exodus 12:37, which mentions "about six hundred thousand men on foot, besides women and children," suggesting a total population of approximately two million. See Kenneth A. Kitchen, *On the Reliability of the Old Testament* (Grand Rapids: Eerdmans, 2003), 264.

8 While traditionally translated as "Red Sea," many scholars now recognize "Yam Suph" more accurately means "Sea of Reeds." See Bernard F. Batto, "The Reed Sea: Requiescat in Pace," *Journal of Biblical Literature* 102, no. 1 (1983): 27-35.

9 Bryant G. Wood, "Did the Israelites Conquer Jericho? A New Look at the Archaeological Evidence," *Biblical Archaeology Review* 16, no. 2 (1990): 51.

> you came out of Egypt, and what you did to the two kings of the Amorites who were beyond the Jordan, to Sihon and Og, whom you utterly destroyed."[10]

By God's power, Jericho's supposedly impenetrable walls collapsed without conventional warfare. Joshua ultimately led the Israelites to conquer Canaan, and the land was distributed among the different tribes for settlement.

THE PROMISED LAND

Israel inherited a land of extraordinary abundance, rich in agriculture and livestock. Yahweh had promised that this land would "flow with milk and honey"[11]—a Semitic expression indicating exceptional fertility and prosperity. According to Ezekiel, Yahweh personally selected this territory and declared it to be "the glory of all lands."[12] Moses described it as a land that Yahweh "cares for; the eyes of the LORD your God are continually on it from the beginning to the end of the year."[13]

While Israel journeyed through the wilderness toward the Promised Land, Yahweh instructed Moses to dispatch spies to survey the land—essentially saying, "Go, see for yourselves!" After forty days of reconnaissance, the spies returned to camp, confirming, "It certainly does flow with milk and honey."[14] They brought tangible evidence of the land's bounty, including a cluster of grapes from the Eshcol Valley so enormous that it required two men to carry it.[15] Biblical archaeologist Oded Borowski notes that "the Eshcol Valley, situated in the Hebron region, remains known for its extraordinary viticulture and agricultural fertility to this day."[16]

---

10 Joshua 2:9-10 (New American Standard Bible).

11 Exodus 3:8 (New American Standard Bible).

12 Ezekiel 20:6 (New American Standard Bible).

13 Deuteronomy 11:12 (New International Version).

14 Numbers 13:27 (New International Version).

15 Numbers 13:23 describes how they "cut down a branch with a single cluster of grapes so large that it took two of them to carry it on a pole between them."

16 Oded Borowski, *Agriculture in Iron Age Israel* (Winona Lake, IN: Eisenbrauns, 2002), 102.

Deuteronomy 8:7-9 provides further detail about this abundant land:

> "For the LORD your God is bringing you into a good land—a land with brooks, streams, and deep springs gushing out into the valleys and hills; a land with wheat and barley, vines and fig trees, pomegranates, olive oil and honey; a land where bread will not be scarce and you will lack nothing; a land where the rocks are iron and you can dig copper out of the hills."[17]

The land provided:

- Brooks, streams, and springs
- Wheat and barley
- Grapevines and fig trees
- Pomegranates
- Olive oil and honey
- Iron and copper deposits

This extraordinary territory promised sustenance without scarcity and abundant resources. Historical records confirm Israel's prosperity. During King Solomon's reign, he sacrificed peace offerings of 22,000 oxen and 120,000 sheep at the temple dedication—so many animals "that they could not be counted or numbered."[18] The Jewish Talmud describes the land's fertility: "Our Sages saw goats eating from fig trees. The figs were so luscious that they were dripping with juice; the goats' udders were so full that the milk simply flowed out. These two liquids mingled into a sweet stream creating a land that was literally 'flowing with milk and honey.'"[19]

THEY PROVOKED HIM TO JEALOUSY

"They provoked him to jealousy with strange gods, with abominations provoked they him to anger."[20]

---

17 Deuteronomy 8:7-9 (New International Version).

18 1 Kings 8:63 (New American Standard Bible).

19 Babylonian Talmud, Ketubot 111b, trans. Adin Steinsaltz (Jerusalem: Koren Publishers, 2012).

20 Deuteronomy 32:16 (King James Version).

From His initial promises to Abraham through Israel's occupation of Canaan, Yahweh demonstrated unwavering faithfulness to His covenant. Israel, however, wavered in their commitment and devotion, vacillating between worshiping Yahweh and the deities of neighboring peoples. If the greatest commandment is wholehearted love for God, then the greatest violation is idolatrous worship of other gods. The book of Judges records this precise pattern of infidelity. Their recurring attraction to foreign gods provoked the jealousy of a God who had given them His deepest devotion.

Biblical theologian Moshe Weinfeld explains that "ancient Near Eastern covenants invariably included both blessings for loyalty and curses for disloyalty. Israel's covenant with Yahweh followed this pattern, with idolatry representing the supreme act of covenant violation."[21] The prophet Hosea uses marriage as a powerful metaphor for this relationship: "And the LORD said to me, 'Go again, love a woman who is loved by her husband, yet an adulteress, even as the LORD loves the sons of Israel, though they turn to other gods.'"[22] Idolatry was not merely religious unfaithfulness but a personal betrayal of Yahweh's love.

Repeated idolatry was the ultimate covenant breaker that inflamed God's jealousy. Whenever Israel strayed into serving other gods, Yahweh would plead with them to repent and return their love to Him. When Israel delayed their return, He would send warnings of impending judgments. These warnings were for Israel's benefit. When ignored, and Israel persisted in idolatry, Yahweh was compelled to execute the judgments He had pronounced. These judgments ranged from agricultural devastation to famine to foreign invasion and ultimately captivity.

THE ULTIMATE JUDGMENT

Israel's cyclical relationship with foreign gods and inability to maintain fidelity to Yahweh eventually resulted in the judgment of exile—being severed from the land they so cherished. The Lord scattered them

---

21 Moshe Weinfeld, *Deuteronomy and the Deuteronomic School* (Oxford: Clarendon Press, 1972), 116.

22 Hosea 3:1 (New American Standard Bible).

among the nations "from one end of the earth to the other."[23] Biblical scholar Daniel I. Block observes that "exile represented not only physical displacement but theological crisis—separation from the land was understood as separation from God's presence."[24]

God's chosen ethnic group experienced four major dispersions. Conventional historical accounts typically acknowledge only three: the Assyrian exile (722 BCE), the Babylonian exile (586 BCE), and the Roman dispersion following the destruction of Jerusalem in 70 CE. Most historians focus exclusively on these three diaspora events, suggesting that scattered Israel eventually reappeared in Western Europe without melanin in their skin. However, this narrative obscures a fourth dispersion—one that has been largely erased from mainstream historical accounts.

What conventional history fails to acknowledge is that a significant portion of the Hebrew population was forcibly displaced during the Inquisition period, particularly from Iberia in the late 15th century. Many of these displaced Hebrews were not "white" but rather dark-skinned peoples who were shipped to West African coastlands and eventually to the Americas.[25] Historian Tudor Parfitt notes that "genetic evidence increasingly supports connections between certain African populations and ancient Hebrew peoples, challenging traditional European-centric narratives of Jewish diaspora."[26]

The following chapters will reveal a substantially different history than what our conquerors have presented. I will demonstrate how history was rewritten to accommodate those who conquered and colonized the world. Historian Eric Williams observes that "much of what we consider 'objective history' regarding African peoples and their connections

---

23 Deuteronomy 28:64 (New American Standard Bible). See also Leviticus 26:33, Deuteronomy 4:27, 1 Kings 14:15, Nehemiah 1:8, Psalm 106:27, Jeremiah 9:16, Ezekiel 12:15; 20:23, 22:15.

24 Daniel I. Block, *The Gods of the Nations: Studies in Ancient Near Eastern National Theology* (Grand Rapids: Baker Academic, 2000), 123.

25 José V. Malcioln, *The African Origins of Modern Judaism: From Hebrews to Jews* (Trenton, NJ: Africa World Press, 2012), 178-189.

26 Tudor Parfitt, *Black Jews in Africa and the Americas* (Cambridge: Harvard University Press, 2013), 87.

to ancient Israel has been intentionally obscured to justify European colonization and the transatlantic slave trade."[27] So, reserve your energy; our journey for historical truth is only beginning.

27 Eric Williams, *Capitalism and Slavery* (Chapel Hill: University of North Carolina Press, 1944), 43.

Section 2

THE TIMES OF THE GENTILES

"The rise of gentile empires following the Babylonian conquest represented a fundamental shift in the Near Eastern power structure, as non-Hebrew nations achieved unprecedented dominion over the known world, fulfilling what many Hebrew prophets had foretold as both judgment and divine purpose in history."

Toynbee, Arnold J. *A Study of History.* Oxford: Oxford University Press, 1946.

Chapter 3

Biblical Prophecy of Gentile Rule

"For I would not, brethren, that ye should be ignorant of this mystery, lest ye should be wise in your own conceits; that blindness in part is happened to Israel, until the fulness of the Gentiles be come in. And so all Israel shall be saved: as it is written, There shall come out of Sion the Deliverer, and shall turn away ungodliness from Jacob: for this is my covenant unto them, when I shall take away their sins."[1]

THE PROPHECY THAT DRIVES THIS BOOK

The passage above contains a pivotal end-time prophecy that motivates the writing of this book. The Apostle Paul predicts a monumental deliverance that will occur in the end-time for bloodline Israel—that ethnic group Yahweh singled out for Himself. This end-time deliverance represents freedom from the oppression of their conquerors. Biblical scholar N.T. Wright observes that "Paul's vision in Romans 11 is not merely of individual salvation but of the restoration of an entire people to their covenant relationship with God."[2] God has a profound desire to save His people. He cannot renege on the everlasting covenant He made with Abraham. Therefore, Israel must be saved, or Yahweh would be unfaithful to His word.

Before proceeding further, you may wonder, "What does this have to do with African Americans?" If you continue reading, I promise you will discover the connection that binds this end-time prophecy to the African American experience.

1 Romans 11:25-27 (King James Version). Emphasis added.

2 N.T. Wright, *Paul and the Faithfulness of God* (Minneapolis: Fortress Press, 2013), 1156.

For Israel to be saved in the end-times, ethnic Israel must exist in the end-times. And yes, ethnic Israel exists today. Many have been taught that ethnic Israel consists of those who occupy Palestine today and call themselves Jews. However, something worth highlighting in Paul's prophecy is that the ethnic group Yahweh will "save" is an oppressed people. Salvation is never needed for those who are already free. Modern-day Jews of Ashkenazi descent are not an oppressed people group. In the end-time, according to biblical prophecy, ethnic Israel will be an oppressed people requiring deliverance from their oppressors. And who will be ruling over oppressed Israel? According to the prophecy, it will be the Gentiles.

I will explain in the next chapter who the Gentiles are. For now, allow me to highlight three significant aspects of Apostle Paul's prophecy:

1. Israel's partial blindness
2. Gentile rule and its expiration
3. Israel's salvation

Numerous erroneous interpretations of this passage exist, but let us examine the most literal and logical interpretation of this prophecy.

ISRAEL'S BLINDNESS

This prophecy emerges from the overarching theme of Paul's epistle to the Romans—God's grace as it pertains to divine election. As previously mentioned, Israel enjoyed the great privilege of being elected (chosen) by Yahweh as His earthly representative while benefiting from His providential care. Through this election, He established an eternal covenant with Abraham. Abraham and his seed (the Israelites) were required to demonstrate devoted love and obedient faith in Yahweh. Yahweh credited this kind of faith as righteousness.

Over time, Israel corrupted and devalued their relationship with Yahweh. They failed to uphold their covenant responsibilities through gross disobedience and persistent idol worship. They began to excuse their unrighteous behavior while zealously clinging to their knowledge of Yahweh. Their wickedness led them to distort truth, promote immorality, freely worship idols, and murder prophets who dared warn them of impending judgments. They were oblivious to having become as unbelieving as nations who never knew God. This is what Apostle Paul meant by Israel's blindness. Consequently, Yahweh executed His fierce judgment against rebellious Israel. They were "natural branches cut off from the Olive Tree" (Romans 11:20). They were "blinded" (Romans 11:7-8).

Biblical scholar James D.G. Dunn notes that "Paul's concept of Israel's 'blindness' or 'hardening' (porosis) does not indicate permanent rejection but a temporary condition that serves God's larger redemptive purposes."[3] This understanding is crucial to Paul's argument that God has not forsaken His people.

Twice, Israel was led captive to foreign powers—Assyria and Babylon. Remnants returned to the Promised Land after being freed from these captivities. Israel eventually became a Roman province during the period of Roman world dominance. Though they occupied their homeland, the Romans continuously oppressed them. In the Jerusalem Post, Fabio Moretti describes this oppression:

> "After spending several years campaigning against Rome's greatest and most dangerous competitor, the Parthian Empire and her proxies, General Pompey besieged Jerusalem in 63 BCE. In the coming decades, thousands were imprisoned, tortured, and crucified before Jesus was born or started preaching. More Jews died by the sword. Many thousands were sold into slavery. The fittest became gladiators and they fought in arenas throughout the empire."[4]

Israel sought a deliverer to free them from Roman oppression. According to the New Testament, Yahweh sent His only begotten son, Yeshua (Jesus), to deliver His people from both oppression and sin. However, the majority of Israel rejected this Galilean deliverer because they anticipated a political or military savior who could provide

3 James D.G. Dunn, *Romans 9-16, Word Biblical Commentary* (Dallas: Word Books, 1988), 679.

4 Fabio Moretti, "Roman Oppression of Jews in Ancient Jerusalem," *Jerusalem Post*, March 12, 2018.

immediate liberation from their oppressors rather than one who offered salvation from sin. This led to national blindness (with only remnants believing).

The prophets had warned against their rejection of the Messiah: "The stone which the builders rejected has become the chief cornerstone."[5] Yeshua also cautioned them about rejecting their deliverer.[6] The apostles echoed the prophets' sentiments while indicating that Yeshua was indeed that rejected stone.[7] Yeshua warned that their rejection would result in Jerusalem's destruction[8] and the people's dispersion.[9] Jerusalem's destruction was fulfilled around 70 CE at the hands of Roman General Vespasian and his son, Titus. Historian Josephus provides a harrowing account of Jerusalem's fall:

> "The slaughter within was even more dreadful than the spectacle from without. Men and women, old and young, insurgents and priests, those who fought and those who entreated mercy, were hewn down in indiscriminate carnage. The number of the slain exceeded that of the slayers. The legionaries had to clamber over heaps of dead to carry on the work of extermination."[10]

ISRAEL'S BLINDNESS WAS "IN PART"

Israel's blindness was partial. A remnant of Hebrews received Yeshua as their Messiah, and through them, the gospel message spread throughout the world. It became Yahweh's "love message" to humanity.[11] This glorious message proclaimed how Yahweh sent Yeshua of Nazareth into the world through the virgin birth. He came healing the sick, causing blind eyes to see, deaf ears to hear, the paralyzed to walk, and even raising the dead. Yeshua was rejected by His own people "as a sheep

---

5 Psalm 118:22 (New American Standard Bible). See also Isaiah 28:16.

6 Matthew 21:42 (New American Standard Bible).

7 See Acts 4:11, Ephesians 2:20, and 1 Peter 2:7.

8 Matthew 23:37-39; 24:1-2 (New American Standard Bible).

9 Matthew 24:16-21 (New American Standard Bible).

10 Flavius Josephus, *The Jewish War, trans. G.A. Williamson* (New York: Penguin Classics, 1981), 359.

11 John 3:16 (King James Version).

before its slaughter."[12] He was crucified on Calvary for the remission of sins. He died, was buried, and descended into the lowest parts of Hades. On the third day, He rose from the grave. Forty days after His resurrection, He ascended to heaven and sat at God's right hand, from where He will return for His believers.

A remnant of Israel received Yeshua as Messiah. Others chose the more militant social justice leader, Barabbas, whom they believed could liberate them from oppression. Israel could not perceive that they were rejecting Yahweh's only begotten son. This is why Israel's blindness was "in part." Theologian Joseph Shulam, a Messianic Jewish scholar, notes that "throughout history, there has always been a remnant of Jewish believers in Yeshua, maintaining continuity from the first century until today, albeit sometimes as a hidden or suppressed thread within wider Jewish communities."[13]

ISRAEL'S BLINDNESS BECOMES THE WORLD'S OPPORTUNITY FOR SPIRITUAL SALVATION

The Lord used Israel's blindness as an opportunity to extend beyond their borders and bring the good news of His redemption to the Gentiles. All humanity was lost because of Adam's fall, and now reconciliation was extended to Gentile nations through Paul's preaching. Apostle Paul, once a persecutor of Yeshua's followers, was knocked from his mount when encountering Yeshua on the Damascus road.[14] This encounter convinced him that Yeshua was the Messiah and resulted in his commissioning as an apostle to the Gentiles. He embarked on several missionary journeys proclaiming the gospel. Paul firmly upheld his apostolic mandate and preached salvation to the Gentiles (and Hebrews living among them). Paul states, "To the Jew first, and also to the Greek [Gentiles]."[15]

---

12 Isaiah 53:7 (New American Standard Bible).

13 Joseph Shulam, *Jewish Roots of Romans* (Jerusalem: Netivyah Bible Instruction Ministry, 2013), 354.

14 Acts 9 (New American Standard Bible).

15 Romans 1:16 (King James Version).

The Gentiles were pagan nations unfamiliar with Yahweh. Their emperors were deified; they worshiped mythological gods and placed more faith in their philosophers than divine revelation. The Greeks were so spiritually disoriented that they even worshiped Agnostos Theos ("the unknown god"). They constructed a temple dedicated to this deity in Athens. During one journey, Apostle Paul observed an altar with an inscription to this unknown god and informed them that they worshiped "ignorantly."[16] The Gentiles were unaware of the true God—Yahweh. Fortunately for them, because of Israel's blindness, the true and living God was proclaimed to them, and many believed.

Paul cautioned converted Gentiles—who were like branches grafted into the Olive Tree—against pride, warning "if God spared not the natural branches take heed lest He also spare not thee."[17] They had previously followed the same course as other heathens and pagans, influenced by the "prince of the power of the air," that spirit still working in the "children of disobedience (unbelievers)."[18] The mercy shown to the Gentiles will one day return to natural Israel because God's covenant with them is eternal. Paul declares, "As touching the election, they are beloved for the Father's sake. For the gifts [privileges] and calling [election] of God are without repentance [irrevocable]."[19] Here, "the election" refers to the natural branches—ethnic Israel, God's original chosen people—and Yahweh will not revoke His covenant with them because it is everlasting.

To summarize, Israel's partial blindness means that Hebrew remnants receive God's message of salvation through Yeshua. They received the good news through Yeshua's preaching, the apostles' teachings, and the proclamation of believers worldwide through generations. Throughout history, a remnant of Israel has been saved. This will continue until the greatest harvest of Israelites receives sight from their blindness—imposed as judgment for unbelief. Israel's blindness provided Gentile nations the opportunity to be grafted into the Olive Tree.

16 Acts 17:22-31 (King James Version).
17 Romans 11:21 (King James Version).
18 Ephesians 2:2 (King James Version).
19 Romans 11:28-29 (King James Version).

THE FULLNESS OF THE GENTILES (GENTILE RULE AND EXPIRATION)

The second key element of Paul's prophecy concerns Israel under Gentile dominion and when this rule expires. Paul indicates that Israel's blindness will end when "the fullness of the Gentiles" is complete. Biblical scholar Craig Keener explains that "the 'fullness of the Gentiles' represents both the completion of God's purposes among the nations and the end of the current age of Gentile political dominance over Israel."[20] I am convinced that removing Israel's blindness will initiate the greatest spiritual awakening the world has ever witnessed, occurring precisely when the fullness of the Gentiles expires. The expression "fullness of the Gentiles" appears somewhat mysterious. I propose three interpretations that illuminate this phrase.

First, the fullness of the Gentiles refers to Gentile nations having world rulership, which is evident today. Consider Yeshua's statement concerning the fullness of the Gentiles:

> "And they shall fall by the edge of the sword, and shall be led away captive into all nations: and Jerusalem shall be trodden down of the Gentiles, *until the times of the Gentiles be fulfilled.*"[21] The Complete Jewish Bible renders this as *"until the age of the Goyim has run its course."*[22]

Yeshua prophesies a time when Gentile rule will "run its course" or end. Jerusalem will remain under Gentile dominance until their rule expires. To this day, Jerusalem (Israel) is under Gentile influence and control.

Gentile rule has an expiration date! According to Mawuli, author of The Bible is the Black Man's History Book, "Gentile Times" is the Biblical expression describing when the Gentile nations rule supreme over the Earth. During this period, the Israelites would be in exile.[23]

---

20 Craig S. Keener, *Romans: A New Covenant Commentary* (Cambridge: Lutterworth Press, 2009), 137.

21 Luke 21:24 (King James Version).

22 Luke 21:24 (Complete Jewish Bible), trans. David H. Stern (Clarksville, MD: Jewish New Testament Publications, 1998).

23 Mawuli, *The Bible is the Black Man's History Book* (Chicago: African

Second, in Acts, at the Jerusalem Council, Paul and Barnabas reported the miracles Yahweh performed among the Gentiles and how many embraced the gospel of Yeshua. Certain Israelites discouraged many Gentile converts by attempting to impose circumcision as a requirement for belief. Circumcision became the council's focal point. We find a clue to the meaning of the "fullness of the Gentiles" in Apostle James' response: "Simeon hath declared how God at the first did visit the Gentiles, *to take out of them a people for His name.*"[24] The Lord has people He will receive from all nations for His purpose. This purpose will be fulfilled when the number of Gentile souls is reached, after which Israel's blindness will be removed—and the greatest harvest of Hebrews will seek the Lord as never before. When that number of Gentile souls is reached, it constitutes the "fullness of the Gentiles." Only Yahweh knows the exact number of souls He desires from among the Gentiles.

Lastly, the expression "fullness of the Gentiles" relates to when the iniquity of Gentile nations reaches its zenith—when their sin attains a complete level of rebellion against God. We find precedent in Genesis 15:16, which speaks of the appointed time for Israelites returning from bondage, prophesying their return would occur when "the iniquity of the Amorites" reached its "fullness."[25] Similarly, the Gentiles will reach a fullness of iniquity. Theologian Walter Brueggemann observes that "the biblical pattern consistently shows divine patience with sin until it reaches a 'fullness' that inevitably triggers judgment."[26] I believe the Gentiles' iniquity primarily involves their severe mistreatment of bloodline Israelites scattered among them.

Combining these interpretations, the "fullness of the Gentiles" means that while Yahweh calls non-Israelite souls from among the nations, the growing iniquity will reach its peak, precipitating the most extraordinary deliverance of oppressed Israelites worldwide.

American Images, 2018), 143.

24 Acts 15:14 (King James Version). Emphasis added.

25 Genesis 15:16 (New American Standard Bible).

26 Walter Brueggemann, *Theology of the Old Testament: Testimony, Dispute, Advocacy* (Minneapolis: Fortress Press, 1997), 435.

Apostle Paul, writing to the Thessalonian church, mentioned a "mystery of iniquity" at work.[27] This represents a secret (behind-the-scenes) operation of evil powers controlling human affairs to perpetrate wickedness. It will increase until its climactic fulfillment. The "rulers of the darkness of this world"[28] who control Gentile systems will reach heightened evil and severely oppress humanity, particularly ethnic Israel. Many worldwide will awaken to the evil of these deceptive systems and begin efforts to dismantle them. Simultaneously, Yahweh will remove the blindness from ethnic Israel, hidden among the nations, causing them to recognize their true identity and restore their relationship with the everlasting God. Those Gentiles grafted into the Olive Tree will finally recognize and honor true ethnic Israel, assist in their deliverance, and perhaps aid their return to the promised land.

ISRAEL SHALL BE SAVED

> "Oh that the salvation of Israel were come out of Zion! When the Lord bringeth back the captivity of His people, Jacob shall rejoice, and Israel shall be glad."[29]

The final key to Paul's end-time prophecy is Israel's salvation. The Deliverer, whom we emphatically believe to be Yeshua, shall "turn away ungodliness from Jacob (Israel)." Ethnic Israel's salvation will be twofold—spiritual salvation and deliverance from oppression. Their salvation will be divine intervention. Israel is powerless by itself, and without Yahweh's help, it cannot be saved. Whenever Israel, as a nation, repented and cried out for divine assistance, He delivered them. This end-time deliverance will be no different. Ethnic Israel is His beloved, and He awaits their cry. The problem is that they do not know their identity. They are blinded to their true nature. Their oppressors have severely distorted history to the point where they no longer recognize themselves. Meanwhile, others have usurped their identity.

The world now believes that the tribes of Israel are lost. However, substantial evidence is rapidly emerging, revealing startling information

27 2 Thessalonians 2:7 (King James Version).
28 Ephesians 6:12 (King James Version).
29 Psalm 14:7 (King James Version).

pointing to ethnic Israel's true identity. Biblical archaeologist Emanuel Tov notes that "recent archaeological, genetic, and historical discoveries are challenging long-held assumptions about the diaspora and the fate of various Israelite communities."[30] Though God's chosen people are scattered among nations, they are gradually emerging from obscurity. God is also exposing those who deceived the world into believing they are ethnic Israel. They are Gentiles masquerading as ethnic Israel, control media, government, politics, the global economy, education, and more.[31] As true Israel resurfaces, the mystery of iniquity is peaking. This necessitates divine intervention. Apostle Paul prophesies, "Israel shall be saved." Regardless of appearances, Gentile dominance and Israel's oppression have an expiration date. In the end time, Yeshua shall deliver His people from both their sins and their oppressors.

Consequently, Israelites in today's world can be confident that the age of the Gentiles will run its course; it must expire, and a new age will emerge in which the people with whom Yahweh has made an everlasting covenant will rise from the ashes of oppression and become the blessed people Yahweh designed them to be.

No matter how it looks, there is an expiration date on Gentile dominance and Israel's oppression.

---

30 Emanuel Tov, “New Perspectives on Ancient Israelite Identities,” *Journal of Biblical Studies* 45, no. 3 (2020): 217.

31 See Joseph Osei, *Hidden Israel: Finding the Original Chosen People* (Atlanta: Sankofa Press, 2019), 182-189.

Chapter 4

Gentiles Are European Nations

ORIGINS AND IDENTITY

In the end time, Gentile nations will rule. Who are the Gentiles? How did they come to power? This chapter will answer these questions by examining historical, biblical, and archaeological evidence to establish the true identity of the Gentiles.

The first mention of the word "Gentile" in the Bible appears in Genesis 10, commonly known as the "Table of Nations." This chapter delineates seventy peoples—twenty-six from Shem, thirty from Ham, and fourteen from Japheth—born after the flood waters subsided. Biblical scholar Kenneth A. Kitchen describes the Table of Nations as "a unique document in the ancient world, giving an overview of the known major peoples from the Eastern Mediterranean to the Iranian plateau."[1] This genealogy of Noah's sons and their dispersion into various lands after the Flood focuses on the major known societies of the ancient world.

THE TABLE OF NATIONS EXPLICITLY IDENTIFIES WHO THE GENTILES ARE:

"Now these are the generations of the sons of Noah, Shem, Ham, and Japheth: and unto them were sons born after the flood. The sons of Japheth; Gomer, and Magog, and Madai, and Javan, and Tubal, and Meshech, and Tiras. And the sons of Gomer; Ashkenaz, and Riphath, and Togarmah. And the sons of Javan; Elishah, and Tarshish, Kittim, and Dodanim. By these were the isles of the Gentiles divided in their lands; every one after his tongue, after their families, in their nations."[2]

---

1 Kenneth A. Kitchen, *On the Reliability of the Old Testament* (Grand Rapids: Eerdmans, 2003), 439.

2 Genesis 10:1-5 (King James Version). Emphasis added.

Here, the Bible informs us that the regions where Japheth and his descendants settled were known as the *"Isles of the Gentiles."* According to The American Tract Bible Dictionary, the "isles of the Gentiles" in Genesis 10:5 refer to "Asia Minor and the whole of Europe, peopled by the descendants of Japheth."[3] This region was north of the Mediterranean Sea and distinct from Mesopotamia (the land of Shinar), where Abraham originated (Ur of the Chaldeans). This distinction is important since modern-day Jews claim lineage to Abraham. Below, we will examine the sons of Japheth with their possible current locations:

THE SONS OF JAPHETH AND THEIR DESCENDANTS

Gomer: Josephus states, "Gomer founded those whom the Greeks now call Galatians but were then called Gomerites."[4] Gomer had three sons: Ashkenaz, Riphath, and Togarmah.

Ashkenaz: Ashkenaz (from which we derive "Ashkenazi") is believed to have settled in the area now known as Germany. According to historian Paul Kriwaczek, "The term Ashkenaz originally referred to a people living somewhere in the vicinity of Mount Ararat and Upper Mesopotamia... By the medieval period, the designation had shifted to northern Europe, particularly the Rhineland."[5]

Riphath: Flavius Josephus identifies Riphath as the ancestor of the "Riphatheans, now called Paphlagonians."[6] Paphlagonians inhabited an ancient area on the Black Sea coast of north-central Anatolia, situated between Bithynia to the west and Pontus to the east, and separated from Phrygia (later, Galatia) by a prolongation to the east of the Bithynian Olympus. Archaeologist William M. Ramsay notes that "the

---

3 *The American Tract Bible Dictionary* (New York: American Tract Society, 1859), 214.

4 Flavius Josephus, *Antiquities of the Jews,* Book I, Chapter 6, in *The Works of Josephus: Complete and Unabridged,* trans. William Whiston (Peabody, MA: Hendrickson Publishers, 1987), 35.

5 Paul Kriwaczek, *Yiddish Civilisation: The Rise and Fall of a Forgotten Nation* (New York: Alfred A. Knopf, 2005), 173.

6 Josephus, *Antiquities of the Jews,* Book I, Chapter 6.

Paphlagonians were among the most ancient inhabitants of Asia Minor, maintaining their identity through successive empires."[7]

Togarmah: Togarmah is known to have inhabited the Caucasus region, from which we derive the term "Caucasian." In America, "Caucasian" refers to white people generally, though this usage lacks historical precision. Caucasians were specifically the people who dwelt near the Caucasus mountains. The Caucasus region lies between Turkey and Russia, bordering the eastern shore of the Black Sea and the western shore of the Caspian Sea (also called the Khazar Sea). This is also the region of the Khazar Empire, where some scholars believe present-day Ashkenazi Jews originated. Arthur Koestler argues in his controversial work The Thirteenth Tribe that "the large majority of surviving Jews in the world is of Eastern European—and thus perhaps mainly of Khazar—origin."[8]

The term "Ashkenazi Jews" derives from their migration and settlement among Germans (Ashkenaz) after the Mongolian invasions led by Genghis Khan disrupted their original habitat. Even contemporary Jewish scholars acknowledge that Ashkenazi Jews did not originate in Germany or Western Europe. Their traditional histories place their origins in Israel, but mounting evidence suggests the Khazar Empire in the Caucasus region as their more immediate point of origin. As the Jewish historian Shlomo Sand writes, "The assumption that the Yiddish people came from Germany, and not from regions further east, lacks any historical basis."[9]

Do the Ashkenazi Jews look "Caucasian"? According to historical sources including the Khazar Correspondence, they are descendants of Togarmah, as noted by King Joseph of the Khazars in his letter to Hasdai ibn Shaprut around 960 CE: "You ask us also in your epistle: 'Of

---

7 William M. Ramsay, *Historical Geography of Asia Minor* (London: John Murray, 1890), 198.
8 Arthur Koestler, *The Thirteenth Tribe: The Khazar Empire and Its Heritage* (New York: Random House, 1976), 17.
9 Shlomo Sand, *The Invention of the Jewish People,* trans. Yael Lotan (London: Verso, 2009), 241.

what people, of what family, and of what tribe are you?' Know that we are descended from Japhet, through his son Togarmah."[10]

Hence, Gomer was the progenitor of the Galatians (Gauls), Germans, Celts, and Khazars.

Magog: Magog appears several times throughout the Bible. Josephus equates Magog with the Scythians.[11] The Scythians settled in areas now known as Russia, Ukraine, and Crimea. They were nomadic warriors initially occupying the landmass of Siberia, which stretched across Eurasia above China, Mongolia, and Kazakhstan. Archaeological discoveries, particularly the Pazyryk burials studied by Sergei Rudenko, confirm the Scythian presence in these regions.[12] Magog's descendants are the Russians and Ukrainians.

Madai: Biblical scholars have generally identified Madai with the Iranian Medes of later records. The Medes, considered his offspring by Josephus and subsequent writers, were also known as Madai in both Assyrian and Hebrew sources. Additionally, the Kurds maintain traditions of descent from Madai. According to the Book of Jubilees (10:50-51), "Madai had married a daughter of Shem and preferred to live among Shem's descendants rather than dwell in Japheth's allotted inheritance beyond the Black Sea, so he begged his brothers-in-law, Elam, Asshur, and Arphaxad, until he finally received from them the land that was named after him, Media."[13] Media, the land of the Medes, corresponds to modern-day northwestern Iran. Thus, Madai would be the ancestor of the modern-day Iranians. The Cyrus Cylinder, discovered in 1879, confirms the existence of the Median Empire and its eventual absorption into the Persian Empire.[14]

---

10 Norman Golb and Omeljan Pritsak, *Khazarian Hebrew Documents of the Tenth Century* (Ithaca: Cornell University Press, 1982), 106.

11 Josephus, *Antiquities of the Jews*, Book I, Chapter 6.

12 Sergei I. Rudenko, *Frozen Tombs of Siberia: The Pazyryk Burials of Iron Age Horsemen,* trans. M.W. Thompson (Berkeley: University of California Press, 1970), 112-118.

13 *The Book of Jubilees* 10:50-51, trans. R.H. Charles (London: Society for Promoting Christian Knowledge, 1917), 83.

14 Irving Finkel, ed., *The Cyrus Cylinder: The King of Persia's Proclamation from Ancient Babylon* (London: I.B. Tauris, 2013), 44-49.

Javan: Javan (or Yavan) is the Hebrew name for Greece. Under Alexander the Great, the Greeks began to rule the world after defeating the Medo-Persian Empire. Classical historian A.R. Burn notes that "the identification of Javan with the Ionians, the Greek settlers of the western coast of Asia Minor, is linguistically sound and historically justified."[15] Javan had four sons: Elishah, Tarshish, Kittim, and Dodanim.

Elishah: Scholars often identify Elishah (or Eliseus) with Cypriots, as in ancient times, Cyprus or part of it was known as Alashiya. Flavius Josephus connected the descendants of Elishah with the Aeolians, one of the ancestral branches of the Greeks.[16] Archaeological excavations at Enkomi and other sites in Cyprus have revealed evidence of settlements dating to the Late Bronze Age that correlate with the Alashiya mentioned in Egyptian and Hittite texts.[17]

Tarshish: Tarshish is perhaps the most difficult of all the sons to locate precisely. Scholars differ in identifying Tarshish. Various cities in different countries have been suggested, including Tyre on the Phoenician coast; Sardinia, a large Mediterranean island; Tarsus in Cilicia, a coastal area in south-central Turkey; Carthage in Tunisia, North Africa; and Tartessos in ancient Hispania (the Iberian Peninsula). Archaeological evidence, particularly silver artifacts found in Spain and mentioned in association with Tarshish in Ezekiel 27:12, has led scholars like Zorea to suggest that "Tartessos in southwestern Spain is the most likely candidate for biblical Tarshish."[18] We cannot determine if Tarshish and his descendants were nomadic, leaving traces of migration across these various territories throughout the Mediterranean seaboard. Nevertheless, we can conclude that Tarshish, a people of Greek ethnicity, settled somewhere off the Mediterranean Sea west of Israel.

---

15 A.R. Burn, *The Pelican History of Greece* (Harmondsworth: Penguin Books, 1966), 112.

16 Josephus, *Antiquities of the Jews,* Book I, Chapter 6.

17 Vassos Karageorghis, *Excavating at Salamis in Cyprus, 1952-1974* (Athens: A.G. Leventis Foundation, 1999), 123-125.

18 Carlos Zorea, "Tarshish: In Search of a Lost City," *Biblical Archaeology Review* 43, no. 4 (2017): 30-37.

Kittim: Kittim was a settlement in present-day Larnaca on the east coast of Cyprus. Josephus records that "Cethimus [son of Javan] possessed the island Cethima: it is now called Cyprus; and from that it is that all islands, and the greatest part of the sea-coasts, are named Cethim by the Hebrews: and one city there is in Cyprus that has been able to preserve its denomination; it has been called Citius [or Citium/ Κίτιον] by those who use the language of the Greeks, and has not, by the use of that dialect, escaped the name of Cethim."[19] Archaeological excavations at the site of ancient Kition (modern Larnaca) have confirmed a Phoenician settlement dating from the 9th century BCE, which corresponds to the biblical timeline.[20]

Dodanim: Also called Rodanim, this group is associated with the people of the island of Rhodes. They are known for creating one of the seven wonders of the ancient world: the Colossus of Rhodes. Archaeological excavations on Rhodes have revealed extensive settlement dating back to the Mycenaean period (1600-1100 BCE), confirming ancient habitation consistent with biblical chronology.[21]

Tubal: Following Josephus, many scholars have related this name to Iber – Caucasian Iberia. Concerning the ethnic affinity of Tubal's population, Josephus wrote: "Tobal gave rise to the Thobeles, who are now called Iberes"[22] – referring to Caucasian Iberia in Asia Minor, possibly modern-day Georgia. However, Jerome, Isidore of Seville, and the Welsh historian Nennius proposed another tradition that Tubal was an ancestor not only to Iberians but also to the "Italians" [i.e., Italic tribes] and "Spanish" [who were also called Iberians]. Archaeologist Philip L. Kohl notes that "the identification of Tubal with the Tibareni of classical sources and ultimately with Iberian populations is supported

---

19 Josephus, *Antiquities of the Jews*, Book I, Chapter 6.

20 Vassos Karageorghis, *Kition: Mycenaean and Phoenician Discoveries in Cyprus* (London: Thames & Hudson, 1976), 94-96.

21 Anthony M. Snodgrass, *The Dark Age of Greece: An Archaeological Survey of the Eleventh to the Eighth Centuries BC* (Edinburgh: Edinburgh University Press, 2000), 303-305.

22 Josephus, *Antiquities of the Jews*, Book I, Chapter 6.

by both linguistic and archaeological evidence."[23] Conclusively, Tubal was the progenitor of Georgians, Italians, Spaniards, and the Portuguese.

Meshech: Flavius Josephus identified Meshech and his offspring with the Cappadocian Mosocheni (Mushki, also associated with Phrygians or Bryges) and their capital, Mazaca.[24] It was a kingdom in west central Anatolia, now part of Asian Turkey, centered on the Sakarya River. Archaeological excavations at sites like Gordion and Midas City have revealed substantial Phrygian settlements dating from the 8th century BCE, confirming their historical presence in this region.[25] Thus, Meshech and his descendants settled in Anatolia (historic Armenia and Georgia, just east of Turkey).

Tiras: Many scholars trace Tiras and his offspring to the people of Thrace, i.e., the Thracians. The Amazing Bible Timeline with World History provides an interesting account of the Thracians:

"Thracians originated from an area in modern day Turkey and traveled west to the lands of Urartu and Armenia. Thracians dwelt in Thrace bordered by the Dinaric Alps in the west, the Greek plateau on the south, and the Black Sea to the east. It encompasses today's Balkan Peninsula where Romania, Moldova, Bulgaria, East Greece, and West Turkey are located.

Some Thracian nations migrated further north to the Carpathian Mountains and Dniester River, the land named Dacia by the Romans.

Thrace occupied a perfect location connecting Europe and Anatolia, particularly the Dardanelles passage north of Troy and the Bosphorus located just meters from Europe and Asia Minor. Ancient Thracian civilizations flourished near the riverbanks of the Nile, Tigris-Euphrates, Ganges, Hindus, and the Danube. The Danube was the focus of Thraco-Dacian culture.

---

23 Philip L. Kohl, *The Making of Bronze Age Eurasia* (Cambridge: Cambridge University Press, 2007), 193.

24 Josephus, *Antiquities of the Jews*, Book I, Chapter 6.

25 Oscar White Muscarella, "Phrygian Fibulae from Gordion," *Caddos* 4 (1967): 10-27.

Numerous Thracian nations were found in different places. The earliest reference to them appears when they were mentioned as northern conquerors named Tursha during the reign of King Merenptah, who ruled Egypt in the 13th century BCE. Xerxes interacted with seven Thracian tribes of his time: Paeti, Ciconians, Bostonians, Sabaeans, Dersaeans, Edonians, and Satrae. All of these nations except Satrae were conquered.

Satrae maintained their freedom and were never conquered. These fearless warriors lived amid high mountains, rich forests, and snow-covered towering trees.

Thracians were often described as red-haired and blue-eyed. They were among the most populous people on earth. Their lands were difficult to invade until the Roman conquest.

Despite their shared culture, language, and practices, before the Roman invasion, Thracians dwelt in open areas. They wore 'tunic, cloak, cap, and boots.' Their warriors carried shields, spears, and daggers. Their bodies were decorated with tattoos.

They were considered the toughest tribes in Europe—vicious and untamed warriors who lived in the remote mountains of Haimos and Rhodope. Some lived in a more refined manner, mingling peacefully with other settlers at Aegea and Marmara.

Thracians could have had the potential to battle and invade other nations if they had united under one ruler. They were trained combatants, taught only to fight and rob as they grew up. They traded even their own children as slaves or employed them as mercenaries for other nations.

Thracians comprised primitive tribes ruled by different kings who battled against each other. Their kings also performed priestly responsibilities. Their religion focused on fertility, birth, and death. They practiced euphoric rituals and human sacrifices.

Thracians were known for their musical contributions. They are thought to have invented the lyre. They were experts in playing the pan-pipe still played by Romanians today.

Modern Bulgarians claim the Thracians as ancestors. Thracian remnants, including burial tombs, have been excavated throughout

Bulgaria. Some of their rituals, such as fire dancing, are still observed in Strandja.

An excavation at Heraion-Teikhos in Turkey has also exposed an ancient Thracian temple."[26]

Archaeological evidence strongly supports the historical existence of the Thracians. Excavations at sites like Sveshtari and Kazanlak have revealed elaborate tombs and artifacts that confirm their presence in southeastern Europe during the period described in ancient texts.[27]

THE IDENTITY OF THE GENTILES

From the above listing of Japheth's sons and their descendants, as well as the biblical account, we can conclude that the Gentiles are primarily the European and Caucasian ethnic groups. It was only later that "Gentiles" came to mean "anybody who was not a Jew." Before this conceptual shift, people were identified by their specific ethnicity: an Ethiopian was an Ethiopian, an Egyptian was an Egyptian, people from Arabia were called Arabs, and so on. Only the Europeans were originally considered Gentiles. Biblical scholar James D.G. Dunn notes that "the term 'Gentiles' (Greek: ethnē) in its earliest usage designated specifically the non-Jewish peoples of the Greco-Roman world."[28] When Paul said he was commissioned to preach to the Gentiles, he did not go to African nations or Arabia. Paul went explicitly to European countries (including Asia Minor).

One reason why "Gentile" eventually came to denote anyone who was not a Jew is the variety of terms loosely translated as "Gentile(s)" in the Bible. One such term is ethnos. Ethnos had several meanings: "a multitude of people living together," "a multitude of the same nature," or simply "foreigners, especially worshipers of different and strange gods,

---

26 "The Thracians: Ancient History on the Amazing Bible Timeline," *The Amazing Bible Timeline with World History,* accessed February 15, 2025, https://amazingbibletimeline.com/blog/the-thracians.

27 Ivan Marazov, *Thracian Treasures from Bulgaria* (London: British Museum Publications, 1977), 44-52.

28 James D.G. Dunn, *The Theology of Paul the Apostle* (Grand Rapids: Eerdmans, 1998), 129.

i.e., pagans." Ethnos is also translated merely as "nations." The original meaning of Gentile was absorbed into this broader semantic field, giving rise to the concept that all non-Hebraic nations were Gentiles. However, the original Gentiles were specifically the European nations, as stated in Genesis 10:5—the "isles of the Gentiles." When speaking of ethnos, the apostle Paul was referring to those European nations among whom he proclaimed the Gospel of Yeshua (Romans 11:13).

Another word translated as "Gentile" is Héllēn. The primary meaning of Héllēn relates to ethnic Greeks. However, Héllēn acquired an expanded meaning. It came to include any nation (or person) that adopted Greek culture, customs, and language. Even Hebrews living among Gentile nations who adopted the Greek way of life were called Héllēnistai or Grecians, meaning "Greek-like." Acts 6:1 exemplifies this distinction:

> "And in those days, when the number of the disciples was multiplied, there arose a murmuring of the Grecians against the Hebrews, because their widows were neglected in the daily ministration." (KJV)

> "Now at this time while the disciples were increasing in number, a complaint arose on the part of the Hellenistic Jews against the native Hebrews, because their widows were being overlooked in the daily serving of food." (NASB)

Apostle Paul encountered numerous Hebrews living in Gentile nations who spoke the Hellenistic language and adopted their customs. The Hebrews were now scattered among the Gentiles, and over time, as they settled, many embraced Greek culture. Eventually, they began to be called Grecians, meaning "like the Greeks."

One significant reason Paul could distinguish them from the Greeks and other Gentile ethnic groups was not because they served Yahweh but simply because they looked markedly different from the actual Gentiles. These Hebrews were "like the Greeks" culturally but were not Gentiles ethnically.

Consider this: If Abraham originated from the hot climate of southern Mesopotamia, would he have had pale skin? Probably not. The Kingdom of Judah was not a Gentile nation. Evidence indicates that at least seven of the twelve tribes intermarried with people of Hamitic (African) descent. This suggests their physical features more closely resembled African characteristics than European ones. In the first century, the apostle Paul could identify them among the Gentiles primarily by their bronze-colored skin.

Historian Frank M. Snowden Jr., in his comprehensive study Blacks in Antiquity, observes that "the Ethiopians, Egyptians, and other peoples whom the Greeks and Romans characterized as 'black' or 'dark' were an integral part of the Mediterranean world, and distinctions of color, while noted, were seldom the basis of prejudice."[29] This indicates that visible physical differences, including skin color, were recognized and used to distinguish between different peoples in the ancient Mediterranean world.

So why do contemporary Jews appear like Gentiles? Why do they look so European? How does this impact African American identity? Continue reading, and you will discover answers to these questions. For now, we have established that "the times of the Gentiles" refers to the period of European dominance prophesied in Scripture.

---

29 Frank M. Snowden Jr., *Blacks in Antiquity: Ethiopians in the Greco-Roman Experience* (Cambridge, MA: Harvard University Press, 1970), 217.

"The Medes, in their rise to power, displayed a ruthless efficiency in their military campaigns. Their conquest of Assyria was not just a military victory but a demonstration of their willingness to use overwhelming force to achieve their ends."

Briant, Pierre. *From Cyrus to Alexander: A History of the Persian Empire.* Translated by Peter T. Daniels. Winona Lake, IN: Eisenbrauns, 2002.

Chapter 5

The Gentiles Rise to World Power

PRE-GENTILE WORLD POWERS

Other nations were considered world powers before Gentile nations, like Egypt, Assyria, and Babylon. The first known world ruler was a Cushite king named Nimrod. He was the grandson of Ham and the great-grandson of Noah. Biblical scholar David M. Goldenberg notes, "Ham is widely recognized as the progenitor of various African peoples in ancient Near Eastern tradition."[1] What is rarely mentioned is that Mesopotamia and Arabia were both heavily populated with Hamites, even after the dispersing of the nations. Nimrod founded major cities in Mesopotamia, starting with Babel in Shinar and reaching northward into Assyria, where he built the prominent city of Nineveh (Genesis 10:8-12).

Archaeological evidence confirms the historical validity of these early Hamitic civilizations. William F. Albright, pioneering archaeologist of the ancient Near East, observed that "archaeological excavations in Mesopotamia have revealed evidence of early dynastic rulers who may correspond to the biblical Nimrod figure, showing cultural connections between Mesopotamian and African civilizations."[2]

During Nimrod's time, all three sons of Noah and their descendants dwelt in the Mesopotamian region and were under his rule. The distinct separation of Noah's sons and their descendants occurred at the Tower of Babel incident, where Nimrod attempted to lead humanity to heaven

---

1 David M. Goldenberg, *The Curse of Ham: Race and Slavery in Early Judaism, Christianity, and Islam* (Princeton: Princeton University Press, 2003), 142.

2 William F. Albright, *From the Stone Age to Christianity: Monotheism and the Historical Process* (Baltimore: Johns Hopkins Press, 1957), 153.

in a way contrary to God's plan. After the nations were divided on the earth, different groups began to overpower others and became known as world powers. The world's first encounter with Gentile rule was during the Medo-Persian era.

THE MEDO-PERSIAN EMPIRE

Since Madai is the progenitor of the Medes, the earliest rise of European world power would be from the Medo-Persian empire. The Medes were an Indo-European people related to the Persians who entered northeastern Iran probably as early as the 17th century BCE and settled in the plateau land that came to be known as Media.

ShortHistory.org explains, "The oldest tribes of Iran are Persae (Persians) and Madai (Medes), which appeared in the IX century BCE in the Assyrian inscriptions. They inhabited the area of western and southern Iran."[3]

To the Assyrians, Madai's descendants (Madaeans) were Amada, to the Greeks they were Medai, and in Old Persian inscriptions they were called Madai. The earliest surviving secular reference to the Medes, from ca. 858-824 BCE, appears in inscriptions of the Assyrian king Shalmaneser III, who invaded the land of the Medes to plunder them of their fine horses. Greek historians Strabo and Herodotus confirm that the Medes were of Indo-European (Japhetic) origin, and linguists consider Median an Indo-European language.[4] After 631 BCE, the Medes joined with the people of *Askuza (Ashkenazim)* and those of Gomer (Cimmerians) in an attempt to throw off the Assyrian yoke.

During the reign of King Cyaxares, the Median state reached the peak of its power and territorial extent. On the ruins of the Assyrian state, Cyaxares created a powerful Median Empire, which united tribal areas of Persia, Cappadocia, and Armenia. He fought with Libya for five years but failed to conquer it. In the mid-6th century BCE, the

---

3 "Ancient Iran: The Medes and Persians," *ShortHistory.org,* accessed March 10, 2025, https://www.shorthistory.org/ancient-civilizations/ancient-iran/the-medes-and-persians/.

4 Herodotus, *The Histories,* trans. Robin Waterfield (Oxford: Oxford University Press, 1998), 1.101-106.

Median Empire ceased to exist under its last emperor, Astyages. Cyrus conquered Media and turned it into a province of the Persian Empire.

According to historian Maria Brosius, "The unification of the Medes and Persians under Cyrus II created the first true 'world empire' that incorporated diverse peoples, languages, and cultures under a single administrative system."[5]

According to Old Testament records and other historical documents, the Medo-Persian Empire rose to power after King Cyrus II invaded Babylonia around 539 BCE. During this time, the nation of Israel was in bondage in Babylon. The Medo-Persian empire ruled over Israel for more than 200 years, from the overthrow of Babylon in 539 BCE until the Medo-Persians were themselves defeated at the hands of Alexander the Great in 331 BCE.

The Cyrus Cylinder, discovered in 1879 and now housed in the British Museum, confirms the biblical account of Cyrus's conquest of Babylon and his policy of allowing conquered peoples, including the Hebrews, to return to their homelands and practice their traditional religions. This remarkable artifact provides archaeological evidence for the events described in the books of Ezra and Isaiah.[6]

THE GREEKS

According to TimeMaps, the civilization of Ancient Greece emerged into the light of world history in the 8th century BCE. Commonly, it is regarded as ending when Greece fell to the Romans in 146 BCE. However, prominent Greek (Hellenistic) kingdoms lasted longer than this. As a culture (as opposed to a political force), Greek civilization endured and continued to the end of the ancient world.[7]

---

5 Maria Brosius, *The Persians: An Introduction* (London: Routledge, 2006), 11.

6 Irving Finkel, ed., *The Cyrus Cylinder: The King of Persia's Proclamation from Ancient Babylon* (London: I.B. Tauris, 2013), 44-49.

7 "Ancient Greece: From Dark Age to the Rise of Classical Greece," *TimeMaps,* accessed March 12, 2025, https://www.timemaps.com/civilizations/ancient-greece/.

During the late Classical Greek period, the king of Macedonia—Alexander III (later known as Alexander the Great)—expanded the Greek empire from Macedonia to India. At the age of 12, Alexander was tutored by none other than the Greek philosopher Aristotle. The Greeks were strongly influenced by their philosophers. Aristotle is renowned as one of the greatest Greek philosophers of all time. In his book Stamped from the Beginning, Ibram X. Kendi provides insight into what Aristotle may have taught young Alexander:

"Aristotle, who lived from 384 to 322 BCE, concocted a climate theory to justify Greek superiority, saying that extreme hot or cold climates produced intellectually, physically, and morally inferior people who were ugly and lacked the capacity for freedom and self-government. Aristotle labeled Africans 'burnt faces'—the original meaning in Greek of 'Ethiopians'—and viewed the 'ugly' extremes of pale or dark skins as the effect of the extreme cold or hot climates. All of this was in the interest of normalizing Greek slaveholding practices and Greece's rule over the western Mediterranean. Aristotle situated the Greeks, in their supreme, intermediate climate, as the most beautifully endowed superior rulers and enslavers of the world."[8]

"Humanity is divided into two: the masters and the slaves; or, if one prefers it, the Greeks and the Barbarians, those who have the right to command; and those who are born to obey," Aristotle said. For him, the enslaved peoples were "by nature incapable of reasoning and live a life of pure sensation, like certain tribes on the borders of the civilized world, or like people who are diseased through the onset of illnesses like epilepsy or madness."[9]

By the birth of Christ or the start of the Common Era, Romans were justifying their slaveholding practices using Aristotle's climate theory, and eventually, Rome's Christianity began to contribute to these arguments.

---

8 Ibram X. Kendi, *Stamped from the Beginning: The Definitive History of Racist Ideas in America* (New York: Nation Books, 2016), 17-18.

9 Aristotle, *Politics*, trans. Ernest Barker (Oxford: Oxford University Press, 1995), 1254b16-21.

Imagine this kind of rationale psychologically impacting the developing mind of a future world ruler. According to Aristotle's philosophy on human hierarchy, God's chosen people would be characterized as people incapable of reasoning and born for enslavement. The Greeks and Romans had this same ideology toward the Hebrews, having no problem enslaving and killing even the least of them. Does this sound familiar?

At 16, Alexander was left in charge of Macedonia as his father, King Phillip II, went off to battle. His first battle was with the supposedly unconquerable army, the Sacred Band of Thebes, and he defeated them. After his father's death, Alexander assumed the throne as king of Macedonia at 20 years of age. He commenced one of the most outstanding military campaigns, eventually spreading Hellenistic influence worldwide. His most notable conquests were those of Persia and Egypt, vastly expanding the Greek empire. The great Egyptian city of Alexandria was named after Alexander the Great.

Archaeological evidence from Alexandria confirms the spread of Hellenistic culture into Egypt. Excavations have revealed Greek-style architecture, art, and inscriptions throughout the city, demonstrating the powerful cultural influence that accompanied Greek military conquest.[10]

Before they fell to the Roman Empire, the Greek empire stretched from Macedonia to Yavanarajya (modern-day Afghanistan). Greek culture influenced the entire ancient world during and after their period of world dominance. Even the Romans who conquered the Greeks adopted much of Greek culture and philosophy. We see a spinoff of Hellenistic culture and world influence in Western civilization today.

THE ROMANS

In the 8th Century BCE, the Roman empire began to take shape. Among the different clans of the Italian territory, the Latins of Latium, the Etruscans, and even some Greek colonies in the plains of Campania

---

10 Judith McKenzie, *The Architecture of Alexandria and Egypt, c. 300 B.C. to A.D. 700* (New Haven: Yale University Press, 2007), 32-45.

played an essential part in Roman empire development. Because of their interactions with those of the Mediterranean region and the Far East, the Etruscans lived in cities, unlike the Latins, who were more rural village dwellers. The Etruscans developed a sophisticated urban culture. The Latins could not help but feel the influences radiating from north and south, and slowly, they merged their farming villages into urban settlements. Many of them came under the political domination of Etruscan lords.

Archaeological evidence supports this historical narrative. Mary Beard, classical scholar and author of SPQR: A History of Ancient Rome, notes, "Excavations at early Roman sites show a gradual transition from simple hut settlements to more complex urban arrangements, with clear influences from both Etruscan and Greek architectural styles."[11]

Rome's significant rise to power began to emerge after their wars with the Carthaginian military. Carthage was the leading military power along the Mediterranean Sea. Their maritime forces were second to none. The two wars between the Romans and Carthaginians are known as the Punic Wars. They were called Punic Wars because the Romans identified the Carthaginians as Phoenicians. During the second Punic War (218-204 BCE), Rome was outwitted and bested by the world's greatest war general, Hannibal. Hannibal is well-known for his military strategy of carrying war to Italy by crossing the Alps with his North African war elephants. Hannibal occupied southern Italy for 15 years. He was eventually defeated by Scipio Africanus.

By 205 BCE, Scipio Africanus had gained control of Spain, and three years later, Hannibal was finally defeated at the battle of Zama. The Romans' victory over the Carthaginians catapulted them into becoming the ruling power of the western Mediterranean.

From Scipio to Octavian (later named Caesar Augustus), Rome spread its wings and established provinces over the conquered world. During Caesar Augustus's reign, the Roman Empire was enlarged by annexing Egypt, expanding possessions in Africa, conquering Hispania,

11 Mary Beard, *SPQR: A History of Ancient Rome* (New York: Liveright Publishing, 2015), 91.

and conducting diplomacy with the Parthian Empire. He restored the Roman senate but convinced them to make him the sole ruler.

From 30 BCE to 270 CE, different Caesars ruled the Roman empire. They helped in its world expansion campaign, starting with Augustus and followed by Tiberius, Caligula, Claudius, Nero, Vespasian, Titus, Domitian, Trajan, Septimius Severus, Caracalla, and Aurelian.

The Roman Empire's territorial rule over the known world was at its greatest extent under Trajan in 117 CE. Archaeological evidence, including boundary markers, military installations, and administrative centers, confirms the vast extent of Roman territorial control during this period.[12]

By the 5th Century CE, the Western Roman Empire was fragmented, weakened, and collapsed, but the Eastern Roman Empire (also known as the Byzantine Empire) continued with Constantinople as its capital. The Byzantine Empire was defeated by the Ottoman Empire (a Turkish empire), which captured Constantinople in 1453.

HEROD – ROME'S PUPPET KING IN JUDAH

The Bible recounts an interesting character named Herod. Herod was a son of Antipater, who had become procurator of Judaea. They were Edomites (or, as the Romans called them, *Idumaean*). Antipater became a powerful official under the later Hasmonean kings and became a client of the Roman general Pompey the Great when Pompey conquered Judah in the name of the Roman Republic. After Julius Caesar defeated Pompey, Antipater rescued him from Alexandria, and Caesar appointed him procurator of Judaea. Later, Antipater appointed two of his sons, Phasael and Herod, into positions of power. Phasael became commander of the military region of Jerusalem, while Herod was given command over the northern military region (Galilee). Antipater was detested by the non-Hellenistic Hebrews because of his pro-Roman politics. He was eventually poisoned.

12 Anthony R. Birley, *Hadrian: The Restless Emperor* (London: Routledge, 1997), 123-125.

Herod avenged his father's death and succeeded to his position. Mark Antony and Octavian gave Herod the title of king after he returned from refuge in Rome. Herod (the Great), king of the Roman vassal state of Judaea, was ruthless. In 29 BCE, Herod had his mother-in-law and his wife, Mariamne, killed. In 11 BCE, he also had his sons, Alexander and Aristobulus, killed. Then, he had another of his sons, Antipater, killed before his own death.

Archaeological excavations at Herodium, Masada, and other Herodian sites confirm the historical reality of Herod's rule and his extensive building projects. Historian Jodi Magness observes, "The archaeological remains of Herod's building projects, including the Temple Mount in Jerusalem, reflect his attempt to legitimize his rule through monumental architecture that combined Roman and Jewish elements."[13]

Herod committed perhaps his most cynical act shortly before his death. This deadly event is called "The Massacre of the Innocent." This incident is recorded in the Holy Bible (Matthew 2:1-23) and centered around Yeshua's birth. King Herod was troubled when he heard about wise men from the east coming to Jerusalem to find the child they deemed King of the *Ioudaios* (Judaeans). He gathered all the religious leaders to find out where Yeshua would be born. Next, he called for the wise men and sent them to Bethlehem, instructing them to bring Yeshua to him so he could also worship him. Yahweh warned the wise men in a dream not to return to Herod. Then, the Lord warned Joseph in a dream to take Yeshua and Mary to Egypt because Herod sought to kill him. They stayed in Egypt (Africa) until Herod's death. Herod became livid once he realized that the wise men had deceived him. He was so enraged that he ordered all the Hebrew children in Bethlehem and its vicinity who were 2 years old and younger to be killed.

This is a prime example of how Roman authorities treated Hebrews during the days of Yeshua. Hebrews were living in a relatively hostile environment because of Roman soldiers and, at the same time, burdened by the demands of religious leaders such as the Pharisees and Sadducees.

---

13 Jodi Magness, *The Archaeology of Qumran and the Dead Sea Scrolls* (Grand Rapids: Eerdmans, 2002), 45.

Their only hope was in the prophecy of the coming of a Messiah—one who could deliver them from their oppression.

This led to constant Hebrew revolts against the Roman occupation of Judaea during Yeshua's time. Revolts were not uncommon against oppressive systems. The Roman military was undoubtedly on guard against any possible uprisings that could mimic the famous Maccabean Revolt. Josephus gives us an account as to why the Maccabean revolt was initiated against the Greeks:

> "Now Antiochus was not satisfied either with his unexpected taking the city [Jerusalem], or with its pillage, or with the great slaughter he had made there; but being overcome with his violent passions, and remembering what he had suffered during the siege, he compelled the Jews [Hebrews] to dissolve the laws of their country, and to keep their infants uncircumcised, and to sacrifice swine's flesh upon the altar; against which they all opposed themselves, and the most approved among them were put to death."[14]

Typically, these Hebrew uprisings were launched against systems that countered their cultural and religious practices, especially those demanding that they submit to a god other than Yahweh. For example, a Hebrew revolutionary named Mattathias started a revolt against the Greek Seleucid Empire to resist the demand to worship the Greek gods. He murdered a Greek officer who was sent to Judah to enforce the decree to worship only the Greek gods. He also killed a Grecian (a Hebrew who adopted the Greek way of living) who tried to commence sacrificing to these Greek gods in his stead. After his death, his son, Judah Maccabee, retaliated by going from village to village and dismantling altars erected to worship these Greek gods. This revolt continued for years until Judah's brothers were able to break the Seleucid's rule. This allowed the rise of the Hasmonean dynasty, a Hebrew ruling dynasty independent of Hellenistic rule until the Roman Republic conquered

---

14 Flavius Josephus, *Antiquities of the Jews,* Book XII, Chapter 5, in *The Works of Josephus: Complete and Unabridged,* trans. William Whiston (Peabody, MA: Hendrickson Publishers, 1987), 324.

them. The Romans set the Edomite political figure, Herod the Great, as king when displacing the short-lived independent Judaean kingdom.

Archaeological evidence from the Maccabean period, including coins minted by the Hasmonean rulers and fortifications at sites like Modi'in (the hometown of the Maccabees), confirms the historical reality of this period of Hebrew independence before Roman conquest.[15]

Revolts like the Maccabean revolt against the Greeks put the Romans on high alert. Revolts of any kind caused the Roman authorities in that region to deal more harshly with the Hebrews, especially any suspected revolutionary sects. Two of the more prominent sects were the Zealots and the Sicarii. Perhaps Roman authorities had their surveillance on the Messiah (Yeshua) and his followers since it was prophesied that he would be king of the Judaeans. They speculated that this Hebrew king would also deliver his people from Roman oppression. We can now see why Pontius Pilate allowed the crowd to choose between Yeshua and Barabbas since they were both considered to be messiahs/deliverers. The Hebrews were looking for an immediate deliverer to overthrow their oppressors. So, they chose the militant activist Barabbas instead of the nonviolent spiritual revivalist. Barabbas is freed from prison while the miracle-working evangelist, Yeshua, is sentenced to death by crucifixion. The Romans mocked him, stripped him of his garments, pierced him in his side, and watched him take his last breath as he hung upon the cross on Golgotha's Hill.

EARLY HEBREW-MESSIANIC BELIEVERS WITHIN THE ROMAN EMPIRE AND BEYOND

The early church began in an upper room in Jerusalem as 120 people were filled with the Holy Spirit and began to speak in unknown languages. Devout Hebrews who lived in foreign countries were also in Jerusalem to partake of the annual feast of Pentecost. These out-of-town Hebrews heard those in the upper room speaking in their language. There were Parthians, Medes, Elamites, people from Mesopotamia,

15 Andrea M. Berlin and J. Andrew Overman, eds., *The First Jewish Revolt: Archaeology, History, and Ideology* (London: Routledge, 2002), 113-120.

Cappadocia, Pontus, Asia, Phrygia, Pamphylia, Egypt, Libya (Cyrene), Rome, Crete, and Arabia that heard the upper room gatherers speaking in these foreign languages. Many were amazed, while others thought they were drunk from too much wine. This sparked the apostle Peter to preach to these Hebrews the gospel of Yeshua—that He was Elohim manifested in an earthly body reconciling the world to Himself. Three thousand people received Peter's message and were baptized into the Hebrew-Messianic faith.

Biblical scholar Larry Hurtado notes, "The Jerusalem church represented the original nucleus of the Jesus movement, comprised primarily of Jewish believers who maintained their Jewish identity while proclaiming Jesus as Messiah."[16]

The apostles went throughout Judaea, Arabia, and Africa, preaching the good news of the resurrection of Yeshua. Acts 8:26-40 records, before Paul's conversion and missionary ministry to the Gentiles, Phillip's evangelizing of an Ethiopian (Hamitic/African) Eunuch who was Queen Candace's treasurer. This proves that the gospel of Yeshua ha Mashiach (Jesus the Messiah) spread throughout African regions outside the Roman Empire. Ethiopia was not under Gentile rule during this time. Only the northern parts of Africa, such as Egypt, Cyrene (Libya), and Mauritania, were under Gentile rule. We must also note that before the gospel of Yeshua was preached, the law of Moses and faith in Yahweh had already spread throughout the continent, mainly because of Hebrew migration centuries before the birth of the Messiah.

The Hebrew faith significantly influenced Ethiopia because of Solomon. His relationship with the Queen of Sheba (Makeda) lends credence to the Hebrew presence in Ethiopia and starts the first Hamitic-Hebrew dynasty. Historical evidence suggests that Makeda bore Solomon's son, Menelik. Menelik I was made king by his father, thus founding the royal Solomonic dynasty of Ethiopia, which ruled until the deposition of Haile Selassie I in 1974.

---

16 Larry W. Hurtado, *Lord Jesus Christ: Devotion to Jesus in Earliest Christianity* (Grand Rapids: Eerdmans, 2003), 175.

Historian Harold G. Marcus writes, "The Kebra Nagast, Ethiopia's national epic, describes the Queen of Sheba's visit to Solomon and the subsequent birth of Menelik I, establishing a historical narrative that connected Ethiopia directly to the biblical heritage of Israel."[17]

The purpose of the Ethiopian Eunuch's travel to Israel indicates Ethiopia's national belief in the God of the Hebrews, i.e., Yahweh. The eunuch traveled to pay tribute to Yahweh on behalf of Queen Candace (Kandake). The queen was a believer in Yahweh and the laws of Moses. Now, through her treasurer's encounter with Phillip and his gospel, the Ethiopian empire embraced faith in Yeshua as the unique son of Yahweh, embodied in the flesh to reconcile the world unto Himself.

Before Phillip's encounter with the Ethiopian eunuch, he preached the gospel in Samaria. He was in Samaria because the church was experiencing persecution in Jerusalem. Thus, they scattered throughout Judaea and Samaria. Saul (later named Paul) was the ringleader of the persecution. He had evangelist Stephen stoned to death for preaching the gospel of Yeshua. Saul requested letters from the high priest allowing him to arrest and bring back to Jerusalem any Hebrew in the synagogues in Damascus found proclaiming Yeshua as the Messiah. While Saul headed north to Damascus, Phillip headed south toward Gaza and encountered the Ethiopian eunuch. When Saul neared Damascus, he had a supernatural encounter that led to his conversion. There were already believers in Damascus when Saul arrived. Instead of arresting them, he was discipled by them, especially Ananias. He quickly found himself preaching in the synagogues that Yeshua was indeed the Son of God.

Saul (now Paul), after his conversion to faith in the Messiah, was commissioned to preach the gospel to the Gentiles. The gospel of Yeshua ha Mashiach—his crucifixion, burial, and resurrection—spread throughout the Roman Empire under the preaching of Apostle Paul. Paul was a Benjamite Hebrew born in Tarsus (Southeastern Turkey), which made him a Roman citizen. Paul had three missionary journeys that significantly spread the gospel of Yeshua throughout the Roman

17 Harold G. Marcus, *A History of Ethiopia* (Berkeley: University of California Press, 1994), 17.

Empire. He preached in his hometown of Tarsus, Ephesus, Galatia, Corinth, Cyprus, Iconium, Lystra, Derbe, Lycaonia, Troas, Philippi, Thessalonica, Berea, Athens, Miletus, Macedonia, Antioch and other cities within Asia Minor. It is interesting to note that Paul, although a Hebrew born in Gentile territory, was mistaken as an African from Egypt:

> "Aren't you the Egyptian who started a revolt and led four thousand terrorists out into the wilderness some time ago?" (Acts 21:38)

This misidentification suggests that Paul's physical appearance was consistent with that of an Egyptian, highlighting the visual similarities between Hebrews and North Africans during this period. Anthropologist Shomarka Keita notes, "Physical anthropological studies of ancient Egyptian and Levantine populations show significant overlap in physical characteristics, which helps explain such cases of mistaken identity in the ancient world."[18]

ROMAN EMPERORS, PAGANISM AND PERSECUTION

Paganism was deeply rooted throughout the Roman Empire. It was a primary source of persecution against the Hebrew faith and the fast-growing Hebrew-Messianic faith that converted many Gentiles. Paganism and mythology did not escape the practices of the hierarchal authorities of Rome. Many wealthy and prominent figures were deeply involved in pagan rituals. Some citizens even hailed the emperors as divine. This was in direct conflict with the Hebrew faith and followers of Yeshua.

The emperor Gaius Caligula demanded to be worshiped as a god, which alienated the Hebrews in his realm. Caligula ordered his Syrian legate to erect his statue in the temple at Jerusalem, but his death prevented this issue from coming to a crisis.[19]

---

18 Shomarka Keita, "Studies of Ancient Crania from Northern Africa," *American Journal of Physical Anthropology* 83, no. 1 (1990): 35-48.

19 Anthony A. Barrett, *Caligula: The Corruption of Power* (New Haven: Yale University Press, 1990), 188-195.

Caligula's successor, Claudius, having a hatred for foreign cults, tried to restore the ancient Roman religion—a religion of mythological gods, such as Jupiter, Mars, and the Roman twin gods of Romulus and Remas. The goddess Diana became an essential central deity figure in the Empire and united the Romans and their neighbors regarding worship. Judaism became a problem for Claudius. According to Suetonius, Claudius expelled the Jews [Hebrews] from Rome because of some riots that had taken place "at the instigation of one Chrestus (Christus)."[20]

Nero, indulging in revelries, emptied the public treasury and became a tyrannical emperor, resulting in violence and oppression. His excessive behavior became so extreme that even the Senate was terrified, not knowing if any of them would be subjected to his cruelty, especially after he had his own mother murdered. In 64 CE, a great fire broke out in Rome, destroying a large part of the city. Nero was suspected of having deliberately set it to make room for his new Golden House, a splendid 125-acre palace he had built on the Esquiline hill. However, Nero accused the Christians of having caused the disaster. Many of them were brought to trial and were tortured to death.

Historian Tacitus provides a firsthand account of Nero's persecution:

> "Nero fastened the guilt and inflicted the most exquisite tortures on a class hated for their abominations, called Christians by the populace. Christus, from whom the name had its origin, suffered the extreme penalty during the reign of Tiberius at the hands of one of our procurators, Pontius Pilatus, and a most mischievous superstition, thus checked for the moment, again broke out not only in Judæa, the first source of the evil, but even in Rome."[21]

In 69-70 CE, the Roman empire came under the rule of Titus Flavius Vespasianus (known as Vespasian). He had a successful military career, commanding the second legion in the invasion of Britain in 43 CE and conquering the southwest of England. He later rose in the senate

---

20 Suetonius, *The Twelve Caesars,* trans. Robert Graves (London: Penguin Classics, 2007), "Claudius," 25.4.

21 Tacitus, *Annals,* Book XV, Chapter 44, trans. Alfred John Church and William Jackson Brodribb (New York: Random House, 1942), 304-305.

to become consul in 51 CE and governor of Africa a decade later. He became a trusted aide of the emperor Nero and was put in charge of the suppression of the Jewish [Hebrew] Revolt (66-70 CE). After the death of Nero, the Roman senate made Vespasian emperor. He left his son Titus in charge of Hebrew revolt suppression as he traveled to Rome. Titus laid siege to Jerusalem in the spring of 70 CE with at least four legions and numerous auxiliaries.

According to the information provided independently by Josephus and Tacitus, more than 600,000 Jews [Hebrews, God's chosen ethnic group] were killed during the military occupation, about twenty-five percent of the population, and many others were taken prisoner and sold as slaves. Thus, it would seem possible that something like half the Jewish [Hebrew] population had been physically eliminated.[22] In his book, From Babylon to Timbuktu, Rudolph R. Windsor informs us that during the period from Pompey to Julius, it has been estimated that over one million Jews [Hebrews] fled into Africa, fleeing from Roman persecution and slavery.[23] The Jewish philosopher Philo, a resident of Alexandria, Egypt (about 40 BCE - 40 CE), said that one million Jews [Hebrews] resided in Libya and Egypt from the Catabathmos to the borders of Ethiopia.[24] Thus, before Jerusalem's destruction, millions of Hebrews were already living in Africa. With over a million Hebrews fleeing persecution in 70 CE, the continent of Africa became a central hub of refuge for God's chosen people.

Archaeological evidence from the Jewish [Judaean] Diaspora confirms this massive migration. Excavations at sites like Leontopolis in Egypt have revealed significant Jewish [Judaean] communities with synagogues and distinctive burial practices dating to this period.[25]

---

22 Martin Goodman, *Rome and Jerusalem: The Clash of Ancient Civilizations* (New York: Alfred A. Knopf, 2007), 387-390.
23 Rudolph R. Windsor, *From Babylon to Timbuktu: A History of the Ancient Black Races Including the Black Hebrews* (Atlanta: Windsor's Golden Series, 2003), 105.
24 Philo of Alexandria, *In Flaccum,* trans. F.H. Colson (Cambridge, MA: Harvard University Press, 1941), 43-44.
25 Joseph Mélèze Modrzejewski, *The Jews of Egypt: From Rameses II to Emperor Hadrian* (Philadelphia: Jewish Publication Society, 1995), 161-173.

In 115-117 CE, exiled Hebrews in Egypt, Cyrene, Cyprus, and Mesopotamia revolted against the Roman empire. Thousands of Hebrews were killed during these two years until the Roman military was able to suppress the rebellion. This became known as the Kitos War. Another major revolt led by Simon Bar Kochba occurred between 132-136 CE. The proximate reasons seem to be the construction of a new city, Aelia Capitolina, over the ruins of Jerusalem and the erection of a temple to Jupiter on the Temple Mount.[26] The Church Fathers and rabbinic literature emphasize the role of Rufus, governor of Judaea, in provoking the revolt.[27] Whenever ethnic Hebrews were unwilling to bow to false gods and laws that situated them against their faith, there was an eventual uprising, unfortunately, met by an overpowering destructive force.

This chapter was merely a glimpse of world history, particularly the history of the Gentiles rising to world power and how God's chosen ethnic group—the Hebrews—was affected by it. You may ask, "What does all this history have to do with the African American?" If you keep reading this book, you will find the answer and be left with a significant challenge. The plot thickens. It's heating up, so take a drink of fresh water from your canteen as we continue on this trail of hidden truth.

With over a million Hebrews fleeing persecution in 70 CE, the continent of Africa became a central hub of refuge for God's chosen people.

26 Werner Eck, "The Bar Kokhba Revolt: The Roman Point of View," *Journal of Roman Studies* 89 (1999): 76-89.

27 Peter Schäfer, *The Bar Kokhba War Reconsidered: New Perspectives on the Second Jewish Revolt Against Rome* (Tübingen: Mohr Siebeck, 2003), 22-30.

Chapter 6

A Stolen World

"The white man is very clever. He came quietly and peaceably with his religion. We were amused at his foolishness and allowed him to stay. Now he has won our brothers, and our clan can no longer act like one. He has put a knife on the things that held us together, and we have fallen apart."

Chinua Achebe
Achebe, C (1958). *Things Fall Apart.* Heinemann. p. 176.

THE CONTINUING GENTILE DOMINANCE

Gentile rule continued with the Romans. God's chosen ethnic group (the Hebrews) and their practice of faith in Yahweh never suited well within the Roman Empire. The Hebrews experienced centuries of torture. Their belief in Yahweh, juxtaposed to the way of life of most of the empire's populous who practiced paganism or gave homage to the mythological gods of Rome or cherished Greek philosophies, was either ridiculed or made illegal. Often met with cruelty, anyone found practicing or proclaiming their Hebrew faith would be persecuted.

Similarly, from its inception until the 4th Century CE, the Hebrew-Messianic faith also underwent extreme persecution and, in many cases, was disallowed. Mostly, those who believed in this new Hebrew doctrine—whether Hebrew, Grecian, or Gentile—assembled in homes to avoid Gentile cruelty. It was only until the time of the Roman emperor Constantine's assumed conversion that followers of the Way found some ease from the ongoing torture of the pagan world.

As we've traced in previous chapters, the rise of Gentile powers fundamentally altered the course of world history, particularly for God's chosen people. The Medo-Persian, Greek, and Roman empires each expanded their influence across the known world, subjugating nations and reshaping cultures in their wake. The prophet Daniel foresaw this succession of Gentile powers in his vision of four beasts, representing four kingdoms that would arise from the earth.[1] Biblical scholar John J. Collins notes that "Daniel's vision of four successive empires established a framework for understanding world history as a progression of dominant powers leading to an ultimate divine intervention."[2] This prophetic vision aligns remarkably with the historical succession from Babylonian to Persian to Greek to Roman rule, with European nations emerging as the inheritors of this Gentile dominance.

1 Daniel 7:1-28 (King James Version).

2 John J. Collins, *The Apocalyptic Vision of the Book of Daniel* (Cambridge, MA: Harvard University Press, 1977), 152.

CONSTANTINE THE GREAT AND THE TRANSFORMATION OF THE FAITH

History records an eventful battle in Rome that took place in 312 CE and paved the way for what is now known as the Roman Catholic Church. Two emperors, Constantine the Great and Maxentius, faced off at the Milvian Bridge to claim the imperial throne. The winner would become the sole ruler of the Roman Empire. Constantine was the victor in this battle and began to rule the empire along with his brother-in-law, Licinius. Constantine ruled the west, while Licinius ruled the east.

Eusebius of Caesarea, the bishop of Caesarea Maritima and a historian of Christianity, and Lactantius, a Christian author who became Constantine's advisor for his Christian religious policy in its early stages of emergence, both claim that Constantine had converted to Christianity. His conversion stemmed from a vision before the Milvian Bridge battle, where he was commanded to mark his soldiers' shields with a sign denoting Christ. Eusebius says it was the "Chi-Rho" cross. The story goes that Constantine had a vision of the words in *hoc signo vinces* ("in this sign you will conquer") upon a cross, and he swore that, should he triumph against great odds, he would pledge himself to Christianity.[3] According to Eusebius and Lactantius, Constantine held to his vow of submitting to the Christian God.

Constantine's victory and conversion were quintessential to the toleration and legalization of Christianity. In 313 CE, Constantine and Licinius issued the *Edict of Milan*—an agreement to treat "Christians" benevolently within the Roman Empire. This edict helped shape the Roman Empire and, eventually, the European world. As historian Peter Brown notes, "The Edict of Milan represented not merely religious tolerance but the beginning of Christianity's transformation from a persecuted sect into the dominant religion of the empire."[4]

A feud began between the brothers-in-law when Constantine decided to build a city in his honor. This city is Constantinople (now Istanbul).

---

3 Eusebius, *Life of Constantine,* trans. Averil Cameron and Stuart G. Hall (Oxford: Clarendon Press, 1999), 81.

4 Peter Brown, *The Rise of Western Christendom: Triumph and Diversity, A.D. 200-1000* (Oxford: Wiley-Blackwell, 2013), 60.

They remained rivals over a decade of uneasy truces before their animosity culminated in the Battle of Chrysopolis in 324. Licinius was routed, and Constantine became the sole Emperor of Rome.

In 325 CE, slightly over a decade after his supposed conversion, Constantine summoned the bishops of the "Christian" Church within the Roman Empire to Nicaea as a first attempt to address divisions in the Church and to attain a consensus of the faith that could be agreed upon by all believers. The Council formulated what is known as the Nicene Creed, which became the tenets of the Christian doctrine, especially the relationship between God the Father (Yahweh) and Yeshua the Messiah, concluding that they were *Homoousion* (same in being, essence, or substance).

It is believed that Constantine used this ecumenical council of bishops at Nicaea, with its resulting creed, to integrate the Christian faith into the imperial government, making it the religion of the state (although not all the bishops were in total agreement with the creed). Theologian Jaroslav Pelikan observes that "the Nicene settlement transformed not only the doctrine of the church but its relationship to imperial power, creating a template for church-state relations that would endure for centuries."[5]

THE RISE OF POPES AND THE ROMAN CATHOLIC CHURCH

Again, before Constantine's conversion and the Edict of Milan, Hebrews suffered for exercising faith in Yahweh, and the Hebrew-born Messianic faith became a mere underground operation. These Hebrew belief systems were outlawed in the Roman Empire. Those who assumed the bishopric and apostolic role in the early Church did so with the understanding that their lives were an easy target for martyrdom.

Most of what we know as the teachings and practices of the Roman Catholic Church began to emerge after the Council of Nicaea, especially

5 Jaroslav Pelikan, *The Christian Tradition: A History of the Development of Doctrine, Vol. 1: The Emergence of the Catholic Tradition (100-600)* (Chicago: University of Chicago Press, 1971), 200.

when Constantine made Christianity the religion of the state. At this point, most, if not all, Hebrew cultural observances were dissolved away from the church as many Greco-Roman pagan practices were interwoven into the fabric of the Hebrew-Messianic faith. Although the Hebrew-Messianic faith, now known as Christianity, became the religion of the state, anti-Hebrew sentiment was still widespread. Anything associated with Hebrew culture was still widely frowned upon throughout the Roman Empire. Hebrew belief systems, both Old and New, required a way of living that was foreign to much of the pagan practices throughout the Empire. The Hebrew faith required one to abandon the worship of idols and immorality.

Shortly after Constantine's conversion, keeping the Sabbath was substituted with Sunday worship as Mithraism or sun worship was the Roman Empire's official religion. There was no scriptural basis for the change. The Hebrew apostles never declared a change from keeping the Sabbath. We even see in the New Testament where the apostles kept the Sabbath. Sabbath Truth's article reports:

> "You see, at that time [321 CE, during the time of Constantine's reign] the cult of Mithraism or sun-worship was the official religion of the Roman Empire. It stood as the greatest competitor to the new Christian religion. It had its own organization, temples, priesthood, robes—everything. It also had an official worship day on which special homage was given to the sun. That day was called 'The Venerable Day of the Sun.' It was the first day of the week, and from it we get our name Sunday. When Constantine pressed his pagan hordes into the church they were observing the day of the sun for their adoration of the sun god. It was their special holy day. In order to make it more convenient for them to make the change to the new religion, Constantine accepted their day of worship, Sunday, instead of the Christian Sabbath which had been observed by Jesus and His disciples. Remember that the way had been prepared for this already by the increasing anti-Jewish feelings against those who were accused of putting

> Jesus to death. Those feelings would naturally condition many Christians to swing away from something which was held religiously by the Jews [Hebrews]. It is therefore easier to understand how the change was imposed on Christianity through a strong civil law issued by Constantine as the Emperor of Rome."[6]

Constantine, the Gentile world ruler, had the power to change Biblical practices to appeal to the people's satisfaction. After a while, the once Hebrew-led, Hebrew-cultured Messianic faith became a shell of what the apostles and the early church practiced. Christianity was too Hebrew and became syncretized by Constantine to fit within his pagan world.

Religious historian Justo L. González observes that "Constantine's adoption of Christianity as the favored religion of the empire led to a massive influx of nominal converts and a corresponding dilution of the faith's distinctive character, particularly its Hebrew roots."[7] This transformation represents a critical moment in the alienation of Christianity from its Hebrew origins—a process that would continue and intensify in subsequent centuries.

THE POWER OF THE POPE

The papacy (order of the Popes) became one of the most powerful forces in world history, especially during the Middle Ages. Their power grew significantly from a forged document called *The Donation of Constantine.*

The Donation of Constantine was a forged document pretending to have been written in the early fourth century. In it, Constantine authorizes and gives large areas of land, political power, and religious authority to Pope Sylvester I (in power from 314–335 CE) and his papal successors. The document reports that Sylvester healed Constantine of leprosy, which was the reason for the gifts to the Pope.

---

6 "How Sunday Became the Popular Day of Worship," *Sabbath Truth,* accessed March 15, 2025, https://www.sabbathtruth.com/free-resources/article-library/id/916/how-sunday-became-the-popular-day-of-worship.

7 Justo L. González, *The Story of Christianity, Vol. 1: The Early Church to the Dawn of the Reformation* (New York: HarperOne, 2010), 124.

The Donation begins with a narrative: Sylvester I was supposed to have cured Roman Emperor Constantine of leprosy before the latter gave his support to Rome and the Pope as the heart of the church. It then moves into the granting of rights, a 'donation' to the church: the Pope is made the supreme religious ruler of many great capitals—including the newly expanded Constantinople—and given control of all the lands given to the church throughout Constantine's empire. The Pope is also given the Imperial Palace in Rome and the western empire, and the ability to appoint all kings and emperors ruling there. What this meant, if it had been true, was that the Papacy had the legal right to rule a large area of Italy in a secular fashion, which it did during the medieval period.

The Donation of Constantine appears to have been written around 750-800 CE. No one is certain who forged the Donation. However, the purpose was to give the papacy complete religious authority and political influence, especially in appointing kings and emperors. This is one of the reasons why kings felt that God appointed them, because the supreme religious authority, the Pontiff himself, said so. Eventually, as the masses accepted this fake document, the power and wealth of the Pope and the Roman Catholic Church grew exponentially. They literally became world rulers. Kings rarely made decisions without the confirmation of the papacy. Papal Bulls (authoritative proclamations) were written by Popes and valued to the highest degree, almost as though God himself wrote them. By the time Lorenzo Valla proved the Donation's forgery in 1440 CE, the Roman Catholic Church was a religious and political behemoth having a major influence on the known world and playing a vital role in shaping the world as we know it today.

Historian Johannes Fried notes that "despite being a forgery, the Donation of Constantine profoundly shaped medieval political theory and practice, legitimizing papal claims to temporal power and establishing a paradigm for church-state relations that would endure for centuries."[8] The document's influence, despite its fraudulent nature,

8 Johannes Fried, *Donation of Constantine and Constitutum Constantini: The Misinterpretation of a Fiction and Its Original Meaning* (Berlin: Walter de Gruyter, 2007), 53.

exemplifies how European powers constructed legitimacy through fabricated connections to ancient authority—a pattern that would be repeated in their claims to Israelite heritage and their justifications for colonial expansion.

THE DOCTRINE OF DISCOVERY

Why do people say that Christopher Columbus and other explorers "discovered" places already populated with people? Our history books never tell the dark secret of the Roman Catholic Church. One reason why most African Americans do not know their identity is because of the power of the Papacy and what took place in the 15th century. Gentile rule is what it is today because of the power of the Papacy. Nothing greater signifies the level of their power than that of their Papal Bulls. Papal bulls were used since the 6th century. A papal bull is an official edict from the Pope. It got its name from the bulla, a device that created a bubble-like shape that formed the stamped seal on the Pope's official documents. Kings and Queens would treat papal bulls as if they were decrees honored by God.

There were three significant papal bulls in the 15th century that authorized explorations, slavery, and annihilation of indigenous people. These 15th-century papal bulls are referred to as the Doctrine of Discovery. It is the gateway to Gentile rule of Africa and the Americas. Maria Theresa Stadtmueller shares:

"The Doctrine of Discovery is 'a series of three 15th century Papal Bulls that granted ownership of everything—and everyone—on planet Earth to Christians. And since we're talking about Renaissance Christians, we're mostly talking about white Europeans.'"[9] The three Papal Bulls are Dum Diversas (1452), Romanus Pontifex (1455) and Inter Caetera Divinae (1493).

The first of the papal bulls was Dum Diversas written by Pope Nicholas V. It was written in 1452, declaring that the first European Christians to land on any territory anywhere in the world, in the name of a Christian

9 Maria Theresa Stadtmueller, "The Doctrine of Discovery," *Grassroots Economic Organizing,* March 4, 2013, https://geo.coop/story/doctrine-discovery.

king, became owners of the land no matter if people were occupying the land or not. The king owned the land, the people on it, and all their stuff, in perpetuity.[10] It (Dum Diversas) authorized Alfonso V of Portugal to reduce any "Saracens (Muslims) and pagans and any other unbelievers" to perpetual slavery.[11] This facilitated the Portuguese slave trade from West Africa.

In the Papal Bulls of 1493, Pope Alexander explicitly granted Spain and Portugal authority over governmental relations, diplomacy, trade, and economic activities with indigenous peoples and governments worldwide.[12] The bulls authorized Spanish and Portuguese attacks on pagans around the world, the capture of their goods and territories, and ordered that they be placed into "perpetual slavery."[13]

Legal scholar Robert J. Miller explains, "The Doctrine of Discovery was the legal principle that European nations used to claim superior rights over Indigenous nations. Under this principle, Europeans claimed that their monarchs had acquired property rights and sovereignty over non-Christian nations merely by sailing along coasts or planting a flag."[14] This doctrine would have profound implications for both Native Americans and the millions of Africans who would be transported to the Americas through the transatlantic slave trade.

THE NEW WORLD

Gentile rule expanded into the New World. In 1492, Christopher Columbus voyaged across the Atlantic into the New World, assuming he

10 Steven T. Newcomb, *Pagans in the Promised Land: Decoding the Doctrine of Christian Discovery* (Golden, CO: Fulcrum Publishing, 2008), 84-85.

11 "Dum Diversas," *Papal Encyclicals Online,* accessed March 20, 2025, http://www.papalencyclicals.net/nichol05/dumdiver.htm.

12 Robert J. Miller et al., *Discovering Indigenous Lands: The Doctrine of Discovery in the English Colonies* (Oxford: Oxford University Press, 2010), 9.

13 Robert A. Williams Jr., *The American Indian in Western Legal Thought: The Discourses of Conquest* (New York: Oxford University Press, 1990), 72.

14 Robert J. Miller, *Native America, Discovered and Conquered: Thomas Jefferson, Lewis & Clark, and Manifest Destiny* (Westport, CT: Praeger Publishers, 2006), 12.

reached India, but arriving in the Antilles. He arrived in Hispaniola, being confronted by Taíno chieftains. The Taíno (meaning "good people") were indigenous to the Antilles. So, you wonder how Columbus was crowned with the honor of discovering the land? The Papal Bulls! To the European explorers, they "discovered" the land because no "believers" were present, only "heathens." To them, heathens (unbelievers) had no rights to any land. Therefore, the so-called Christian explorers had the right to claim the land on behalf of their king, the land annexed to their nation, including the people in it. And they had the right to kill or enslave anyone who rebelled against them. With the high authority of the Pope, Columbus was deemed the discoverer of the New World. The conquerors narrate the history!

The Spaniards' exploitation of the Taíno was diabolical. The Spaniards brought over new infectious diseases. It is recorded that 90% of the Hispaniola natives were killed by the smallpox epidemic in 1518, and by 1548 CE, the native population was reduced to a mere 500.[15]

Spanish settlement caused a deterioration in Taíno culture as well. Women were raped and taken by the Spaniard men producing *mestizo* children. The Taino Museum records:

"The Spaniards, who first arrived in the Bahamas, Cuba, and Hispaniola in 1492, and later in Puerto Rico, did not bring women in the first expeditions. They took Taíno women for their common-law wives, resulting in mestizo children. Sexual violence in Haiti with the Taíno women by the Spanish was also common. Scholars suggest there was substantial *mestizaje* (racial and cultural mixing) in Cuba, as well, and several Indian pueblos that survived into the 19th century."[16]

Eventually, this plundering of the New World expanded across the Caribbean islands and North and South America. Historian Tzvetan Todorov characterizes the European conquest of the Americas as "the greatest genocide in human history," noting that the combination

---

15 Noble David Cook, *Born to Die: Disease and New World Conquest, 1492-1650* (Cambridge: Cambridge University Press, 1998), 202.

16 "Spanish Impact on Taíno Culture," *The Taíno Museum,* accessed March 18, 2025, http://www.tainomuseum.org/spanishimpact.html.

of violence, disease, and cultural destruction resulted in population declines of up to 90% in many indigenous societies.[17]

THE TRANSATLANTIC SLAVE TRADE

When the foreigners saw that they could gain much wealth and benefit economically from sugar, they forced the natives to try and produce an overreaching amount of product to export back to Europe. So, the natives were not only dying from diseases but also from the hard, laborious tasks of their conquerors on the sugar plantations on the islands. European indentured servants could not bear the hot, tropical climate and workloads, and many were dying, while others feared crossing the Atlantic Ocean (formerly called the Ethiopian Ocean). A labor shortage became a new world dilemma.

The Dominican friar, Bartolomé de las Casas, saved the day for the Europeans. He was the Protector of the Indians, an administrative office of the Spanish colonies responsible for attending to the wellbeing of the native populations, including speaking on their behalf in courts and reporting back to the King of Spain. As Protector of the Indians, he came up with the labor solution. Ironically, the solution benefited one group of people while bringing devastation to another. De las Casas' solution was to bring Africans to the West Indies to replace the natives in the fields since Africans were accustomed to working in tropical climates.

> "Initially, as a result of his first conversion in 1514, while a secular cleric, Las Casas embraced the cause of the indigenous people. However, one of the remedies for the plight of the indigenous people in his 1516 reform plan included bringing African slaves to the Indies; its purpose was to free and save the lives of the natives of La Española, who were held in *encomienda* and worked in mines and fields."[18]

---

17 Tzvetan Todorov, *The Conquest of America: The Question of the Other, trans. Richard Howard* (Norman: University of Oklahoma Press, 1999), 133.

18 Lawrence A. Clayton, *Bartolomé de las Casas: A Biography* (Cambridge: Cambridge University Press, 2012), 146.

Soon after De las Casas' labor solution was accepted, the Portuguese devised a plan to trade their products for human beings. In 1518, through special licenses with the Spanish emperor Charles V, called *"Asientos,"* the Portuguese shipped 250 Africans living in Lagos, Portugal, to Santo Domingo (present-day Haiti). By 1538, Europeans began enslaving Africans from their own continent to the New World.[19] The Portuguese were the first to initiate the Transatlantic Slave Trade.[20] From the Congo to Senegambia, the most heinous crimes against humanity were executed as the Gentile power of the Portuguese stormed across West Africa, enslaving, killing, raping, and plundering. It didn't take long for other European nations to jump into exploiting the African continent.

Between the 16th and 19th centuries, approximately 12.5 million Africans were forcibly transported to the Americas, with about 10.7 million surviving the infamous Middle Passage.[21] This mass displacement represents one of history's greatest crimes against humanity and had profound implications for the identity and heritage of those enslaved. It is also estimated that nearly 2 million Africans died during the Middle Passage. What is not commonly recorded are the captives who did not survive the hinterland shackled journey. In some cases, trails from the interior to the slave dungeons were 200+ miles long. Those who were weak from exhaustion, injury, sickness, starvation, etc., would be tied to trees for wild beasts to come and devour them, or an impatient kidnapper may have killed them.

What people do not realize is that found within the DNA of many of the captives was Hebrew blood being freighted across the Atlantic to the New World. This fact, which we will discuss in later chapters, is the reason for this book—to enlighten those of African descent that there is a link between the Africans in the Americas and the Hebrews of the Scriptures! While we honor and value our West African, Hamitic heritage, for many of us, our heritage dates further back eastward into

---

19 Herbert S. Klein, *The Atlantic Slave Trade* (Cambridge: Cambridge University Press, 2010), 37.

20 John Thornton, *Africa and Africans in the Making of the Atlantic World, 1400-1800* (Cambridge: Cambridge University Press, 1998), 72.

21 David Eltis and David Richardson, *Atlas of the Transatlantic Slave Trade* (New Haven: Yale University Press, 2010), 23.

the Promised Land. Even speaking with some of my West African brothers, the oral traditions of some tribes testify to their migration from the East.

The slave trade targeted West African regions that, as we've established, had become significant centers of Hebrew settlement following dispersions from Israel. Historian John Henrik Clarke notes that "many areas of West Africa targeted by slave traders had long-standing connections to ancient Hebrew communities."[22] These regions included areas that had been influenced by Hebrew religious practices, either through direct migration or through cultural diffusion across trade routes.

When Europeans arrived on Africa's west coast, they encountered diverse societies with complex religious systems, many incorporating elements recognizable as Hebraic in origin. Anthropologist Melville J. Herskovits documented numerous cultural practices among West African peoples that paralleled Hebrew traditions, including dietary restrictions, purification rituals, and naming ceremonies.[23] These parallels suggest that many of those captured and enslaved may have indeed been descendants of the dispersed Israelites who had found refuge in Africa centuries earlier.

The slave trade systematically destroyed these connections to Hebrew identity. Anthropologist Sterling Stuckey explains, "The process of enslavement deliberately severed cultural and historical ties, forcing enslaved Africans to abandon their names, languages, and religious practices—the very markers of their identity and heritage."[24] This severance was not incidental but strategic, as it facilitated control over enslaved populations by disconnecting them from sources of identity and resistance.

---

22 John Henrik Clarke, "The African Heritage of White America," in *African Presence in Early America,* ed. Ivan Van Sertima (New Brunswick, NJ: Transaction Publishers, 1992), 109.

23 Melville J. Herskovits, *The Myth of the Negro Past* (Boston: Beacon Press, 1990), 75-89.

24 Sterling Stuckey, *Slave Culture: Nationalist Theory and the Foundations of Black America* (New York: Oxford University Press, 1987), 43.

Upon arrival in the Americas, enslaved Africans faced a comprehensive program of cultural erasure. Their names were replaced with European ones, their languages forbidden, their family structures disrupted, and their religious practices suppressed. In place of their ancestral traditions, they were often forcibly converted to Christianity—ironically, the faith that had emerged from their own Hebrew ancestors, albeit in a form now shaped by European interpretation and control.

Historian Sylviane A. Diouf observes that "despite these systematic attempts at erasure, elements of Hebrew identity persisted in the religious practices, folklore, and cultural expressions of enslaved communities."[25] These persistent elements—including rituals around childbirth, burial practices, and dietary customs—suggest a resilient connection to Hebrew origins that could not be completely extinguished even through generations of bondage.

THE SCRAMBLE FOR AFRICA

After nearly 300 years of accumulating wealth from chattel slavery, many anti-slavery movements began to formulate by the mid-1800s. The abolitionists protested slavery and its horrors, helping to dissolve the legalization of slavery in most countries. Slavery was so lucrative that many beneficiaries fought against the protestors with their self-centered rationalizations. European nations continued their economic exploitations on the continent of Africa despite the outlawing of slavery in most countries. Gentile nations were still on their on-the-ground hunt for more wealth, power, and control.

European explorers and missionaries began mapping the interior of Africa in the nineteenth century. Adventurers like Henry Stanley revealed that Africa was full of raw materials that could be exploited to fuel the industrial revolution. They saw it as a new place to invest the money made in industry.[26]

---

25 Sylviane A. Diouf, *Servants of Allah: African Muslims Enslaved in the Americas* (New York: New York University Press, 1998), 152.

26 Thomas Pakenham, *The Scramble for Africa: White Man's Conquest of the Dark Continent from 1876 to 1912* (New York: Random House, 1991), 22.

In 1884, a conference was convened in Berlin, Germany, between thirteen European countries, including the United States, to discuss European control of Africa. The Europeans customized boundaries as marked territories for themselves and customized rules of competition as they pursued control and extraction of raw materials and other resources out of Africa. The Berlin Conference is known as the Scramble for Africa (also called the Conquest of Africa). The Europeans divided Africa among themselves as each claimed ownership of specific areas.

The imaginary boundaries brought more conflict to African kingdoms and tribes that had their own distinct territories. Some of the new boundaries split tribes in half. Others made huge territories that were difficult to control. This led to conflicts in the twentieth century when the colonized countries became independent.[27] Colonization is the action or process of settling among and establishing control over the indigenous people of an area. Today, although many African nations claim independence from the colonizing countries, they are still colonized. The world is still feeling the impact of colonialism today. During slavery and colonization, conquered ethnicities were oppressed not only by the stripping away of raw materials and conflicting boundaries but also by culture and arts, names and languages, belief systems, and identity. For control of the people, Europeans plotted to make the oppressed believe they were, by nature, inferior to the conquerors. To do this, history had to be whitewashed.

Historian Walter Rodney argues in his seminal work How Europe Underdeveloped Africa that "European colonialism in Africa was not merely exploitative but systematically destructive of African political, economic, and social systems, creating dependencies that would persist long after formal independence."[28] This systematic underdevelopment ensured that even after the end of direct colonial rule, African nations would remain economically dependent on European powers—extending Gentile dominance into the modern era.

---

27 A. Adu Boahen, *African Perspectives on Colonialism* (Baltimore: Johns Hopkins University Press, 1987), 95-96.

28 Walter Rodney, *How Europe Underdeveloped Africa* (London: Bogle-L'Ouverture Publications, 1972), 149.

IDENTITY THEFT: THE EUROPEAN APPROPRIATION OF ISRAELITE HERITAGE

While the descendants of Hebrews who had found refuge in Africa were being disconnected from their ancestral identity through slavery, a parallel process was unfolding in Europe. Through a complex historical process, European religious authorities increasingly positioned themselves as the true inheritors of the Israelite covenant.

The adoption of Christianity as the official religion of the Roman Empire under Constantine in the 4th century CE marked a crucial turning point. What had begun as a Hebrew faith movement, led by a Hebrew Messiah and Hebrew apostles, was gradually transformed into a European religion that positioned itself against the Way rather than within it. Theologian James H. Cone notes that "European Christianity developed a supersessionist theology that claimed God had abandoned the Jews and transferred the covenant to the Church."[29]

This theological supersessionism laid the groundwork for later European claims to be the "New Israel." When European nations embraced Christianity, they often interpreted their national histories through biblical paradigms, casting themselves as chosen peoples with divine mandates for expansion and dominance. Historian Linda Colley documents how "Britain increasingly saw itself as a new Israel with a providential role in world history, particularly during its imperial expansion."[30]

The Reformation intensified these tendencies, with Protestant nations particularly eager to identify themselves as new manifestations of biblical Israel. This ideological framework would prove especially influential in the American colonies, where Puritan settlers explicitly understood their project as establishing a "New Jerusalem" or a "City upon a Hill."[31]

---

29 James H. Cone, *God of the Oppressed* (Maryknoll, NY: Orbis Books, 1997), 117.

30 Linda Colley, *Britons: Forging the Nation 1707-1837* (New Haven: Yale University Press, 2009), 30.

31 Sacvan Bercovitch, *The Puritan Origins of the American Self* (New Haven: Yale University Press, 1975), 108.

These claims to Israelite heritage were not merely theological abstractions but had profound political and social implications. By positioning themselves as the new chosen people, European powers could justify their dominance over others as divinely ordained. Those subjugated—including the descendants of actual Israelites now enslaved in the Americas—were recast as modern-day Canaanites or Egyptians, peoples whose subjugation was sanctioned by biblical precedent.

The ultimate irony of this appropriation became apparent as European Jewish communities themselves faced persistent persecution throughout the medieval and early modern periods. Historian Jonathan Israel observes that "while European nations increasingly adopted Hebraic self-understanding, they simultaneously marginalized and persecuted actual Jewish communities within their borders."[32] This contradiction reveals the selectivity of European appropriation of Israelite identity—embracing the status and promise while rejecting the actual people and their practices.

CONCLUSION: A STOLEN WORLD

As we've traced throughout this chapter, the world stolen through European colonialism and the transatlantic slave trade included not just land and resources but identity itself. The descendants of Hebrews who had found refuge in Africa were stripped of their connection to this heritage, while European powers simultaneously appropriated Israelite identity for themselves.

This historical process aligns remarkably with the prophecy examined in Chapter 3 concerning "the times of the Gentiles." The dominance of European (Gentile) powers over the past five centuries has indeed fulfilled the biblical prediction of Israel's subjugation under Gentile rule. But the prophecy also promises an end to this period and the restoration of Israel.

The awakening of African Americans to their potential Israelite heritage may represent the beginning of this prophesied restoration.

32 Jonathan Israel, *European Jewry in the Age of Mercantilism, 1550-1750* (Oxford: Clarendon Press, 1998), 67.

Biblical scholar Walter C. Kaiser suggests that "the recognition of Israelite heritage among populations not traditionally identified as Jewish could be part of the ingathering promised in biblical prophecy."[33]

As we move forward in subsequent chapters, we will examine more specific evidence for the Israelite heritage of African Americans, including linguistic connections, cultural practices, and genetic markers. This evidence will strengthen the case that when we speak of God's chosen people in the modern world, we must look not only to those who have maintained a continuous religious tradition but also to those whose connection to ancient Israel has been obscured through historical forces of oppression and identity theft.

The reclamation of this stolen identity is not merely a matter of historical interest but has profound implications for understanding biblical prophecy and God's ongoing work in the world. As we continue to trace the connections between ancient Israel and African Americans, we are witnessing nothing less than the fulfillment of divine promises made thousands of years ago.

33 Walter C. Kaiser Jr., *Mission in the Old Testament: Israel as a Light to the Nations* (Grand Rapids: Baker Academic, 2012), 92.

Chapter 7

Whitewashing History

"The most effective way to destroy people is to deny and obliterate their own understanding of their history. Whitewashing history is an attempt to erase the memory of the oppressed and to control the narrative of the present."

Orwell, George. *1984*. London: Secker & Warburg, 1949.

"Then they fasted that day, and put on sackcloth, and cast ashes upon their heads, and rent their clothes, and laid open the book of the law, wherein the heathen had sought to paint the likeness of their images."[1]

THE ERASURE OF MEMORY

As George Orwell astutely observed, "The most effective way to destroy people is to deny and obliterate their own understanding of their history. Whitewashing history is an attempt to erase the memory of the oppressed and to control the narrative of the present."[2] This profound insight illuminates the mechanisms by which Gentile powers, as examined in preceding chapters, have maintained their dominance. From the first known Gentile rule until now, whitewashing history has aided Gentile powers in making European colonizers appear superior to all others.

The whitewashing of history refers to the practice of altering or manipulating historical facts, typically to make them appear more favorable or less offensive, often at the expense of accuracy and truth. This can involve omitting inconvenient truths, downplaying negative aspects of history, or glorifying events and figures in a way that does not reflect the complexity and reality of the historical record. Whitewashing can lead to a skewed understanding of history, impacting how societies remember their past and understand their present. History has been altered significantly by European enslavers and colonizers. The hunter became the hero while the lion's story was buried.

The Hebrew scripture quoted at the beginning of this chapter reveals how heathens sought to paint the likeness of Hebrew images, providing an example of whitewashing history as far back as the Maccabean revolt. The "heathens" referred to in this case would be those of the Seleucid (Greek) empire that oppressed the Hebrews during the Maccabean period (2nd century BCE). Scholar John J. Collins notes that "the Hellenization campaign of Antiochus IV Epiphanes included not only political and religious oppression but also cultural appropriation, attempting to replace Hebrew identity with Greek representations."[3]

---

1 1 Maccabees 3:47-48 (King James Version).

2 George Orwell, *1984* (London: Secker & Warburg, 1949), 37.

3 John J. Collins, *Between Athens and Jerusalem: Jewish Identity in the*

Much of history has been whitewashed for centuries, mainly due to the dark sin of racism. People who have been indoctrinated with the evils of racism have committed unparalleled atrocities against humanity. The colonization of Africa, the Americas, and the Caribbean did not come without vices. Chattel slavery, the stripping of African lands and their rich resources, and forcing Indigenous people of the Americas and the Caribbean to be displaced are the world's biggest crimes. These heinous crimes have been glossed over and covered up far too long, so long that anytime anyone attempts to utilize the turpentine of truth to strip away that cheap, white paint, they are labeled as heretics, conspiracy theorists, and so on. These labels often come when uncovering the whitewashed criminal history of the Euro-centric doctrine of White Superiority. There will always be controversy when challenging inaccuracies and traditions that men hold dear to their hearts. They will always attempt to discredit the work of those who confront their deceptions.

As we continue our examination of how the world was stolen from God's chosen people, as detailed in Chapter 6, we must now confront how the very memory and identity of these people were systematically erased through the whitewashing of history.

THE ORIGIN OF RACISM

During slavery times, Europeans everywhere adopted the doctrine of superiority, separating people groups into White and Slave (Blacks). This social construct is called *racism*. Racism is defined as a belief that race is the primary determinant of human traits and capacities and that racial differences produce an inherent superiority of a particular race.[4] The origin of modern scientific racism has been linked to the comparative anatomy teachings of Johann F. Blumenbach, a German physiologist who Europeans ultimately deemed as the father of physical anthropology. His teachings in comparative anatomy were applied to his classification of human races, of which he claimed there were five—

Hellenistic Diaspora (Grand Rapids: Eerdmans, 2000), 145.

4 Merriam-Webster, *Merriam-Webster's Collegiate Dictionary,* 11th ed. (Springfield, MA: Merriam-Webster, Inc., 2003), s.v. "racism."

Caucasian, Mongolian, Malayan, Ethiopian, and American [Native].[5] He considered Caucasians to be the original race. He grouped all white Europeans into the Caucasian classification. He used "Caucasian" because he thought the purest white people originated from the Caucasus Mountains, between the Black and Caspian Seas.

However, in England, throes of racism, separating ethnic groups with prejudice, existed before Blumenbach's 1795 theory. The English had a long history of separating themselves from others and treating foreigners, such as the Irish, as alien "others."[6] By the 17th century, their policies and practices in Ireland had led to an image of the Irish as "savages" who were incapable of being civilized.[7] Calling someone "Savage" is like calling an African American a "Nigger." Labeling an entire ethnic group as Savage depicted them as wild beasts—violent, uncivilized, and unintelligible. It was the perfect way of dehumanizing other humans for the psychological purpose of making one race superior to the other. This psychological impact helped rationalize the deploring treatment of other humans, especially those taken in the diaspora.

Historian Winthrop D. Jordan observes that "the English sense of distinctiveness, already well established before their encounter with Africans, provided a psychological framework for viewing darker peoples as fundamentally different and inferior."[8] This predisposition to view themselves as superior would prove instrumental in the development of racialized slavery and colonialism.

RELIGIOUS RACIAL IDEOLOGIES

The Europeans (this includes White Americans) muddied their

---

5 Johann Friedrich Blumenbach, *On the Natural Varieties of Mankind,* trans. Thomas Bendyshe (New York: Bergman Publishers, 1969), 209.

6 Nicholas Canny, *The Elizabethan Conquest of Ireland: A Pattern Established, 1565-76* (New York: Barnes & Noble Books, 1976), 74.

7 Michael Hechter, *Internal Colonialism: The Celtic Fringe in British National Development, 1536-1966* (Berkeley: University of California Press, 1975), 56.

8 Winthrop D. Jordan, *White Over Black: American Attitudes Toward the Negro, 1550-1812* (Chapel Hill: University of North Carolina Press, 1968), 240.

bigotry and biases with religion, especially in Christianity. In his book, The Bible is the Black Man's History Book, Mawuli points out the infiltration of racism into religion:

> "In 1900, Charles Carroll wrote a book entitled, 'The Negro a Beast or In the Image of God.' Using the Bible to support his racist bigotry, the book opens with this short poem:
>
> 'The Negro a beast, but created with articulate speech and hands, that he may be of service to his master the White man.'[9] This verse crystallizes Carroll's heavily biased view of Black people."
>
> He concludes: "The White race is in the image and likeness of God. Adam gave birth to only the white race. The Negro, on the other hand, is a pre-Adamite beast. Negroes could not possibly have been made in God's image and likeness because they are beastlike, immoral, and ugly."[10]

Mawuli cites other Europeans who used the Bible to contextualize and justify their racist beliefs. A Swiss physician named Paracelsus taught that Black people are descended from Cain and apes. He argued that white people descended from Adam and Eve while Negroes descended from the apes.[11] The Italian Dominican friar and philosopher Giordano Bruno and his 1591 theory believed that since no one could accept that the Ethiopians had similar ancestry as the Jews, God must have created more than one Adam. Africans were descendants of pre-Adamic races.[12] Italian Lucilio Vanini (1619) theorized that Black people descended from apes, and apes once upon a time walked on all fours.[13] Frenchman Isaac de La Peyrere (1655) theorized that the pre-Adamic races had given rise to the people of Africa.[14]

---

9 Charles Carroll, *The Negro a Beast or In the Image of God* (St. Louis: American Book and Bible House, 1900)

10 Ibid., 87.

11 Mawuli, *The Bible is the Black Man's History Book* (Chicago: African American Images, 2018), 54.

12 Ibid., 55.

13 Ibid., 56.

14 Ibid., 56-57.

Mawuli further reveals the hideous doctrine of the Mormons:

"From 1848 to 1978 (130 years), the Mormon Church had an official 'Curse of Cain Doctrine,' which stated as follows:

'There was a War in Heaven; two-thirds of God's angels fought for Jesus, and one-third for Lucifer. The two-thirds became humans on Earth, and the one-third became demons without bodies.

- Those angels who fought for Christ but were less valiant were punished. These were the lineage of Cain.
- Cain, son of Adam and Eve, was born a White man. But because he killed Abel, God put a mark on him. This turned him into the first Negro. He married his sister, and she became Negro number 2. They became the parents of the Negro race.
- Negroes are descendants of Cain. Therefore, they cannot receive the priesthood. They go to the Celestial Kingdom as servants.
- Ham was a non-Negro who married a woman who was descended from Cain the Negro. She was already pregnant when Ham married her. She gave birth to Canaan the progenitor of the Black African race.'"[15]

Religious historian Colin Kidd notes that "these theological justifications for racial hierarchy represent not just isolated aberrations but a systematic attempt to align the emerging racial ideologies of European colonialism with biblical authority."[16] By claiming divine sanction for racial hierarchies, European powers could present their dominance not as a product of human violence and greed but as the fulfillment of a cosmic order.

THE CURSE OF CAIN DEBUNKED

The two curses that the Europeans used to oppress Blacks are the

15 Ibid., 58.

16 Colin Kidd, *The Forging of Races: Race and Scripture in the Protestant Atlantic World, 1600-2000* (Cambridge: Cambridge University Press, 2006), 29.

curse of Cain and the curse of Ham. They are both superficial, quite ridiculous, and can be easily debunked.

The curse of Cain is found in Genesis 4 after he murders his brother, Abel:

> "And now you [Cain] are cursed from the ground, which has opened its mouth to receive your brother's blood from your hand. When you work the ground, it shall no longer yield to you its strength. You shall be a fugitive and a wanderer on the earth."
>
> "Cain said to the Lord, 'My punishment is greater than I can bear. Behold, you have driven me today away from the ground, and from your face I shall be hidden. I shall be a fugitive and a wanderer on the earth, and whoever finds me will kill me.'"
>
> "Then the Lord said to him, 'Not so! If anyone kills Cain, vengeance shall be taken on him sevenfold.' And the Lord put a mark on Cain, lest any who found him should attack him. Then Cain went away from the presence of the Lord and settled in the land of Nod, east of Eden."[17]

We can clearly debunk the myth of Cain's curse being one of eternal enslavement:

1. First, as we can easily see, the actual curse God put on Cain was personally for Cain. There is no mention of the curse being passed to his descendants.
2. Second was the phrase, "Cursed from the ground...when you work the ground, it shall no longer yield to you its strength." Cain was particularly a great farmer. So, God's curse to Cain was not allowing the ground to produce crops when he farmed the land.
3. Third, God told Cain he would be "a fugitive and wanderer on the earth." God was to make him a vagabond, a drifter on the earth.

---

17 Genesis 4:11-16 (English Standard Version).

Cain responds, "This punishment is too much for me to bear!" (paraphrased). He recites the curse back to God as he heard it, "Behold, you have driven me today away from the ground, AND from your face I shall be hidden." What? Wait. Did God tell him that? Cain added that God would "hide His face" from him. In other words, "Lord, wherever I'll end up, your presence won't be there with me (paraphrased). Cain must've known that when God says, "You got to go from here" (paraphrased), that must have included being away from His divine presence, too. That was the part of the curse that was the most unbearable to Cain.

Biblical scholar David M. Goldenberg observes that "the identification of the 'mark of Cain' with black skin appears nowhere in the biblical text or in early Jewish or Christian interpretation. This association developed much later as a justification for racial hierarchy and slavery."[18]

What About the Mark?

The big question is, "What about the mark?" It's funny how 'the mark' is the highlight of the mythological curse of Cain when the mark wasn't about being cursed at all. It was about God's mercy on Cain. The mark was for Cain's protection, not for him and his seed being enslaved or subservient to anyone. Nowhere in the Bible does it mention Cain or his descendants being enslaved to Seth and his descendants. Nowhere in the Bible does it mention that the mark was the darkening of his skin for his entire body, i.e., becoming a Black man. It was a mark, not some total skin makeover. The mark protected him from being attacked or killed. Does that sound like the mark allowed slavery? Does that sound like the mark allowed lynching or being gunned down by police officers because of your skin color? Debunked!

THE CURSE OF HAM DEBUNKED

Next, we have the curse of Ham which supposedly came from the Genesis 9 story where Noah got piss-drunk from his blessed vineyard and woke up cursing. The story reads:

---

18 David M. Goldenberg, *The Curse of Ham: Race and Slavery in Early Judaism, Christianity, and Islam* (Princeton: Princeton University Press, 2003), 178.

> "And he drank of the wine, and was drunken; and he was uncovered within his tent. And Ham, the father of Canaan, saw the nakedness of his father, and told his two brethren without. And Shem and Japheth took a garment, and laid it upon both their shoulders, and went backward, and covered the nakedness of their father; and their faces were backward, and they saw not their father's nakedness. And Noah awoke from his wine, and knew what his younger son had done unto him. And he said, cursed be Canaan; a servant of servants shall he be unto his brethren. And he said, blessed be the LORD God of Shem; and Canaan shall be his servant. God shall enlarge Japheth, and he shall dwell in the tents of Shem; and Canaan shall be his servant."[19]

Now, where in the Holy Bible did Noah declare a curse over his son Ham? There was never a curse on Ham! Why is this important? If Ham is the progenitor of all Africans or all Black people, which some proclaim without fact, then the curse does not relate to ALL people who have Black skin. That simple. Slavery was not a product of the fictitious curse of Ham. Slavery was a product of the evils that men do.

Ham was not cursed. Ham had four sons – Mizraim, Cush, Put, and Canaan. Only Canaan was cursed. Canaan was to be a servant of servants to his brethren and Shem, and when God enlarged Japheth, he was to serve him, too. Three of Ham's "Black" sons and their descendants were not cursed, i.e., Mizraim (Egypt), Cush (Ethiopia), and Put (known in history as Libya). Their descendants spread throughout Africa, Arabia, the Levant, and Mesopotamia, especially the Cushites. Canaan had his portion of land eventually conquered and occupied by Abraham's seed, the Israelites (Hebrews). So, all Black people are not cursed.

Biblical scholar Stephen R. Haynes notes that "the 'curse of Ham' represents one of the most profound misinterpretations in biblical history, one that persisted precisely because it served the ideological needs of those who benefited from racial slavery."[20] This distortion exemplifies

---

19 Genesis 9:21-27 (King James Version).

20 Stephen R. Haynes, *Noah's Curse: The Biblical Justification of American*

how biblical texts were manipulated to align with the economic and political interests of European powers.

This Curse of Ham is a diabolical myth and was used along with other racist doctrines to justify slavery. I guess the whiskey wasn't strong enough to chase away the conscience's guilt of the maltreatment and cruelty of the people they enslaved, so the alternative was to create an erroneous biblical teaching.

"Let's put God in it. Let's say God condemned them to eternal servitude to the White man. Let's say God made us superior to all races. Let's say God didn't make them humans at all. They are apes. They are savages. They are cursed. Yeah, that's it! Go ahead, throw nets over their heads, whip them with whips, put hooks in their noses and chains upon their feet, pack them in unclean ships until death from dysentery or suicide becomes their only relief, strip them of their clothing and put them on auction tables, separate their families, rape their women (and men), commit them to hard labor, feed them with the slob of pigs, feed their babies to alligators, and hang them by their necks if they get out of line – it's okay, God cursed them."

America, from sea to shiny sea, was shaped by this mindset. That is why justice and equality are a constant struggle for African Americans. Racism has been deeply rooted in the fabric of our society and ultimately became a global movement. From slavery to this present age, where we see the unwarranted, unjustifiable shooting of Black people, this dark Euro-centric attitude is deeply embedded in the fabric of our legislative, judicial, political, socioeconomic, and religious landscape. It has led to a privileged persona among white people, whether they know it or not.

White privilege tells us, "Get over it. Slavery ended centuries ago." White privilege says, "We've prayed for forgiveness for the sins of our past," but fail to act against the injustice and inequities of the present.

Sociologist Eduardo Bonilla-Silva observes that "contemporary racial inequality is reproduced through 'new racism' practices that are subtle, institutional, and apparently nonracial, yet maintain the racial status

---

Slavery (New York: Oxford University Press, 2002), 12.

quo."[21] This persistence of racial hierarchy, despite the formal end of slavery and legal segregation, reveals the deep-rooted nature of the whitewashing process and its ongoing impact on society.

THE SLAVE BIBLE

These distorted religious views tainted the actual narrative of history and humanity. These views shaped America. Other whitewashing of history were such things as handing slaves bibles with missing scriptures. I remember December 29, 2017, when I visited the Museum of the Bible in Washington, D.C. I recall seeing an exhibit of the Slave Bible. I had heard about it before, but seeing a copy right before my eyes froze me in my steps. I was captivated by its existence, which all the more revealed the truth about history's distortion. This is what the Museum of the Bible says about the Slave Bible:

> "The Slave Bible, as it would become known, is a missionary book. It was originally published in London in 1807 on behalf of the Society for the Conversion of Negro Slaves, an organization dedicated to improving the lives of enslaved Africans toiling in Britain's lucrative Caribbean colonies. They used the Slave Bible to teach enslaved Africans how to read while at the same time introducing them to the Christian faith. Unlike other missionary Bibles, however, the Slave Bible contained only 'select parts' of the biblical text. Its publishers deliberately removed portions of the biblical text, such as the Exodus story, that could inspire hope for liberation. Instead, the publishers emphasized portions that justified and fortified the system of slavery that was so vital to the British Empire."[22]

This Euro-centric, racially motivated, incomplete version of the Bible was meant to teach the Negro slaves how to read [in English] and to

---

21 Eduardo Bonilla-Silva, *Racism without Racists: Color-Blind Racism and the Persistence of Racial Inequality in America,* 5th ed. (Lanham, MD: Rowman & Littlefield, 2018), 3.

22 "The Slave Bible: Let the Story Be Told," Museum of the Bible, accessed March 25, 2025, https://www.museumofthebible.org/exhibits/slave-bible.

introduce them to their Christian faith. However, it only had selected parts of the bible, excluding parts they felt may incite rebellion and liberation. Anthony Schmidt, associate curator of Bible and Religion in America at the museum, says, "About 90 percent of the Old Testament is missing [and] 50 percent of the New Testament is missing. Put another way, there are 1,189 chapters in a standard protestant Bible. This [Slave] Bible contains only 232."[23]

Schmidt says passages that could have prompted rebellion were removed, for example:

> "There is neither Jew nor Greek, there is neither bond nor free, there is neither male nor female: for ye are all one in Christ Jesus."[24]

And verses that reinforced the institution of slavery, including "the most famous pro-slavery verse that many pro-slavery people would have cited," says Schmidt, were kept:

> "Servants, be obedient to them that are your masters according to the flesh, with fear and trembling, in singleness of your heart, as unto Christ."[25]

This blatant manipulation of the scriptures to make slavery appear to be God's will is just another example of the whitewashing of history and how our society glosses over it. Historian Sylvester A. Johnson notes that "the selective editing of scripture for enslaved populations represents one of the most egregious examples of how religious texts were weaponized as tools of domination rather than liberation."[26]

---

23 Anthony Schmidt, quoted in Adelle M. Banks, "Museum of the Bible Displays Slave Bible That Focuses on Servitude, Leaves Out Freedom," *Religion News Service,* November 28, 2018, https://religionnews.com/2018/11/28/museum-of-the-bible-displays-slave-bible-that-focuses-on-servitude-leaves-out-freedom/.

24 Galatians 3:28 (King James Version).

25 Ephesians 6:5 (King James Version).

26 Sylvester A. Johnson, *The Myth of Ham in Nineteenth-Century American Christianity: Race, Heathens, and the People of God* (New York: Palgrave Macmillan, 2004), 137.

WHITE JESUS

One of the ways that the White race has manipulated history was by the repainting of biblical characters from people of color to White, especially the paintings of Yeshua (Jesus). White superiority could not allow God to be in the image of a Black man! In the 1500s, Michelangelo and other European artists began to paint pictures of a white Jesus. The Catholic Church started to plaster these paintings throughout Vatican City buildings. Soon, the painting of White Jesus became mainstream throughout the world. Jesus did not come from Japheth or any European nation, so why portray Him as such? The obvious answer is to make Him appear like the conquerors whose narrative is to convince the world that White is the original race and superior to all others.

Art historian James H. Cone observes that "the Europeanization of Christ's image was not merely an artistic choice but a theological statement asserting white spiritual supremacy."[27] This visual whitewashing served to reinforce the notion that divine favor rested with European peoples rather than with the actual descendants of biblical Israel.

After all the dehumanizing misconceptions of Black people, it is highly improbable that one would be convinced that the original ethnic group chosen by God, the Hebrews, were bronze-skinned people. Racism and its false narrative served its demonic purpose for centuries.

However, many early paintings and sculptures of Jesus, his apostles, and even the patriarchs like Abraham depicted people of color, i.e., Black. The picture of The Healing of the Paralytic, dated circa 235 CE, is known as the oldest painting of Jesus. It depicts a black Jesus.

Anthropologist Sheila S. Walker notes that "early Christian iconography from North Africa, Syria, and Byzantium frequently depicted Jesus and other biblical figures with features and coloration consistent with the populations of the Near East and Mediterranean, not the fair features later standardized in European art."[28]

---

27 James H. Cone, *A Black Theology of Liberation* (Maryknoll, NY: Orbis Books, 2010), 121.

28 Sheila S. Walker, *African Roots/American Cultures: Africa in the*

CONCLUSION: THE PURPOSE OF WHITEWASHING

Whitewashing history effectively aided in the continual rule of Gentile nations as the mindset of many enslaved and oppressed people fainted into the delusion of being less in value, inferior, weak, and less than human. This was its purpose—to maintain power and control.

The systematic distortion of history—from the misrepresentation of biblical texts to the visual whitewashing of religious imagery—served a crucial function in maintaining Gentile dominance over God's chosen people. By divorcing African Americans from their potential Israelite heritage and simultaneously positioning Europeans as the spiritual heirs of biblical promises, this whitewashing created a theological framework that sanctioned racial hierarchy and colonial exploitation.

However, as we have seen throughout this book, the truth cannot remain buried forever. The prophecy examined in Chapter 3 assures us that "the times of the Gentiles" will come to an end, and God's people will recognize their true identity and heritage. The increasing recognition that many African Americans may indeed be descendants of the dispersed tribes of Israel represents a powerful challenge to centuries of historical whitewashing.

Let me remind you again that Yeshua promised an expiration of Gentile rule. As the scales of historical distortion fall from our eyes, we come closer to the fulfillment of that divine promise.

Creation of the Americas (Lanham, MD: Rowman & Littlefield, 2001), 256.

Chapter 8

Gentiles in the Holy Land

"The Europeans claiming to be Jews are nothing more than Hebrew-speaking Gentiles. You (the Jews) will never be able to live here in peace because you left here black but came back white. We cannot accept you!"[1]

THE QUESTION OF IDENTITY

These powerful words by Egyptian President Gamal Abdel Nasser encapsulate a profound challenge to the conventional understanding of Jewish identity in modern Israel. What message was he trying to convey? Perhaps what he saw did not match the evidence of history. History leaves trails and track records. Even more so, if we believe that the Bible is an accurate historical record, it also has evidence conflicting with what we see in Israel today.

As we've traced throughout the preceding chapters, Gentile nations have systematically colonized much of the world, whitewashed history, and appropriated the identity of God's chosen people. With the help of other Gentile nations, there was an entrance of Gentiles into the Holy Land to gain occupancy, control, and rulership of the land that originally belonged to God's chosen ethnic group. This Promised Land settlement would validate the idea that God's chosen ethnic group strikingly resembles Europeans and amplify the psychological effect of White superiority.

When speaking of prophecy about End-time events, many Christian teachers and prophets look at what's happening in the land of Israel today or even with the people-group who call themselves Israeli as a

1 Gamal Abdel Nasser, quoted in Joel Carmichael, *The Satanizing of the Jews: Origin and Development of Mystical Anti-Semitism* (New York: Fromm International Publishing, 1992), 163.

timetable for when the Messiah shall return. In addition to this, an overwhelming number of resources is funneled into Israel, especially from the predominantly White evangelical churches, to assist them in their development as a nation. The reason behind this massive support is based upon God's promise to Abraham to give Israel that portion of land (Canaan, also known as the Promise Land) and prophecies of Israel's return to their land from being scattered throughout the nations in fulfillment of End-time events.

In his Washington Post article, Phillip Bump records, "The LifeWay poll also asked evangelical respondents what factors contribute to their support for the state of Israel. More than 6 in 10 cited God's pledge to Abraham. The third-most-cited reason was that the existence of Israel was necessary for fulfilling prophecy. More than half of evangelicals said that was a reason they supported Israel's existence."[2]

Pastor Nate Pyle told Newsweek, "What kick-starts the end times into motion is Israel's political boundaries being reestablished to what God promised the Israelites according to the Bible."[3]

This supporting role of Christendom is a direct result of Christian Zionism, which is a belief among some Christians that the return of the Jews to the Holy Land and the establishment of the state of Israel in 1948 was following Bible prophecy. This term began to be used in the mid-20th century. As historian Stephen Spector notes, "Christian Zionism emerged as a significant political force in the United States during the latter half of the twentieth century, shaping American foreign policy toward Israel in profound ways."[4]

---

2 Phillip Bump, "Half of Evangelicals Support Israel Because They Believe It Is Important for Fulfilling End-Times Prophecy," *Washington Post,* May 14, 2018, https://www.washingtonpost.com/news/politics/wp/2018/05/14/half-of-evangelicals-support-israel-because-they-believe-it-is-important-for-fulfilling-end-times-prophecy/.

3 Nate Pyle, quoted in Nina Burleigh, "Evangelical Christians Helped Elect Donald Trump, but Their Time as a Major Political Force Is Coming to an End," *Newsweek,* December 13, 2018, https://www.newsweek.com/2018/12/21/evangelicals-republicans-trump-millenials-1255745.html.

4 Stephen Spector, *Evangelicals and Israel: The Story of American Christian Zionism* (New York: Oxford University Press, 2009), 23.

Christian Zionism stems from Jewish Zionism, which is the national movement of the Jewish people that supports the re-establishment of a Jewish homeland in the territory defined as the historic Land of Israel. Historian Walter Laqueur observes that "Jewish Zionism developed in the late nineteenth century as a response to European antisemitism, drawing on religious connections to the land but functioning primarily as a secular nationalist movement."[5]

BIBLICAL SUPPORT FOR ISRAEL'S RETURN

Supporting Israel's return is biblical and not invalid – it unequivocally should be done based on several scriptures. Among such scriptures are:

> "And he shall set up an ensign for the nations, and shall assemble the outcasts of Israel, and gather together the dispersed of Judah from the four corners of the earth."[6]
>
> "And I will be found of you, saith the Lord: and I will turn away your captivity, and I will gather you from all the nations, and from all the places whither I have driven you, saith the Lord; and I will bring you again into the place whence I caused you to be carried away captive."[7]
>
> "I will accept you with your sweet savour, when I bring you out from the people, and gather you out of the countries wherein ye have been scattered; and I will be sanctified in you before the heathen. And ye shall know that I am the Lord, when I shall bring you into the land of Israel, into the country for the which I lifted up mine hand to give it to your fathers."[8]

Biblical scholar Walter C. Kaiser Jr. notes that "the prophetic promise of Israel's return to their land is one of the most consistently reiterated themes in the Old Testament, appearing in virtually every prophetic

---

5 Walter Laqueur, *A History of Zionism: From the French Revolution to the Establishment of the State of Israel* (New York: Schocken Books, 2003), 40.

6 Isaiah 11:12 (King James Version).

7 Jeremiah 29:14 (King James Version).

8 Ezekiel 20:41-42 (King James Version).

book."[9] The scriptural foundation for Israel's restoration to their homeland is undeniable.

However, the problem does not lie in the support of biblical prophecy concerning Israel's return but in the identity of the people who were transported to the Palestinian region. Suppose the people occupying Israel today are indeed the descendants of Abraham, Isaac, and Jacob. There is no quarrel; the evangelicals are on track, and the end-time events are upon us. On the contrary, the end-time clock must be reset if they are not true Israel. This, my friend, is our dilemma.

THE NEED FOR CRITICAL RESEARCH

We must pose the question, "Did the Evangelical church (or any Zionist supporter) do their homework to validate the origin and real ethnicity of the 'Jews' who are in Palestine today?" What research was conducted to conclude that they are indeed of Semitic-Abrahamic blood? We believe there was more assumption than research and that their universally accepted history of the Jews is theorized. I will show in this book that another theory is probable and needs to be thoroughly examined as well. This additional historical inquiry includes scholarly content that brings validity to its claim.

In our humble opinion, the church automatically assumed the traditional theory of Jewish history theory merely because of their belief in Judaism. However, belief alone is not the qualifier for validating ethnicity. Belief and bloodline are two different things. To be an ethnic Israelite, Hebrew, or Judah should be based upon ancestry, bloodline, and lineage. This will be the Israel that shall be gathered from the four corners of the globe and receive salvation from their oppression in the End-times.

Theologian James D. Smart observes that "the tendency to conflate religious adherence with ethnic identity has created significant confusion in understanding biblical promises concerning Israel's restoration."[10]

---

9 Walter C. Kaiser Jr., *The Promise-Plan of God: A Biblical Theology of the Old and New Testaments* (Grand Rapids: Zondervan, 2008), 246.

10 James D. Smart, *The Divided Mind of Modern Theology: Karl Barth and Rudolf Bultmann, 1908-1933* (Philadelphia: Westminster Press, 1967), 178.

This distinction between religious conversion and biological descent is crucial for understanding the prophecies concerning Israel's future.

Some truth about the people in Israel today is startling. Why is it important? It is essential because if we are to look at Israel as the barometer for End-time events according to biblical prophecy, then we must know precisely who Israel really is. Besides, if we are going to support Israel (God's chosen people), then we want to support the Israel of the Bible.

The intent of this book is to provide enough evidence to prove who Israel may be in the world today. We live in the age of knowledge because of the advancement of technology and science. There is little that you cannot find today. Along with technology, scientific studies, such as DNA, help in the discovery of truths that have been hidden for centuries. Isn't that exciting? We believe Yahweh is allowing new truths to be unearthed and revealed because He's setting the stage for the Great Awakening and the Messiah's return.

This book is written to spark a dialogue within Christendom concerning truths rarely discussed and traditions upheld and practiced without any meeting of the minds or deep dive discussions on what is true. Sadly enough, Christianity is a hotbed for syncretism because we never confront and dismiss the fallacies and false narratives that it has embraced. From the changing of the Sabbath to the Doctrine of Discovery to syncretized pagan practices to forced conversions to modern-day Christian nationalists' views, Christianity has accumulated layers of cultural, political, and philosophical influences that have often obscured its original teachings. Throughout history, these additions have sometimes served power structures more than they've served truth, creating divisions rather than unity, and leaving many believers practicing traditions whose origins they don't fully understand. This book aims to invite honest examination of these elements not to tear down faith, but to strengthen it through greater alignment with genuine biblical teachings.

I believe that the church can reclaim its moral authority and prophetic voice only when spiritual shepherds courageously excavate and repudiate the theological distortions and syncretized rituals that have infiltrated sacred spaces—rituals often unknowingly perpetuated generation after generation. The church must not merely acknowledge but actively atone for its historical complicity in the subjugation and dehumanization of African Americans and the systematic decimation of Indigenous cultures throughout the Americas, moving beyond performative gestures toward substantive reparation and the dismantling of structural inequities. This reconciliatory journey, though arduous and humbling, will catalyze an unprecedented spiritual renaissance—a divine ingathering that will eclipse all previous revivals in both magnitude and authenticity. Among those drawn to this purified expression of faith will undoubtedly be the descendants of ancient Israel, fulfilling the prophetic declaration that has reverberated through millennia: "And so all Israel shall be saved," as the veil of historical distortion finally lifts and God's redemptive purposes come into crystal clarity.

ASHKENAZI JEWS: HEBREW SPEAKING GENTILES?

Let's proceed with our historical inquiry as it pertains to who the Jews that we see today. Our posing question is, "Where did the modern-day 'Jews' come from?" There are approximately 15 million Jews today. Interestingly, 83% of the Jewish population either live in Israel or the United States.[11] Why are the majority of Jews living in Israel and the United States of Ashkenazi descent? Ashkenazi Jews make up over 80% of the Jewish people.[12] Approximately 90-95% of American Jews are Ashkenazi.[13] These are those among the Jewish community whose features are pale and strikingly resemble other European people groups.

At what point did the Semitic people, those originating from a hot climate region of Mesopotamia and the Levant, no longer need melanin in their skin for the geographical location they lived in? Ironically, the Israel Cancer Association reported that the Jews of today have the second

---

11 Sergio DellaPergola, "World Jewish Population, 2019," in *American Jewish Year Book 2019,* ed. Arnold Dashefsky and Ira M. Sheskin (Cham: Springer, 2020), 263-353.

12 Ibid., 278.

13 Ira M. Sheskin and Arnold Dashefsky, "United States Jewish Population, 2019," in *American Jewish Year Book 2019,* ed. Arnold Dashefsky and Ira M. Sheskin (Cham: Springer, 2020), 135-239.

highest rate of skin cancer disease in the world since 2000. At the end of 2000, there were 3,631 skin cancer patients in Israel, and around 200 die every year from the disease.[14] The Jerusalem Post reports, "Prof. Eli Sprecher, chairman of the hospital's (Tel Aviv Sourasky Medical Center) dermatology department, and colleagues here and abroad recently discovered that 'peeling skin syndrome' results from abnormal function of a large protein (due to a mutated gene) called filaggrin 2. Persons with the condition suffer from fragile and continuously peeling skin, especially in very warm weather and following physical trauma to the skin."[15]

These biological vulnerabilities raise legitimate questions about the genetic compatibility of Ashkenazi Jews with the climate of the Middle East. Anthropologist Shomarka Keita observes that "populations indigenous to the Levant historically exhibited physical adaptations to the region's climate, including increased melanin production as protection against intense solar radiation."[16] The high rates of skin cancer among modern Israeli populations seem inconsistent with a population that evolved in this region.

THE KHAZAR THEORY

According to the Table of Nations, Ashkenaz and Togarmah were Gomer's sons and the grandson of Japheth. On the contrary, Abraham and his descendants are from the lineage of Shem, not Japheth. I don't think that the Bible made an error.

In his book The Thirteenth Tribe, Arthur Koestler cites the historical origin of the people we now know as [Ashkenazi] Jews. Many of us have never heard of a Khazar Empire, but according to Koestler, this is precisely where today's Holy Land occupiers are from.

---

14 "Cancer Rates in Israel," Israel Cancer Association, accessed March 28, 2025, https://www.cancer.org.il/template_e/default.aspx?PageId=7635.

15 Judy Siegel-Itzkovich, "Israeli Scientists Find Cause of Rare Skin Disease," *Jerusalem Post,* May 8, 2011, https://www.jpost.com/health-and-science/israeli-scientists-find-cause-of-rare-skin-disease.

16 Shomarka Keita, "Studies of Ancient Crania from Northern Africa," *American Journal of Physical Anthropology* 83, no. 1 (1990): 35-48.

The Khazar Kingdom was an Eastern European kingdom located in the Caucasus region and situated between the Byzantine Empire and the Persian Empire. The Khazars were a coalition of strong Turkic or Hunnic-Bulgar clans who, as they began to settle down, mingled with the Scythians who had inhabited these mountains and steppes between the Black Sea and the Caspian Sea, which was known for a long time as the Khazar Sea.[17] If Ashkenazi Jews are indeed Khazars, then they are a mixed Gentile ethnic group originating from the Caucasus Mountains.

Koestler's book shares the story of the exchange of letters between King Joseph ben Aaron of the Khazars and Hasdai Ibn Shaprut, a physician and important statesman, the Jewish chief minister of the Caliph of Cordoba, 'Abd ar-Rahman III.

The exchange of letters took place sometime between 954 and 961 CE.[18] Hasdai Ibn Shaprut was said to be perhaps the most brilliant figure in the "[Sephardic] Golden Age" (900-1200 CE) of the Jews in Spain. According to his account, Hasdai first heard of the existence of an independent Jewish kingdom from some merchant traders from Khurasan in Persia. Still, he doubted the truth of their story. Later, he questioned the members of a Byzantine diplomatic mission to Cordoba, and they confirmed the merchant's account, contributing a considerable amount of factual detail about the Khazar kingdom, including the name—Joseph—of its present King. Thereupon, Hasdai decided to send couriers with a letter to King Joseph.[19]

Hasdai's letter contained a list of questions about the Khazar state. One of the main questions in his letter to King Joseph was the inquiry to which of the twelve tribes he belonged to: what is the monarchy system? Is it passed from father to son, as the ancestors did in the Torah? In King Joseph's response letter, he provides Hasdai with an answer regarding Khazar's genealogy.

Historian D.M. Dunlop, one of the leading authorities on Khazar history, confirms the authenticity of this correspondence, noting that

---

17 Arthur Koestler, *The Thirteenth Tribe: The Khazar Empire and Its Heritage* (New York: Random House, 1976), 19.
18 Ibid., 75.
19 Ibid., 76-77.

"while some details may have been embellished in transmission, the core elements of the Khazar conversion to Judaism and their non-Israelite origins are historically reliable."[20]

King Joseph shares the genealogy of the Khazars, "We have found in the family registers of our fathers that *Togarma* had ten sons, and the names of their offspring are as follows: Uigur, Dursu, Avar, Huns, Basilii, Tarniakh, *Khazars,* Zagora, Bulgars, Sabir. *We are the sons of Khazar,* the seventh..."[21] According to Genesis 10:2-3, Togarmah is the son of Gomer and the grandson of Noah's son, Japheth. However, the people of Israel came from Noah's son, Shem. The Khazars were not Semitic; they did not come from Shem, Abraham, Isaac, or Jacob! Their own King validates this truth that Khazars, the European Jews, are indeed Gentiles and have no bloodline connection with the Hebrews of the Bible.

JEWS BY CONVERSION

King Joseph further reveals that they became "Jews" by conversion. He gives a eulogizing narrative of his predecessor, King Bulan. He shares how King Bulan was a great conqueror and a wise man who "drove out the sorcerers and idolaters from his land." Subsequently, an angel appeared to him in a dream, exhorting him to worship the only true God, promising that in exchange, he would "bless and multiply Bulan's offspring and deliver his enemies into his hands, and make his kingdom last to the end of the world."[22] King Bulan replies to the angel about his people having pagan minds and if the angel could also appear to their "Great Prince" to make him support him – in which we are told that the angel did just that.

In addition to this dream, King Bulan must have needed confirmation. King Joseph's letter narrates probably the real drama that led to their conversion to Judaism. Seemingly after his feat against Armenia, King

20 D.M. Dunlop, *The History of the Jewish Khazars* (Princeton: Princeton University Press, 1954), 132.
21 Norman Golb and Omeljan Pritsak, *Khazarian Hebrew Documents of the Tenth Century* (Ithaca: Cornell University Press, 1982), 106.
22 Koestler, *The Thirteenth Tribe*, 66.

Bulan's fame spread to all the countries. Joseph tells how the King of Edom [Byzantium] and the King of the Ishmaelim [the Muslims] heard the news and sent to him [Bulan] envoys with precious gifts and money and learned men to convert him to their beliefs, but the king was wise and sent for a Jew with much knowledge and acumen and put all three together to discuss their doctrines.

The letter explains that King Bulan confers with all three men separately. When they were alone, he asked the Christian which of the other two religions was nearer the truth, and the Christian answered, "The Jews." Then, he asked the Muslim the same question and got the same reply. From this, Bulan made his decision to convert to Judaism. This was about 740 CE, approximately 200 years before King Joseph's reign.[23]

Shlomo Sand, in his International Bestseller book, "The Invention of the Jewish People," pens:

> "The desire to remain independent in the face of might, grasping empires—in this case, the Orthodox Byzantine Empire and the Abbasid Muslim Caliphate—impelled the rulers of Khazaria to adopt Judaism as a defensive ideological weapon. Had the Khazars adopted Islam, for example, they would have become the subjects of the caliph. Had they remained pagan, they would have been marked for annihilation by the Muslims, who did not tolerate idolatry. Christianity, of course, would have subordinated them to the Eastern Empire for a long time. The slow and gradual transition from the ancient shamanism of the region to Jewish monotheism probably also contributed to the consolidation and centralization of the Khazar realm."[24]

The mass conversion of the Khazars to Judaism proved to be progressive. King Joseph also notes in his letter that one of King Bulan's offspring, Obadiah, continued the reformation:

---

23 Ibid., 67.

24 Shlomo Sand, *The Invention of the Jewish People,* trans. Yael Lotan (London: Verso, 2009), 219.

> "Then rose a king of his offspring, named Obadiah, a righteous and honest man, who reformed the kingdom and set the Law in the proper order, and built synagogues and seminaries and brought in many of the sages of Israel..."[25]

Obadiah reformed the kingdom by setting in place the Law and building synagogues and seminaries with the assistance of the sages of Israel. Interestingly, King Joseph mentions Obadiah bringing in sages of Israel. To me, this signifies that the Khazar kingdom needed help with not only the teachings of the Hebrews but also Israel's history and lineage; this help could only come from ethnic Israel and not from among the proselytes of Obadiah's own people. Solomon Schecter writes, "Now they say in our land that our ancestors came from the tribe of Simeon, but we are not able to prove the truth of the matter."[26] By the testimony of one of Khazars' own kings (Joseph ben Aaron), we can very well conclude that Ashkenazi Jews are proselytes at best.

Historian Peter B. Golden, a specialist in Khazar studies, confirms that "the Judaization of the Khazars was primarily a conversion of the elite, with varying degrees of adoption among the general population, representing one of the most significant mass conversions to Judaism in history."[27]

THE FALL OF KHAZAR AND ASHKENAZI MIGRATION

In the tenth century, the alliance between the first Russian kingdom and the Eastern Roman Empire, which attacked Khazaria around 965 CE, caused the initial collapse of the Khazar empire.[28] A successive event of war that dealt Khazaria another blow took place in the early eleventh century. British scholar Douglas Dunlop writes:

25 Koestler, *The Thirteenth Tribe*, 68.

26 Solomon Schechter, quoted in Norman Golb and Omeljan Pritsak, *Khazarian Hebrew Documents of the Tenth Century* (Ithaca: Cornell University Press, 1982), 119.

27 Peter B. Golden, *Khazar Studies: An Historico-Philological Inquiry into the Origins of the Khazars* (Budapest: Akadémiai Kiadó, 1980), 123.

28 Koestler, The Thirteenth Tribe, 142.

> "Prince Vladimir I of Kiev, Sviatoslav's young son, expanded the boundaries of his principality as far as the Crimea, and in a significant step for the future of Russia, converted to Christianity. His alliance with the Eastern Roman Empire undermined its long connection with Khazaria, and in 1016 CE, a joint Byzantine-Russian force attacked and defeated the Jewish kingdom."[29]

The final destruction of the Khazarian kingdom came at the hands of the Mongols, led by the great war General, Genghis Khan, in the early thirteenth century. After the first half of the thirteenth century, there are no more mentions of Khazaria: the kingdom sank into historical oblivion.

These wars caused Khazar to migrate to other surrounding countries for refuge. There, they began to make settlements. Salo Wittmayer Baron, who taught at Columbia University, described as "the greatest Jewish historian of the 20th century," wrote in his literary work, "A Social and Religious History of the Jews":

"After Sviatoslav's victories and the ensuing decline of the Khazar empire, on the other hand, refugees from the devastated districts, including Jews, sought shelter in the very lands of their conquerors. Here they met other Jewish groups and individuals migrating from the west and south. Together with these arrivals from Germany and the Balkan, they began laying the foundation for a Jewish community, which, especially in sixteenth-century Poland, outstripped all the other contemporary areas of Jewish settlement in population density as well as in economic and cultural power."[30]

The migration of these proselyte Jews from Khazaria was met with the migration of Jews from the west and south. We are not told whether these Jews who migrated from the west and south were ethnic Judah/Israel, proselytes, or both since there were several migrations of

---

29 D.M. Dunlop, *The History of the Jewish Khazars* (Princeton: Princeton University Press, 1954), 239.

30 Salo Wittmayer Baron, *A Social and Religious History of the Jews, Vol. 3: Heirs of Rome and Persia* (New York: Columbia University Press, 1957), 207.

Judah/Israel from their Babylonian and Assyrian captivities and exile from Emperor Titus' siege on Jerusalem in 70 CE. Judah/Israel was dispersed throughout the nations as far west as modern-day Mauritania (Northwest Africa), Portugal, and Spain and as far east as India, Malaysia, and China. Scripture also bears evidence of proselytes in the Roman empire during the days of Yeshua; they were zealously proselytized by the Pharisees (Matthew 23:15).

In 1867, the great Jewish scholar Abraham Harkavy had written in the introduction of his book, "The Jews and the Languages of the Slavs," that "the first Jews who came to the southern regions from Russia did not originate in Germany, as many writers tend to believe, but from the Greek cities on the shores of the Black Sea and from Asia, via the mountains of the Caucasus."[31] This sounds like Harkavy is emphatically concluding that European Jews originated from the Khazar region.

Yitzhak Schipper, a senior socioeconomic historian and a prominent Zionist in Poland, believed for a long time that the "Khazar thesis" accounted well for the massive demographic presence of Jews in Eastern Europe. In this, he was following a series of Polish scholars, Jewish and non-Jewish, who had written about the first settlements of Jewish believers in Poland, Lithuania, Belorussia, and Ukraine.[32]

INQUIRY INTO THE TRADITIONAL ZIONIST HYPOTHESIS

Traditional Zionist historiography had always maintained that the Jews of Eastern Europe had come from Germany (before that, they had spent "some time" in Rome, to which they had been driven from "the Land of Israel").[33] We have substantial evidence to that presents a different historical origin for Ashkenazim. This theory claims that the Jews of Eastern Europe were mainly the converted Jews of Khazaria and not ethnic Judah. It was they who, because of their conquered

---

31 Abraham Harkavy, *The Jews and the Languages of the Slavs,* trans. Judah H. Levin (New York: YIVO Institute for Jewish Research, 1969), 8.

32 Yitzhak Schipper, *Toldot ha-Kalkalah ha-Yehudit* [History of Jewish Economy] (Tel Aviv: Dvir, 1975), 74-76.

33 Sand, *The Invention of the Jewish People,* 233.

kingdom, spread throughout the regions of Europe and are the people group we know today as "Ashkenazi Jews"—a Caucasian ethnic group who converted to the religion of Talmudic Judaism, integrating some of its laws and customs.

Traditionally, Jews are taught the Zionist hypothesis that Eastern European Jews are a population isolate that emerged from a small group of German Jews who migrated eastward from the Rhine River and expanded rapidly. They want the world to believe this and have done an incredible job convincing the world with this theory. Any other theory of their origin that contradicts their hypothesis is deemed as mere speculation and heresy. Concerning challenging the traditional [Ashkenazi] Jewish history, Evan Goldstein once wrote, "No one wants to go looking under stones when venomous scorpions might be lurking beneath them, waiting to attack the self-image of the existing ethnos and its territorial ambitions."[34] Notwithstanding, the once neglected and ostracized Khazar theory is being re-examined and studied closely today.

Historian Eric Hobsbawm observes that "all nationalist movements construct 'invented traditions' and mythologized histories to legitimize their claims to territory and status."[35] The Jewish nationalist movement's construction of a direct lineage from ancient Israel to modern Ashkenazi Jews may represent such an invented tradition, one that merits critical historical examination.

Eran Elhaik, PhD, an Israeli American geneticist, bioinformatician, and associate professor of bioinformatics at Lund University in Sweden, argues for a non-Levantine origin of the Ashkenazi and favors the hypothesis that they are of mixed Irano-Turkish-Slavic and southern European descent.[36]

---

34 Evan Goldstein, "Where Do Jews Come From?" *The Wall Street Journal,* January 15, 2010.

35 Eric Hobsbawm, "Introduction: Inventing Traditions," in *The Invention of Tradition,* ed. Eric Hobsbawm and Terence Ranger (Cambridge: Cambridge University Press, 1983), 1-14.

36 Eran Elhaik, "The Missing Link of Jewish European Ancestry: Contrasting the Rhineland and the Khazarian Hypotheses," *Genome Biology and Evolution* 5, no. 1 (2013): 61-74.

There is a collective article by Ranajit Das, Paul Wexler, Mehdi Pirooznia and Eran Elhaik that suggests the Khazarian hypotheses is more valid than the assumed Rhineland theory. On the genetic structure of Ashkenazi Jews it states:

> "Ashkenazi Jews were localized to modern-day Turkey and found to be genetically closest to Turkic, southern Caucasian, and Iranian populations, suggesting a common origin in Iranian 'Ashkenaz' lands. These findings were more compatible with an Irano-Turko-Slavic origin for Ashkenazi Jews and a Slavic origin for Yiddish (language) than with the Rhineland hypothesis, which lacks historical, genetic, and linguistic support. The findings have also highlighted the strong social-cultural and genetic bonds of Ashkenazic and Iranian Judaism and their shared Iranian origins."[37]

I conclude that this scientific evidence makes it difficult to believe that modern-day European Jewry has a bloodline connection with the Hebrews of the Bible—God's chosen ethnic group. Ashkenazi Jews like Professor Eran Elhaik, Arthur Koestler, Best-Seller author Shlomo Sands, and others bring to light scientific and historical evidence that supports a history different from the traditional historical theory.

I can also see why Egyptian president [Nasser]—whether right or wrong—asserted, "The Europeans claiming to be Jews, are nothing more than 'Hebrew-speaking Gentiles. You (the Jews) will never be able to live here in peace, because you left here black but came back white?"

IMPLICATIONS FOR BIBLICAL PROPHECY

The implications of this historical and genetic evidence are profound for our understanding of biblical prophecy and the fulfillment of God's promises to Israel. If the majority population of modern Israel consists primarily of converted Gentiles rather than biological descendants of

37 Ranajit Das, Paul Wexler, Mehdi Pirooznia, and Eran Elhaik, "Localizing Ashkenazic Jews to Primeval Villages in the Ancient Iranian Lands of Ashkenaz," *Genome Biology and Evolution* 8, no. 4 (2016): 1132-1149.

Abraham, Isaac, and Jacob, how should we interpret the prophetic promises of Israel's restoration?

Biblical scholar Craig A. Evans notes that "the prophetic promises of restoration are consistently addressed to the physical descendants of Jacob, not merely to those who adopt Jewish religious practices."[38] This raises serious questions about whether the establishment of the modern state of Israel represents the fulfillment of biblical prophecy.

Furthermore, if biological descendants of ancient Israel are to be found primarily among populations that have been historically oppressed—such as the African Americans whose ancestors were brought to the Americas through the transatlantic slave trade—then we must reconsider our understanding of God's end-time work of restoration and deliverance.

As we have seen in Chapter 3, Romans 11:25-27 prophesies that "blindness in part is happened to Israel, until the fulness of the Gentiles be come in. And so all Israel shall be saved." If Israel has been blind to its true identity, and if Gentile powers have dominated not only politically and economically but also through the appropriation of Israelite identity, then the prophesied salvation of Israel may involve a reclamation of identity by those who have been most oppressed by Gentile rule.

Right now, I have you in the middle of the jungle with a half-filled water canteen and a half-empty bag of Trail Mix. Unfortunately, we cannot camp here if we are going to find the link between God's chosen ethnic group and the African Americans of today.

38 Craig A. Evans, *Ancient Texts for New Testament Studies: A Guide to the Background Literature* (Peabody, MA: Hendrickson Publishers, 2005), 210.

Chapter 9

The Creation of a Jewish State

"I do not care what puppet is placed on the throne of England to rule the Empire...The man who controls Britain's money supply controls the British Empire. And I control the money supply."[1]

ZIONISM AND THE PATH TO STATEHOOD

In the preceding chapters, we've traced how Gentile powers have systematically dominated the world, whitewashed history, and appropriated Israelite identity. We've examined substantial evidence suggesting that the Ashkenazi Jews who now occupy the land of Israel lack authentic genealogical connections to ancient Israel. As we continue our investigation, we must now examine how these Gentiles managed to establish a Jewish state in Palestine—a development that many Christians interpret as the fulfillment of biblical prophecy.

Nahum Sokolow, known as one of the early architects of modern Zionism, played a significant role in the Zionist movement, particularly in promoting the idea of a Jewish homeland in Palestine and in securing international support for the Zionist cause. He defined Zionism as "the endless dream and the stubborn will to rebuild the land of Israel and to secure its future."[2] This romantic characterization obscures the calculated political maneuvering that made the movement successful.

1 Nathan Mayer Rothschild, quoted in Eustace Mullins, *The Secrets of the Federal Reserve* (Carson City, NV: Bridger House Publishers, 1991), 59. While this quote is widely attributed to Rothschild, some historians question its authenticity.

2 Nahum Sokolow, *History of Zionism, 1600-1918,* Vol. 1 (London: Longmans, Green and Co., 1919), xxi.

As mentioned in the previous chapter, some Christians, especially White evangelicals, support Jewish entry into Palestine to claim it as a Jewish State, citing prophetic passages of the Bible as their justification. However, their support piggybacks off a political plot from affluent Ashkenazi Jews called Zionists. It was through the Zionist movement that the Jews were able to create a Jewish State in Palestine.

THE DEVELOPMENT OF POLITICAL ZIONISM

According to the Oxford English Dictionary, Zionism is a movement for (originally) the re-establishment and the development and protection of a Jewish nation in what is now Israel.[3] It was established as *a political organization* in 1897 under Theodor Herzl and was later led by Chaim Weizmann, who also became the first president of Israel. Historian Howard M. Sachar notes that "Herzl transformed Zionism from a vague cultural and spiritual notion into a modern political movement with specific goals and organizational structure."[4]

Zionism was established with the political goal of creating a Jewish state in order to create a nation where Jews could be the majority rather than the minority, which they were in a variety of nations in the diaspora. Theodor Herzl, the ideological father of Zionism, considered antisemitism to be an eternal feature of all societies in which Jews lived as minorities and that only a separation could allow Jews to escape eternal persecution. "Let them give us sovereignty over a piece of the Earth's surface, just sufficient for the needs of our people, then we will do the rest!" he proclaimed, exposing his plan.[5]

What is particularly revealing, however, is that Herzl proposed two possible destinations to colonize: Argentina and Palestine. He preferred Argentina for its vast and sparsely populated territory and temperate climate but conceded that Palestine would have greater attraction

---

3 Oxford English Dictionary, s.v. “Zionism,” accessed April 1, 2025, https://www.oed.com.

4 Howard M. Sachar, *A History of Israel: From the Rise of Zionism to Our Time* (New York: Alfred A. Knopf, 2007), 47.

5 Theodor Herzl, *Der Judenstaat* [The Jewish State], trans. Sylvie D’Avigdor (New York: American Zionist Emergency Council, 1946), 38.

because of the historical ties of Jews with that area. He also accepted to evaluate Joseph Chamberlain's proposal for possible Jewish settlement in Great Britain's East African colonies.[6]

Herzl considered other lands besides Palestine, i.e., the Promised Land? Argentina is in South America, and the Great Britain East African colony that Herzl considered was Uganda. Those two regions, and quite frankly, any other region of the earth, should never have been considered if the return to Palestine represented a genuine fulfillment of biblical prophecy. The Promised Land is the Promised Land! Here is why Uganda was considered:

> "In 1903, British Colonial Secretary Joseph Chamberlain offered Herzl 5,000 square miles in the Uganda Protectorate for Jewish settlement. Called the Uganda Scheme, it was introduced the same year to the World Zionist Organization's Congress at its sixth meeting, where a fierce debate ensued. Some groups felt that accepting the scheme would make it more difficult to establish a Jewish state in Palestine, the African land was described as an 'antechamber to the Holy Land.' It was decided to send a commission to investigate the proposed land by 295 to 177 votes, with 132 abstaining. The following year, congress sent a delegation to inspect the plateau. A temperate climate due to its high elevation, was thought to be suitable for European settlement. However, the area was populated by a large number of Maasai, who did not seem to favor an influx of Europeans. Furthermore, the delegation found it to be filled with lions and other animals."[7]

Perhaps, if the Uganda Protectorate was not filled with lions and other animals, the Ashkenazi Jews may have been a people group settled in East Africa and not Palestine, the real Promised Land. Would that be contradictive of biblical prophecy? I wonder if evangelicals would support Jews living in Uganda instead of the Holy Land. After all, known

---

6 Walter Laqueur, *A History of Zionism: From the French Revolution to the Establishment of the State of Israel* (New York: Schocken Books, 2003), 118.
7 Michael Berkowitz, *Zionist Culture and West European Jewry Before the First World War* (Cambridge: Cambridge University Press, 1993), 112.

Jews living in other parts of Africa do not receive the same support as Ashkenazi Jews living in Israel.

Political scientist Ian S. Lustick observes that "the willingness of early Zionist leaders to consider alternatives to Palestine demonstrates that their movement was fundamentally a modern nationalist enterprise rather than the fulfillment of an ancient religious imperative."[8] This pragmatic approach to territory selection raises serious questions about the theological interpretation of Israel's founding as the fulfillment of biblical prophecy.

SELECTIVE "RETURN": THE CASE OF ETHIOPIAN JEWS

Thank God for Operation Moses in 1984, which rescued Ethiopian Jews [Hebrews] living in Sudan refugee camps during the Sudanese Civil War, and Operation Solomon in 1991, which rescued Ethiopian Jews [Hebrews] within 36 hours.[9] However, countless Jews are living in Africa. Some of these Jews wish to return to the land of their origin but are disallowed and even treated as though they have no link or heritage with Abraham, Isaac, and Jacob.

Historian Tudor Parfitt notes that "the selective application of Israel's Law of Return, which theoretically grants automatic citizenship to any Jew, reveals underlying racial biases in how Jewish identity is recognized."[10] While Ethiopian Jews were eventually recognized and airlifted to Israel, other African groups claiming Jewish heritage—such as the Lemba of Zimbabwe or various communities in West Africa—have faced skepticism and rejection of their claims.

RACISM IN THE HOLY LAND

Even the Ethiopian [Black] Jews living in Israel today (perhaps the

---

8 Ian S. Lustick, *Unsettled States, Disputed Lands: Britain and Ireland, France and Algeria, Israel and the West Bank-Gaza* (Ithaca: Cornell University Press, 1993), 34.

9 Tudor Parfitt, *Operation Moses: The Story of the Exodus of the Falasha Jews from Ethiopia* (London: Weidenfeld & Nicolson, 1985), 87.

10 Tudor Parfitt, *Black Jews in Africa and the Americas* (Cambridge, MA: Harvard University Press, 2013), 121-122.

children of those who were rescued in Operations Moses and Solomon) suffer from racism and over-policing. This treatment stands in stark contrast to the biblical vision of Israel as a just and compassionate society.

Etta Prince Gibson, in her August 3, 2020 Haaretz article, "Racism Is Everywhere in Israel, Even at anti-Netanyahu Protests, Ethiopian Israeli Activist Says," shares an interview with activist Shula Mola, founder of the Association of Ethiopian Jews. Mola reveals:

> "I've given up on the illusion that the police, or the government, will ever do anything to fight racism. They haven't done anything to change the situation. The report showed that the police open files against Ethiopians at a rate five times greater than their proportion in the country," Mola says.
>
> "There's still over-policing in Ethiopian neighborhoods. Crime by white teenagers, like rowdiness or drugs, is normalized for whites and criminalized for Ethiopians, so they over-police our neighborhoods. I want all brown children to be free to walk wherever they want, and no policeman should hunt them down."

Mola says this situation could only exist in a country that supports racism in all its institutions, especially through the educational system.

> "When we Ethiopians came here, the establishment treated our parents as the desert generation that would live here and die out. As if our story began when the whites came to Ethiopia to save us, as if we hadn't lived in Ethiopia for more than 2,000 years with a wonderful culture and religion and wisdom," she says.
>
> "The whites wanted to raise us, the children, to be the hewers of wood and the carriers of water. The white establishment has spent lots of money on the Ethiopian community but never to make us equals. They sent us to boarding schools that offered us no academic horizon, where we learned vocations that would never allow us to advance in the marketplace or

fulfill our abilities, no matter how smart or talented any of us were."[11]

Sociologist Hanna Herzog observes that "the treatment of Ethiopian Jews in Israel reveals how racial hierarchies persist even within Jewish Israeli society, with European Jews maintaining privileged positions economically, politically, and culturally."[12] The structural racism experienced by Ethiopian Jews contradicts the egalitarian vision of the prophets for restored Israel.

The political Zionist movement was initially designed for Ashkenazim or White Jews and not necessarily for Black Jews or Jews living in Africa. This is evident by the racism inflicted upon people of color in Israel today. It's similar to the founding of America; its Constitution and laws were never meant for descendants of the Transatlantic Slave trade.

In a May 11, 2021 Pew Research Center survey, 92% of Jews of European descent [Ashkenazim] living in the United States identify as White.[13] Ashkenazim in America are blood relatives of those who control the Jewish State and take advantage of White American privileges.

THE FATHER OF ASHKENAZI JEWISH SETTLEMENT

Etan Bloom shares that Arthur Ruppin was the central figure in the Zionist colonization project in Palestine-Land of Israel, in the decades preceding the establishment of the state of Israel. Ruppin's immense contribution gave him the title of 'Father of Jewish settlement in Palestine' in Zionist historiography.[14]

---

11 Etta Prince Gibson, "Racism Is Everywhere in Israel, Even at anti-Netanyahu Protests, Ethiopian Israeli Activist Says," *Haaretz,* August 3, 2020, https://www.haaretz.com/israel-news/.premium-racism-is-everywhere-in-israel-even-at-anti-netanyahu-protests-activist-says-1.9043907.

12 Hanna Herzog, *Gendering Politics: Women in Israel* (Ann Arbor: University of Michigan Press, 1999), 87.

13 Pew Research Center, "Jewish Americans in 2020," May 11, 2021, https://www.pewforum.org/2021/05/11/jewish-americans-in-2020/.

14 Etan Bloom, *Arthur Ruppin and the Production of Pre-Israeli Culture* (Leiden: Brill Academic Publishers, 2011), 3.

Opinion editor of the Jerusalem Post, Seth J. Frantzman, in his Forward article entitled, "Israel's Uncomfortable History of Racist Engineering," lays out what Etan Bloom reveals about Ruppin and his approach to Jewish settlement:

> "A little-noticed 2011 book by academic Etan Bloom revealed that the father of Israeli sociology and a leading Zionist of the British Mandate named Arthur Ruppin was a believer in eugenics. In 1919 he argued that the Jewish race should be 'purified' and that it was 'desirable that only the racially pure come to the land.' As head of the Palestine Office of the Zionist Executive (later the Jewish Agency for Israel), he put his purity schemes into practice, arguing that Ethiopian Jews should not be permitted to immigrate because 'they have no blood connection' and arguing that Yemenite Jews should be brought only for menial labor."[15]

Ruppin and his fellow travelers were able to influence the Zionist movement, tragically in retrospect, to view non-Europeans as a different caste and to back up their arguments with outdated theories of eugenists. For instance, Chaim Sheba, who became director general of the Health Ministry in 1950, argued, according to a 2005 report, that "a high concentration of those ill in body and soul would jeopardize the future of Jewish community in Israel. To support his argument, he used examples from genetic theories which purported to show national gene pools weakened through a lack of genetic vigilance."[16] Sheba was influential in temporarily preventing Cochin Jews from immigrating.

Frantzman adds:

> "Since the 1950s, this legacy of ethnocentrism has haunted Israel. When the philosopher Hannah Arendt visited Israel in 1961, she described her fear of Jews who 'looked Arab but spoke Hebrew,' calling them 'an Oriental mob.' In 1981, singer Dudu Topaz castigated non-Ashkenazi Jewish voters

15 Seth J. Frantzman, “Israel’s Uncomfortable History of Racist Engineering,” *Forward,* April 29, 2013, https://forward.com/opinion/176043/israels-uncomfortable-history-of-racist-engineering/.

16 Ibid.

> as *'chachachim,'* a derogatory term. In 1983, Shulamit Aloni lambasted Sephardic Shas supporters as 'barbarous tribal forces.' Shmuel Schnitzer, a journalist, described in 1995 Ethiopian Jews as 'thousands of apostates bearing disease.' Noted author Amos Elon pondered in 1953 what effect Moroccan Jews' 'uncontrolled fertility would have on the Jewish people's genetic robustness,' and in a 2004 interview, he was still claiming that 'political primitiveness' came from immigrants to Israel."[17]

This narrative of what Ehud Barak called a "villa in the jungle" has cast an immense shadow over the ability to confront racism in Israel.

In an earlier Haaretz article, Tom Segev points out that Ruppin's belief that the realization of Zionism demanded "racial purity" is less known among the Jews and that his views were inspired by the works of anti-Semitic thinkers, including some of the original Nazi ideologists.[18] Segev explains that after the Holocaust, Israeli historiography tended to play down this embarrassing information as much as possible—or even ignore it totally.[19] Segev also cites:

> "Bloom discovered that Ruppin had a 'definitive influence' on the German view of the Jews as a race. For example, Ruppin's own research, some of it carried out at the Hebrew University, offered an explanation for Jews' supposed avarice: He posited that the Jews who originally lived in the Land of Israel before the destruction of the First Temple, and engaged in agriculture, actually belonged to non-Semitic tribes. At a certain stage, they began mixing with Semitic tribes, something that compromised their racial purity and weakened them. As the Semitic element began to become dominant, it prompted the Jews to leave agriculture and to develop commercial instincts, a heightened lust for money, and uncontrollable greed."[20]

---

17 Ibid.

18 Tom Segev, "The Makings of History / Punching a Hole in the Narrative," *Haaretz,* March 18, 2010, https://www.haaretz.com/1.5052916.

19 Ibid.

20 Ibid.

These articles reveal the hidden history behind establishing the Jewish state of Israel. Ruppin, the father of Zionist colonization, customized a settlement project where he just wanted Ashkenazi Jews to make up the land of Israel as one race of people, excluding all other Jews, i.e., Mizrahi, Sephardic, Ethiopian, Arabian-born, Oriental, Cochin, etc.

In the 1970s, Jewish immigrants from North Africa and Middle Eastern countries founded the Black Panthers of Eretz Israel movement in reaction to the discrimination against Mizrahi Jews, which had existed since the establishment of the state.[21] So, racism and discrimination were at the inception of the formulation of the Jewish state. It has never left the land. Now, we see why it is so hard for non-Ashkenazim to gain citizenship in Israel. Many non-Ashkenazi Israelis have left Israel because of the discrimination and inequities in Israel. Can you imagine the pushback that Jews from Africa or Black Jews from other countries receive for claiming Jewish ancestry and desiring to practice Aliyah and return to Israel? Now can you see why African Americans are discredited for claiming Hebrew heritage no matter how much significant evidence they have to validate their claim? The sick condition of racism always manipulated narratives. The world has been gaslighted by Zionist social engineering. Anytime someone who doesn't look White says that they are a Jew, the world makes them feel as though they are confused and borderline insane for even thinking that way simply because of the narrative that was painted by Ruppin and Jewish historiographers who fell for his racist tactics attempting to purify Israel with only Ashkenazim, not doing a thorough and honest research of history. Instead of having a deep-dive conversation with those who have researched Israel's history and can prove a Black existence, Zionism screams "Anti-Semitism" and has half the world screaming with them! The Holy Bible itself proves that Israel was an ethnic group with much melanin. And as we see, history favors the blackness of Israel and casts a shadow over Ashkenazi's true connection with ancient Israel.

21 Sami Shalom Chetrit, *Intra-Jewish Conflict in Israel: White Jews, Black Jews* (London: Routledge, 2010), 74.

Jewish historian and author of The Invention of the Jewish People, Shlomo Sand, quotes, "How can we return to Israel when we (the Ashkenazi Jew) were never there to begin with?"[22]

ASHKENAZI ECONOMIC HISTORY AND INFLUENCE

Zionism was birthed from Ashkenazi political and economic heads. Their political wit and economic prowess landed them the Jewish State.

The world's biggest and most heinous crime against humanity is undoubtedly the Transatlantic Slave Trade. Perhaps, second to that is the Jewish Holocaust. In January of 2000, while in Jerusalem, I had the opportunity to visit the Yad Vashem Holocaust Museum and learned a lot about the horrific experience that the Jews suffered. This genocide led to a death toll of an estimated six million Jews. I always wondered what would lead a tyrant to plot such a ruthless agenda. Why did the German Führer, Adolf Hitler, and his Nazi cohorts commence the Final Solution, an all-out systematic campaign to annihilate the Jews?

One of the biggest reasons was because of Germany's financial collapse after World War I! Hitler blames the Jews for this defeat.

First, the worldwide economic crisis of 1873 plunged Germany into a six-year depression, and Jewish bankers and financiers, who had played a significant role in amassing the investment capital needed by the new nation, bore the brunt of the blame, with many people embracing the stereotype of the Jew as a manipulator of international finance.[23] This was the initial fuel that sparked antisemitism against the Jews because of [international] financial manipulation. Hitler mimics this blame game after Germany's defeat in World War I. Robert Edwin Hertstein writes:

> "After World War I and the establishment of the Weimar Republic in 1919, anti-Semitic orators again took to the hustings. During the early 1920s, Adolf Hitler and other Nazis blamed Jewish bankers and industrialists for Germany's

---

22 Shlomo Sand, *The Invention of the Jewish People,* trans. Yael Lotan (London: Verso, 2009), 289.

23 Fritz Stern, *Gold and Iron: Bismarck, Bleichröder, and the Building of the German Empire* (New York: Vintage Books, 1979), 162.

humiliating defeat. In the winter of 1916-1917, Hitler later charged, 'nearly the whole production was under the control of Jewish finance. The spider was slowly beginning to suck the blood out of the people's pores.'"[24]

"When Hitler began preaching anti-Semitism, he might have taken his text from the 16th Century German theologian Martin Luther, who, in railing against the many groups that opposed his new church, declared that the Jews were 'like a plague, pestilence, pure misfortune.' Luther charged: 'They let us work in the sweat of our noses, to earn money and property for them, while they sit behind the over, lazy, let off the gas, bake pears, eat, drink, live softly and well from our wealth.'"[25]

JEWISH FINANCIAL INFLUENCE: THE ROTHSCHILD DYNASTY

Did the Jews actually have financial power?

Some people are left to believe that all Jews lived in ghettos. This may have been their start, as some Western European countries gave them grace to live among them. But they soon excelled and were very industrious. One particular Jewish family rose to great financial heights and became the marquee family for the development of the Zionist State of Israel. That family is none other than the Rothschilds. It is hard to write about the Rothschilds because controversy always seems to follow. There is a great debate about whether some things about the Rothschilds are factual. My only point in writing about them in this book is highlighting Jewish economic power. No one can doubt the economic wealth that the Rothschilds amassed. Along with great wealth comes great power and influence.

---

24 Robert Edwin Hertstein, "The Enigma of German Antisemitism," in *The Legacy of Nazi Occupation: Patriotic Memory and National Recovery in Western Europe, 1945-1965,* ed. Pieter Lagrou (Cambridge: Cambridge University Press, 2000), 57.

25 Martin Luther, *On the Jews and Their Lies (1543),* trans. Martin H. Bertram, in Luther's Works, vol. 47 (Philadelphia: Fortress Press, 1971), 137.

Encyclopedia Britannica states, "The Rothschilds family, the most famous of all European banking dynasties, which for some 200 years exerted great influence on the economic and, indirectly, the political history of Europe."[26]

The Rothschilds' story begins in 1743 with Mayer Bauer, a Bavaria, Germany-born Jew. That same year, his father, Moses Amschel Bauer, placed a red hexagram sign above their doorway. This hexagram later became the insignia of the Jewish nation. It somehow amalgamated into being the Star of David and eventually placed onto the nation of Israel's flag instead of the menorah. I tried to find the Star of David in the Bible but to no avail. In 1760, just seventeen years later, Mayer Bauer changed their family name to "Rothschild." The German name Rothschild means "Red Sign." Let me give you a chronological timeline of events that allowed the Rothschilds and the Zionist movement to come into power and ultimately gain control over the land now known as Israel.

Mayer (Amschel Bauer) Rothschild became an apprentice in finance under Jacob Wolf Oppenheimer at Simon Wolf Oppenheimer's banking firm in Hannover. Mayer Rothschild received vast knowledge of the banking system and first-class training in foreign trade and currency exchange. Upon completion of his apprenticeship, Mayer returned home to Frankfurt, Germany, and worked with his brothers' business.

Not long after his return, the Rothschild brothers' family business grew. Mayer specialized in rare coins, which won him the praise of Prince Wilhelm of Hesse, who awarded Mayer with the title of 'Court Factor.' From this, Mayer became involved in prominent financial dealings with other princes and upper statesmen. When the French Revolution took place, Mayer Rothschild was placed in charge of handling payments to Great Britain as they sought to hire mercenaries.

In 1770, Mayer Bauer Rothschild married Guttle Schnapper, the daughter of Wolf Salomon Schnapper. They had five sons and five daughters. All five of his sons became heirs of his business. All of

26 "Rothschild Family," *Encyclopedia Britannica,* accessed March 25, 2025, https://www.britannica.com/topic/Rothschild-family.

his daughters married Jews who occupied positions of influence, importance, and power. He instructed each of his sons to replicate what he did in Frankfurt across five major European cities.[27] The cities they entered were financial centers and hubs of the world's economy during the colonial world.

By the early 1800s, the Rothschilds, who were Ashkenazi Jews, had a strong financial footing across Europe. Even when Napoleon invaded Hesse, although the princely states were stripped of their power, Mayer Rothschild was given permission to continue his banking business and invested a great deal in London. The Rothschilds eventually established their banking system in London, Naples, France, Austria, and Poland. Their banking business became so influential in Europe that they could control the ebbs and flow of wars and politics throughout Europe. Some people, however, would say this is debatable or even a conspiracy. It should be considered since our history books cannot be trusted. It is safe to say that the Rothschilds played a significant role in the strategic maneuvering of many European Jews gaining footing into the high circles of European power structures.

The Encyclopedia Britannica admits, "The Rothschilds were much honored. Mayer's five sons were made barons of the Austrian Empire, a Rothschild was the first Jew to enter the British Parliament, and another was the first to be elevated to the British peerage."[28]

Economic historian Niall Ferguson, in his authoritative work on the Rothschild banking dynasty, notes that "by the middle of the nineteenth century, the Rothschilds had developed from a successful banking enterprise into the most influential financial and political power in Europe, with operations spanning London, Paris, Vienna, Frankfurt, and Naples."[29] Their financial reach and political influence were unprecedented for a Jewish family, especially given the widespread antisemitism of the era.

---

27 Niall Ferguson, *The House of Rothschild: Money's Prophets, 1798-1848* (New York: Viking, 1998), 54-55.

28 "Rothschild Family," *Encyclopedia Britannica.*

29 Niall Ferguson, *The World's Banker: The History of the House of Rothschild* (London: Weidenfeld & Nicolson, 1998), 173.

THE ROTHSCHILDS AND AMERICAN BANKING

The Rothschild-owned banking system reached a new height as it crossed the Atlantic [Ocean] into the New World. By 1791, it had extended its reach to America and set up the First Bank of the United States with a 20-year charter.[30]

When the First Bank of the United States' charter expired in 1811, Congress refused to renew it. Thomas Jefferson and James Madison were opposed to it.

Nathan Mayer Rothschild, son of Mayer Amschel Rothschild, is claimed by some historians to have warned: "...that the United States would find itself involved in a most disastrous war if the bank's charter were not renewed." Coincidently, within five months of the closing of the [First] Bank of the United States, the British declared war, allegedly financed by loans from the Rothschilds, who at this time were already prominent bankers in Europe. The War of 1812 resulted in the first significant issue of treasury notes from the United States of America. These notes differed from bank notes because they were not exchanged for an interest-bearing government bond.[31]

Due to the costs of war, many banks had over-issued their currency from making loans to the government... Soon the entire U.S. banking system was in chaos... The banking system would ultimately be required to honor their obligations. This would result in widespread bankruptcies, as loans must be called in to cover depositor withdrawals. The most politically viable option to prevent this was establishing a central bank to function as the lender of last resort.[32]

The Second Bank of the United States was chartered in 1816 under the administration of U.S. President James Madison. It was founded with a mandate like that of the previous [First] Bank of the United

---

30 G. Edward Griffin, *The Creature from Jekyll Island: A Second Look at the Federal Reserve* (Westlake Village, CA: American Media, 2010), 174.

31 [31] Ibid., 176.

32 Murray N. Rothbard, *A History of Money and Banking in the United States: The Colonial Era to World War II* (Auburn, AL: Ludwig von Mises Institute, 2002), 83.

States, whose charter had expired five years prior.[33] Needless to say, the War of 1812 crippled the young American nation and drew it back into the central banking system that was highly influenced and operated by the Rothschilds, who controlled lending and interest rates. I realize that there were many reasons for the War of 1812, but I cannot negate the fact that the "bank battle" played a big part in the decision to commence intercontinental warfare.

Financial historian Edward S. Kaplan observes that "the establishment of the Second Bank of the United States represented a significant victory for proponents of centralized banking, many of whom had connections to European financial interests including the Rothschilds."[34] This international financial influence would remain a contentious issue in American politics for decades to come.

Other presidents opposed the central banking system. President Andrew Jackson was very adversarial against the central bank. He was said to have "killed" the Second Bank of the United States in 1836. When running his presidential campaign in 1832, Jackson used the slogan "Jackson and No Bank." He said to the bankers, "You are a den of vipers. I intend to expose you, and by the eternal God, I will route you out."[35] President Andrew Jackson "killed" the Second Bank of the United States in 1836 after the debt was paid off.

Many presidents, from Andrew Jackson to Abraham Lincoln to Grover Cleveland, refused to sign a new charter for the foreign central banking system. In fact, Lincoln refused to sign a new central banking charter and ordered the printing of the "Greenbacks" during the Civil War, refusing to borrow money from foreign banks.

---

33 Ralph C. H. Catterall, *The Second Bank of the United States* (Chicago: University of Chicago Press, 1903), 21-22.

34 Edward S. Kaplan, *The Bank of the United States and the American Economy* (Westport, CT: Greenwood Press, 1999), 67.

35 Andrew Jackson, quoted in H.W. Brands, *Andrew Jackson: His Life and Times* (New York: Doubleday, 2005), 498.

PRESIDENT WOODROW WILSON: A HERO AND A SAVIOR TO THE JEWS

It was not until Woodrow Wilson's presidency in 1912 that a third central bank existed in America. That banking system is still the banking system we are under today: the Federal Reserve. Most people are unaware that the Federal Reserve is a privately-owned company. Why is this important? Baron Nathan Mayer Rothschild stated that whoever controls the money supply controls the nation!

The presidents before Woodrow Wilson knew of this concept; it was the very reason they rejected any foreign banking system. For the Rothschilds and other banking partners to get their central bank into the American economy again, they had to find a "puppet on the throne."

History shows that Woodrow Wilson became the puppet that sat on the American presidential throne. His extramarital affair with Mary Peck (Hulbert) made him susceptible to blackmail or attacks from lawyers, elected officials, bankers, etc., who dared to move America forward with their manipulative agenda.[36]

Congressman Charles August Lindbergh of Minnesota declared, "This [Federal Reserve] Act establishes the most gigantic trust on Earth. When the President signs this bill, the invisible government by the Monetary Power will be legalized, and the people may not know it immediately, but the day of reckoning will be only a few years removed. The worst legislative crime of the ages is perpetrated by this banking bill."[37]

The basic plan for the Federal Reserve System was drafted at a secret meeting held in November of 1910 at the private resort of J. P. Morgan on Jekyll's Island off the coast of Georgia. Those who attended represented the great financial institutions of Wall Street and, indirectly, Europe as well.[38] The six men who attended the secret meeting on Jekyll Island, where the Federal Reserve System was conceived, represented an estimated one-fourth of the world's total wealth. They were:

---

36 A. Scott Berg, *Wilson* (New York: G.P. Putnam's Sons, 2013), 318-319.

37 Charles A. Lindbergh, quoted in Griffin, *The Creature from Jekyll Island,* 23.

38 Griffin, *The Creature from Jekyll Island,* 4-5.

1. Nelson W. Aldrich, Republican "whip" in the Senate, Chairman of the National Monetary Commission, father-in-law to John D. Rockefeller, Jr.
2. Henry P. Davison, Sr. Partner of J. P. Morgan Company
3. A. Piatt Andrew, Assistant Secretary of the Treasury
4. Frank A. Vanderlip, President of the National City Bank of New York, representing William Rockefeller
5. Benjamin Strong, head of J. P. Morgan's Bankers Trust Company, later became head of the System
6. Paul M. Warburg, a partner in Kuhn, Loeb & Company, representing the Rothschilds and Warburgs in Europe.[39]

As you can see from this list, there was Jewish representation at that Jekyll Island meeting to draft the banking system that the United States of America uses to this very day!

Economic historian Murray N. Rothbard confirms that "the creation of the Federal Reserve System represented a triumph for banking interests with strong international connections, including significant participation from representatives of European financial houses."[40] This international influence on America's central banking system would prove crucial in shaping both domestic and foreign policy in the decades to come.

The Jews hail Woodrow Wilson as a hero to the Jewish people. Brandeis University Professor Jonathan D. Sarna and Joseph H. & Belle R. Braun, Professor of American Jewish history at Brandeis University and the author of American Judaism: A History, reveals the following about the Jews' high praise of President Woodrow Wilson in a Jewish Virtual Library synopsis:

"Jews long admired Woodrow Wilson for his intellect and political liberalism, as well as for the warm appreciation he displayed toward Jews at a time when so many other Americans were overtly anti-Semitic... In large black letters, the [political] ad (in Boston's Jewish Advocate) listed

39 Ibid., 5

40 Murray N. Rothbard, *The Case Against the Fed* (Auburn, AL: Ludwig von Mises Institute, 1994), 114.

famous Jews who supported Wilson, including financier Jacob H. Schiff, philanthropist Nathan Straus, and ambassador Henry Morgenthau. It urged all 'thinking Jews' to join them.

As president, Wilson, frequently consulted with attorney Louis Brandeis, and in 1916, courageously nominated him as the first Jew ever to serve on the U.S. Supreme Court. He continued to back him in the face of widespread opposition from prominent businessmen and lawyers and succeeded in pushing the nomination through the Senate. The appointment marked a turning point in American Jewish history.

Wilson also befriended a slew of other notable Jews, including Bernard Baruch, Samuel Untermeyer and Rabbi Stephen Wise.

Wilson also pledged support for the aims of the Zionist movement. In 1917, he endorsed the Balfour Declaration that viewed with favor 'the establishment in Palestine of a national home for the Jewish people.' As the son of a Presbyterian minister, he intimated, he considered it 'a privilege to restore the Holy Land to its rightful owners.'

Wilson's championing of both Louis Brandeis and Zionism elevated him to the status of a hero in Jewish history books. Alfred J. Kolatch and David G. Dalin, for example, conclude in their book, The Presidents of the United States and the Jews, published in 2000, that 'perhaps more than any other president, Woodrow Wilson had the utmost respect and admiration for the Jewish people.' They recount that Jews of his day considered him 'a hero and a savior, a man of principle and ethical uprightness.' The twenty-eighth president's legacy, they predicted, 'will loom large in the annals of Jewish history.'"[41]

Wilson's Jewish friends were financiers, philanthropists, attorneys, ambassadors, and even made one a U.S. Supreme Court judge! This reveals Jews have power and influence. Perhaps this is why some people assume that prominent Jewish lawyer Samuel Untermyer, who was well-known in the Democratic Party and advised the government on interpreting and enforcing income tax law and was involved in anti-

41 Jonathan D. Sarna, quoted in "Woodrow Wilson," *Jewish Virtual Library,* accessed March 29, 2025, https://www.jewishvirtuallibrary.org/woodrow-wilson-administration.

trust legislation, and Wilson's Jewish Supreme Court appointee, Louis Brandeis, were very instrumental in Wilson's decision for the United States to join into World War 1 and endorse the Balfour Declaration.

If the Jews were so weak and frowned upon, why would the Rothschilds be represented in the Federal Reserve banking system that runs America today? The Jews have power. With Great Britain and the United States of America on their side, they [Ashkenazi Zionists] had a great chance of their master plan of formulating a Jewish State to come to fruition.

Political scientist Peter Grose notes that "Wilson's support for the Balfour Declaration represented a crucial diplomatic victory for the Zionist movement, lending American legitimacy to the vision of a Jewish homeland in Palestine at a pivotal moment in world history."[42] This American support would prove essential to the eventual establishment of the State of Israel in 1948.

Before I continue, let me pause here to reiterate that I totally disagree with Adolf Hitler and Nazis Final Solution and the murdering and torture of countless Jews. Again, it was diabolical, inhumane, and humanly unjustifiable. Nor will I discount the fact that Blacks living in Germany were also killed during this time because of Hitler's pure race-white supremacy views.

However, we cannot overlook the fact that Jewish Zionism was on the rise, gained substantial influence, and today leveraged its power, especially with the United States. Even world-renowned Christian evangelist Billy Graham had something to say about Jewish control of the news media.

In President Richard M. Nixon's Oval Office, the Rev. Billy Graham did not mince words in describing his feelings about Jewish people and the news media: "This stranglehold has got to be broken or this country's going down the drain."[43]

---

42 Peter Grose, *Israel in the Mind of America* (New York: Schocken Books, 1983), 27.

43 Billy Graham, quoted in James Warren, "Billy Graham's Troubling, Nasty Nixon Moment," *U.S. News & World Report*, February 28, 2018, https://www.usnews.com/opinion/thomas-jefferson-street/articles/2018-02-28/billy-grahams-troubling-legacy-with-jews-and-richard-nixons-anti-semitism.

In his February 28, 2018, U.S. News article, "Billy Graham's Troubling, Nasty Nixon Moment," James Warren, Contributing Editor for Opinion, writes the following about the Graham/Nixon Oval Office conversation about the Jews:

"Graham referenced friends of his own in the press who were Jewish and how they 'swarm around me and are friendly to me.' But, he added, 'They don't know how I really feel about what they're doing to this country.'

It got worse. Nixon brought up a topic of which he said, 'We can't talk about it publicly': the alleged influence of Jews in Hollywood and the press. He references an executive with the 1968-1973 NBC hit show, 'Rowan and Martin's Laugh-in,' as once informing him that 11 of its 12 writers were Jewish. (Nixon surfaced on an episode during the 1968 presidential campaign as part of his attempt at reinvention, famously uttering, 'Sock-it-to-me!' a well-known catchphrase of actress Judy Carne, a show regular.)

'That right?' said Graham. Nixon seamlessly continued by asserting that Life magazine, Newsweek, The New York Times, and the Los Angeles Times were among those 'totally dominated by the Jews.' And, he said, the famous broadcast network anchors Howard K. Smith, David Brinkley, and Walter Cronkite were 'front men who may not be of that persuasion,' but that their writers were '95 percent Jewish.'"[44]

Three decades later, Evangelist Billy Graham apologized for his seemingly anti-Semitic remarks.

JEWISH PARTICIPATION IN AMERICAN ECONOMIC SYSTEMS

Another fact in history validating the wealth of some Jews is the fact that some Jews participated in the slave trade, no matter how minuscule compared to the larger European body of slaveowners.

In the online article by My Jewish Learning entitled, "Where the False Claim That Jews Controlled the Slave Trade Comes From," the question is asked, "Did Jews really own slaves?" The answer:

44 Ibid.

> "Yes. Jacob Rader Marcus, a historian and Reform rabbi, wrote in his four-volume history of American Jews that over 75 percent of Jewish families in Charleston, South Carolina; Richmond, Virginia; and Savannah, Georgia, owned slaves, and nearly 40 percent of Jewish households across the country did. The Jewish population in these cities was quite small, however, so the total number of slaves they owned represented just a small fraction of the total slave population; Eli Faber, a historian at New York City's John Jay College, reported that in 1790, Charleston's Jews owned a total of 93 slaves, and that 'perhaps six Jewish families' lived in Savannah in 1771.
>
> A number of wealthy Jews were also involved in the slave trade in the Americas, some as shipowners who imported slaves and others as agents who resold them. In the United States, Isaac Da Costa of Charleston, David Franks of Philadelphia, and Aaron Lopez of Newport, Rhode Island, are among the early American Jews who were prominent in the importation and sale of African slaves. In addition, some Jews were involved in the trade in various European Caribbean colonies. Alexandre Lindo, a French-born Jew who became a wealthy merchant in Jamaica in the late 18th century, was a major seller of slaves on the island."[45]

From this article alone, we see throughout the Americas, from as far north as Rhode Island down to the southern state of Georgia to the Caribbean, wealthy Jews are found involved in the slave trade as slave owners, slave ship owners, or those reselling slaves.

Historian Seymour Drescher notes that "Jewish participation in the Atlantic slave trade, while numerically small compared to other groups, reflected the broader integration of Jews into the commercial and financial systems of Europe and the Americas."[46] This economic activity,

---

45 "Where the False Claim That Jews Controlled the Slave Trade Comes From," *My Jewish Learning,* accessed March 29, 2025, https://www.myjewishlearning.com/article/jews-and-the-african-slave-trade/.

46 Seymour Drescher, "Jews and the Slave Trade," in *Encyclopedia of the Middle Passage*, ed. Toyin Falola and Amanda Warnock (Westport, CT:

along with other business ventures, helped establish a foundation for Jewish economic influence in Western societies.

Let me reassure you that none of this should have led to the horrible atrocity of the Jewish Holocaust. Again, the purpose is to show that the Nazi panic button and all-out assault stemmed from their phobia of Jewish wealth and political influence, which history does not deny.

ZIONISM AS PART OF GENTILE RULE

I must include the political power and wealth of Jewish Zionism as part of the apostolic prophecy of Gentile rule. This is demonstrated by their ability to obtain and occupy Palestine in 1948 as their homeland by influencing and employing other Gentiles in Europe and America to assist them.

The establishment of the State of Israel in 1948 represents a fascinating case study in the dynamics of Gentile power. As we have seen in previous chapters, the Ashkenazi Jews who spearheaded the Zionist movement were themselves Gentiles—descendants of Japheth rather than Shem, converts to Judaism rather than biological descendants of Abraham, Isaac, and Jacob. Their success in establishing a Jewish state depended entirely on the support of other Gentile powers, particularly Great Britain and the United States.

Historian Mark Mazower observes that "the establishment of Israel represents not the end of European colonialism in the Middle East but its culmination, with a European-derived population establishing political dominance over an indigenous population with the backing of Western powers."[47] This perspective helps us understand how the creation of Israel fits into the broader pattern of Gentile dominance predicted in biblical prophecy.

CONCLUSION: THE FULFILLMENT OF PROPHECY?

As we have seen throughout this chapter, the creation of the Jewish

---

Greenwood Press, 2007), 234-236.

47 Mark Mazower, *Dark Continent: Europe's Twentieth Century* (New York: Vintage Books, 2000), 194.

state in Palestine was not the miraculous return of ancient Israel to their homeland but rather the culmination of a calculated political project by Ashkenazi Jewish elites with the support of Western powers. The fact that this state practices systematic discrimination against darker-skinned Jews from Africa and the Middle East further undermines its claim to represent the fulfillment of biblical prophecy.

If we take seriously the biblical description of ancient Israelites as a people with significant melanin who were dispersed throughout the world—including into Africa and later to the Americas through the slave trade—then we must question whether the establishment of modern Israel truly represents the prophesied restoration of God's chosen people to their land.

The Apostle Paul's prophecy in Romans 11:25-27, which we examined in Chapter 3, speaks of Israel's blindness continuing "until the fullness of the Gentiles be come in" and then "all Israel shall be saved." As we continue to explore the connections between African Americans and ancient Israel in subsequent chapters, we will see how this prophecy may be finding its fulfillment not in the political establishment of the modern state of Israel but in the awakening of scattered Israel to their true identity after centuries of oppression under Gentile rule.

Foreign Office,

November 2nd, 1917.

Dear Lord Rothschild,

I have much pleasure in conveying to you, on behalf of His Majesty's Government, the following declaration of sympathy with Jewish Zionist aspirations which has been submitted to, and approved by, the Cabinet

"His Majesty's Government view with favour the establishment in Palestine of a national home for the Jewish people, and will use their best endeavours to facilitate the achievement of this object, it being clearly understood that nothing shall be done which may prejudice the civil and religious rights of existing non-Jewish communities in Palestine, or the rights and political status enjoyed by Jews in any other country"

I should be grateful if you would bring this declaration to the knowledge of the Zionist Federation.

Yours

Arthur James Balfour

Chapter 10

How Zionists Gained Control of Palestine

THE BALFOUR DECLARATION: A PIVOTAL MOMENT

Having examined the origins of Ashkenazi Jews and their rise to economic and political influence in the previous chapters, we now turn to a critical development in the Zionist movement's quest to establish a Jewish state in Palestine: the Balfour Declaration. This document, more than any other, laid the diplomatic foundation for what would eventually become the State of Israel.

After Theodor Herzl died in 1904, the Zionist movement continued to gain momentum. Chaim Weizmann and Nahum Sokolow played important roles in its ongoing development and were instrumental in securing the Balfour Declaration. Historian Leonard Stein notes that "Weizmann's scientific contributions to the British war effort earned him access to the highest levels of the British government, which he skillfully used to advance the Zionist cause."[1]

On November 2, 1917, British Foreign Secretary Arthur James Balfour wrote a pivotal letter to Britain's most illustrious Jewish citizen, Baron Lionel Walter Rothschild, expressing the British government's support for a Jewish homeland in Palestine. This infamous letter would eventually become known as the Balfour Declaration. Historian Jonathan Schneer describes it as "one of the most important and controversial documents in modern Middle Eastern history, the foundation stone of the state of Israel, and the source of Palestinian grievance for a century."[2]

1 Leonard Stein, *The Balfour Declaration* (London: Valentine Mitchell, 1961), 163.
2 Jonathan Schneer, *The Balfour Declaration: The Origins of the Arab-Israeli Conflict* (New York: Random House, 2010), 5.

Britain's support for the Zionist movement stemmed from its strategic concerns regarding the direction of the First World War. Aside from a genuine belief in the righteousness of Zionism, held by Prime Minister David Lloyd George, among others, Britain's leaders hoped that a statement supporting Zionism would help gain Jewish support for the Allies. As historian Tom Segev explains, "The British believed that the Jews controlled immense power—especially in the United States but also in Bolshevik Russia—and that it was therefore important to receive their support."[3]

It is noteworthy that Balfour sent his letter/declaration to Lord Rothschild, a prominent Zionist and friend of Chaim Weizmann, thus confirming the connections between Zionism and European Jewish banking families that we examined in Chapter 9. In the letter, Balfour stated, "His Majesty's Government view with favor the establishment in Palestine of a national home for the Jewish people."[4]

The influence of the Balfour Declaration on the course of post-war events was immediate. According to the "mandate" system created by the Versailles Treaty of 1919, Britain was entrusted with the administration of Palestine, with the understanding that it would work on behalf of both its Jewish and Arab inhabitants. This arrangement, as historian James L. Gelvin notes, "created a political framework that allowed for increased Jewish immigration to Palestine and the acquisition of land for Jewish settlements, while supposedly protecting the rights of the indigenous Arab population."[5]

---

3 Tom Segev, *One Palestine, Complete: Jews and Arabs Under the British Mandate, trans. Haim Watzman* (New York: Metropolitan Books, 2000), 41.
4 Arthur James Balfour to Lord Rothschild, November 2, 1917, in *Documents on British Foreign Policy, 1919-1939,* ed. E.L. Woodward and Rohan Butler (London: HMSO, 1952), 373.
5 James L. Gelvin, *The Modern Middle East: A History* (New York: Oxford University Press, 2011), 247.

THE TEXT AND IMPLICATIONS OF BALFOUR'S LETTER

The actual Balfour letter reads:

Foreign Office

November 2nd, 1917

Dear **Lord Rothschild**,

I have much pleasure in conveying to you, on behalf of His Majesty's Government, the following declaration of sympathy with Jewish Zionist aspirations which has been submitted to, and approved by, the Cabinet.

His Majesty's Government view with favour the establishment in Palestine of a national home for the Jewish people, and will use their best endeavours to facilitate the achievement of this object, it being clearly understood that nothing shall be done which may prejudice the civil and religious rights of existing non-Jewish communities in Palestine, or the rights and political status enjoyed by Jews in any other country.

I should be grateful if you would bring this declaration to the knowledge of the Zionist Federation.

Yours sincerely,

Arthur James Balfour[6]

Jennifer Rosenberg, in her article "The History of the Balfour Declaration," writes:

> "The Balfour Declaration was a November 2, 1917 letter from British Foreign Secretary Arthur James Balfour to Lord Rothschild that made public the British support of a Jewish homeland in Palestine. The Balfour Declaration led the League of Nations (now called the United Nations) to entrust the United Kingdom with the Palestine Mandate in 1922.
>
> The Balfour Declaration was a product of years of careful negotiation. After centuries of living in a diaspora, the 1894 Dreyfus Affair in France shocked Jews into realizing they

6 Balfour to Rothschild, November 2, 1917.

would not be safe from arbitrary antisemitism unless they had their own country.

In response, Jews created the new concept of political Zionism in which it was believed that through active political maneuvering, a Jewish homeland could be created. Zionism was becoming a popular concept by the time World War I began."[7]

Historian Rashid Khalidi observes that "the Declaration represented a classic example of European imperial powers deciding the fate of non-European territories without consulting the indigenous population."[8] This approach was consistent with the broader pattern of Gentile dominance that we have traced throughout this book.

BRITISH IMPERIAL INTERESTS IN PALESTINE

I fathom the reason Great Britain took an interest in the Zionist movement and the Palestinian territory. Zena Tahhan, an online journalist for Al Jazeera, points out several reasons for Great Britain's issuance of the Balfour Declaration in her "More Than a Century on: The Balfour Declaration Explained." She writes:

"While some argue that many in the British government at the time were Zionists themselves, others say the declaration was issued out of anti-Semitic reasoning, that giving Palestine to the Jews would be a solution to the 'Jewish problem.'

In mainstream academia, however, there are a set of reasons over which there is a general consensus:

- Control over Palestine was a strategic imperial interest to keep Egypt and the Suez Canal within Britain's sphere of influence.
- Britain had to side with the Zionists to rally support among Jews in the United States and Russia, hoping they could

7 Jennifer Rosenberg, "The History of the Balfour Declaration," ThoughtCo, accessed April 5, 2025, https://www.thoughtco.com/balfour-declaration-1778163.

8 Rashid Khalidi, *The Iron Cage: The Story of the Palestinian Struggle for Statehood* (Boston: Beacon Press, 2006), 32.

encourage their governments to stay in the war until victory.

- There was intense Zionist lobbying and strong connections between the Zionist community in Britain and the British government; some of the officials in the government were Zionists themselves.
- Jews were being persecuted in Europe, and the British government was sympathetic to their suffering."[9]

Historian Elizabeth Monroe asserts that "the Balfour Declaration was a classic example of British imperial policy—making commitments to different groups to secure British interests while maintaining plausible deniability about contradictions."[10] This approach would soon manifest in Britain's conflicting promises to Arabs and Jews.

GREAT BRITAIN'S DOUBLE DEALING

The Suez Canal was an important waterway in Egypt and a significant site in the Age of Imperialism. More specifically, European nations such as Britain and France fought over control of the Suez Canal, as it proved to be a strategic waterway for imperialistic campaigns. As such, historians consider the history of the Suez Canal to be significant to European imperialism in Africa (Scramble for Africa) and British Imperialism in India.

Palestine's location was crucial for maintaining British control over the Suez Canal, a vital route for maritime trade and military movements between Europe and the colonies of Asia and Africa. Controlling Palestine helped secure the eastern approaches to the canal. As historian Roger Owen notes, "British policy in the Middle East was driven primarily by imperial concerns, particularly maintaining communication and trade routes to India."[11]

---

9 Zena Tahhan, "More Than a Century on: The Balfour Declaration Explained," Al Jazeera, November 2, 2018, https://www.aljazeera.com/features/2018/11/2/more-than-a-century-on-the-balfour-declaration-explained.

10 Elizabeth Monroe, *Britain's Moment in the Middle East, 1914-1971* (Baltimore: Johns Hopkins University Press, 1981), 43.

11 Roger Owen, *State, Power and Politics in the Making of the Modern Middle East* (London: Routledge, 2004), 8.

During World War I, Britain made conflicting promises to different groups regarding the future of Palestine. The McMahon-Hussein Correspondence (1915-1916) promised Arab leaders support for an independent Arab state, including Palestine, in exchange for their revolt against the Ottoman Empire. Meanwhile, the Sykes-Picot Agreement (1916) secretly divided the Ottoman territories between Britain and France, with Palestine under international administration. The Balfour Declaration (1917) expressed British support for the establishment of a "national home for the Jewish people" in Palestine.

Historian Avi Shlaim characterizes these contradictory commitments as "products of wartime expediency rather than coherent imperial planning,"[12] while Edward Said more critically views them as "deliberate duplicity designed to maintain European control over the region while appearing to support self-determination."[13]

After World War I, Britain sought to maintain and expand its influence in the Middle East. The region was rich in oil, which was becoming increasingly important for the British navy and economy. Controlling Palestine also allowed Britain to counter French influence in neighboring Syria and Lebanon. Historian William Cleveland observes that "the Palestine mandate was a crucial piece in Britain's post-war Middle Eastern strategy, connecting Egypt and the Suez Canal with Iraq and its oil fields."[14]

Following the defeat of the Ottoman Empire, the League of Nations established the mandate system to administer former Ottoman territories. Britain received the mandate for Palestine in 1920, giving it official control and the responsibility to implement the Balfour Declaration while also preparing the region for eventual self-governance. This arrangement, as historian Barbara J. Smith notes, "institutionalized

---

12 Avi Shlaim, *The Politics of Partition: King Abdullah, the Zionists, and Palestine 1921-1951* (Oxford: Oxford University Press, 1990), 5.

13 Edward Said, *The Question of Palestine* (New York: Vintage Books, 1992), 16.

14 William L. Cleveland, *A History of the Modern Middle East* (Boulder: Westview Press, 2016), 163.

the colonial relationship while providing a veneer of international legitimacy."[15]

Palestine held significant religious importance for Christians, Jews, and Muslims. British leaders, influenced by religious and cultural considerations, saw the opportunity to play a role in the region's future, particularly with regard to the Zionist movement and the historical connection of Jews to the land. Lloyd George, the British Prime Minister during this period, was known for his biblical knowledge and believed that restoring the Jews to Palestine would fulfill biblical prophecy.[16]

These factors combined to make Palestine a region of great interest and importance to Great Britain during and after World War I, creating the conditions for the eventual establishment of a Jewish state.

THE ESTABLISHMENT OF ISRAEL

On May 14, 1948, David Ben-Gurion, the head of the Jewish Agency, declared the establishment of the State of Israel. This marked the official creation of a Jewish state in part of the former British Mandate of Palestine. These events, along with the Balfour Declaration, led to the establishment of Israel as a Jewish state, but Palestine itself was never officially designated as such. The declaration of Israel's independence was a unilateral action by the Jewish leadership and was followed by the first Arab-Israeli war.

Historian Benny Morris describes the moment as "the culmination of fifty years of Zionist effort and the beginning of a new chapter in Jewish history, but also the start of the Palestinian refugee problem and decades of Arab-Israeli conflict."[17] This duality—triumph for one people and catastrophe for another—has characterized the region ever since.

---

15 Barbara J. Smith, *The Roots of Separatism in Palestine: British Economic Policy, 1920-1929* (Syracuse: Syracuse University Press, 1993), 85.

16 Donald Lewis, *The Origins of Christian Zionism: Lord Shaftesbury and Evangelical Support for a Jewish Homeland* (Cambridge: Cambridge University Press, 2010), 328.

17 Benny Morris, *1948: A History of the First Arab-Israeli War* (New Haven: Yale University Press, 2008), 75.

KEY EVENTS IN THE ZIONIST ROAD TO STATEHOOD

The events that aided the Zionist movement to gain significant power were:

- The First Zionist Congress (1897): Held in Basel, Switzerland, Zionists established the World Zionist Organization (WZO), which sought to create a home for the Jewish people in Palestine secured by public law. Historian Walter Laqueur notes that "the Basel Congress transformed Zionism from a collection of disparate cultural and settlement movements into a unified political organization with clear goals and strategies."[18]
- The Balfour Declaration (1917): Negotiations with Great Britain for this declaration significantly boosted the Zionist cause and gained international support and recognition. This document, as we have seen, provided crucial diplomatic legitimacy to the Zionist project.
- The British Mandate Period (1920-1948): Under the League of Nations mandate, Britain was responsible for implementing the Balfour Declaration. During this period, Zionist organizations worked to increase Jewish immigration to Palestine and develop the infrastructure of the future Jewish state. Historian Tom Segev describes how "the Yishuv (Jewish community in Palestine) created state-like institutions—including labor organizations, health services, and military forces—well before formal statehood was achieved."[19]
- Jewish Immigration (1920s-1930s): Jewish immigration to Palestine increased, causing tension between Jews and Arabs which led to clashes and revolts. These events highlighted the growing influence and determination of the Zionist movement. The fifth Aliyah (wave of immigration) following Hitler's rise to power in Germany brought many highly educated Central European Jews to Palestine, strengthening

18 Walter Laqueur, *A History of Zionism: From the French Revolution to the Establishment of the State of Israel* (New York: Schocken Books, 2003), 104.
19 Segev, *One Palestine, Complete,* 274.

the Yishuv's economic and intellectual resources.[20]

- World War II and the Holocaust (1939-1945): These events had a profound impact on global opinion regarding the need for a Jewish state. The horrors of the genocide strengthened the resolve of Zionists and garnered international sympathy for their cause. Historian Anita Shapira argues that "the Holocaust transformed Zionism from one solution to the Jewish question to the only solution, giving moral urgency to the establishment of a Jewish state."[21]
- UN Partition Plan (1947): The United Nations proposed a plan to partition Palestine into separate Jewish and Arab states, with Jerusalem under international administration. The plan was accepted by the Jewish community but rejected by the Arab community. The plan's approval by the UN General Assembly marked a significant diplomatic victory for the Zionist movement. Political scientist Ian Lustick notes that "the UN vote represented international recognition of the Jewish claim to statehood, even as it highlighted the fundamental disagreement over Palestine's future."[22]
- Declaration of Independence (1948): David Ben-Gurion's declaration of the establishment of the State of Israel marked the culmination of the Zionist movement's efforts to create a Jewish state. This act, as historian Howard Sachar observes, "transformed a national movement into a sovereign state with all the powers and responsibilities that entailed."[23]

---

20 Anita Shapira, *Land and Power: The Zionist Resort to Force, 1881-1948* (Stanford: Stanford University Press, 1999), 174.

21 Anita Shapira, *Israel: A History* (Waltham, MA: Brandeis University Press, 2012), 94.

22 Ian Lustick, *Unsettled States, Disputed Lands: Britain and Ireland, France and Algeria, Israel and the West Bank-Gaza* (Ithaca: Cornell University Press, 1993), 57.

23 Howard M. Sachar, *A History of Israel: From the Rise of Zionism to Our Time* (New York: Alfred A. Knopf, 2007), 311.

CONCLUSION: ASHKENAZI JEWS AND BIBLICAL PROPHECY

As we close this section of the book, our inquiry has led us to historical and scientific evidence that makes it highly probable that Ashkenazi Jews are a people of European descent, and that they adopted an aspect of the faith of the Hebrews (Talmudic Judaism) and were dispersed among Western European nations by wars that made their forced migration imminent. Ashkenazi Jews, through the political Zionist movement, were able to take control of Palestine and create their own Jewish State. They are descendants of Japheth, not Shem, Abraham, Isaac, and Jacob, and the majority of Jews in America identify as White, along with other Gentiles.

The question remains, "How can the prophecy of Israel's End-time salvation (Romans 11:25) be fulfilled if Ashkenazi Jews are not God's original chosen people, i.e., ethnic Israel?" Does this make Israel nonexistent? For the prophecy to be accurate, Israel cannot be extinct. A thread of their blood must remain on the earth for this prophecy to be fulfilled.

This returns us to the central thesis of our investigation: If the Ashkenazi Jews who control modern Israel are not the biological descendants of ancient Israel, then where are God's chosen people today? As biblical scholar Walter C. Kaiser Jr. observes, "The biblical promises of restoration are consistently directed to the physical descendants of Jacob, not merely to those who adopt Jewish religious practices."[24] Therefore, if we are to understand the fulfillment of biblical prophecy correctly, we must identify those physical descendants.

The evidence we have examined thus far points to a startling possibility: that many descendants of ancient Israel may be found among populations that have experienced centuries of oppression under Gentile rule, including African Americans whose ancestors were brought to the Americas through the transatlantic slave trade. As anthropologist Joseph Holloway notes, "The cultural and genetic connections between

---

24 Walter C. Kaiser Jr., *Mission in the Old Testament: Israel as a Light to the Nations* (Grand Rapids: Baker Academic, 2012), 87.

West Africa and the ancient Near East are stronger than commonly recognized, suggesting historical migrations and population movements that align with biblical accounts of Israelite dispersion."[25]

Therefore, we will take a closer look at who God's original chosen ethnic group is and where they are today. Get your binoculars out of your backpack and get ready to discover more than 400 years of hidden heritage.

---

25 Joseph E. Holloway, ed., *Africanisms in American Culture* (Bloomington: Indiana University Press, 2005), 18.

Section 3

REDISCOVERING GOD'S CHOSEN PEOPLE

"Archaeological evidence, including statuary and frescoes from the ancient Near East, depicts early Semitic peoples with phenotypical features more consistent with African populations than with modern European Jewry. These representations suggest a people who would be considered 'Black' by contemporary racial categorizations."

Van Sertima, Ivan. *African Presence in Early Asia.* New Brunswick: Transaction Publishers, 1988.

Chapter 11

Ethnic Israel

"The ancient Hebrews, who were neighbors to the Egyptians, cannot be divorced from the African context, both culturally and ethnically."[1]

THE QUEST FOR TRUE ISRAEL

In the preceding chapter, we thoroughly analyzed the second component of the threefold eschatological prophecy concerning Israel's liberation from oppression. Our comprehensive historical examination of Ashkenazi Jewish origins provides compelling evidence suggesting their primary genetic lineage differs from that of ancient Israelites. Instead, the historical record indicates a predominantly Japhetic-Ashkenaz ancestry, with foundational settlements established in Khazaria—a medieval kingdom spanning the Caucasus region of Eastern Europe. Furthermore, we have traced how Zionism emerged as a political movement spearheaded by these Ashkenazi Jews, ultimately succeeding in establishing the modern state of Israel through strategic alliances with Western powers, particularly Great Britain and the United States. This geopolitical achievement represents a remarkable fulfillment of historical aspirations, though questions remain about its theological significance within prophetic frameworks.

This revelation presents a profound theological conundrum: If Ashkenazi Jews do not constitute God's chosen people through direct bloodline descent, who then rightfully bears this covenant identity? The contemporary conflation of ethnic Israel with Ashkenazi Jewish communities represents a significant case of mistaken historical identity.

1 John G. Jackson, *Introduction to African Civilizations* (New York: Citadel Press, 1970), 84.

The genesis of this misattribution becomes apparent when examining how Ashkenazi populations adopted the Hebrew faith through conversion, gradually assimilating its liturgical traditions, sacred language, and religious customs into their cultural framework. Thus, while they have legitimately become spiritual Israel through religious conversion and practice, this theological incorporation does not necessarily establish biological continuity with ancient Israelite lineages. This distinction between religious affiliation and genetic heritage is crucial when interpreting eschatological passages such as Romans 11:25-27—which we meticulously analyzed in Chapter 3—where the prophesied salvation specifically pertains to ethnic Israel, those connected through ancestral bloodlines rather than solely through religious observance.

Our investigation now turns toward identifying the authentic descendants of ethnic Israel in the contemporary world. These individuals may currently practice diverse faith traditions—including Islam, Christianity, various forms of Judaism, or even secular philosophies—yet they remain Israel through biological inheritance regardless of their present religious convictions. Historically, there existed an era when all bloodline Israelites worshipped Yahweh exclusively—the God of Abraham, Isaac, and Jacob. Their spiritual practice was originally designated as "The Way," a theological tradition distinct from what would later develop into rabbinic Judaism. Through meticulous examination of scriptural evidence and historical records, we shall endeavor to trace Israel's genetic lineage with the same methodological rigor previously employed to identify the Gentile nations, thereby reconstructing the complete biblical narrative of divine covenant and its modern implications.

TRACING ISRAEL'S LINEAGE

We know from Scripture (Genesis 11) that Israel comes from the lineage of Shem. Although Shem had other children, the following is the specific bloodline from Shem to ethnic Israel:

Shem begat Arphaxad. Arphaxad begat Salah. Salah begat Eber. Eber begat Peleg. Peleg begat Reu. Reu begat Serug. Serug begat Nahor. Nahor begat Terah. Terah begat Abram (Abraham). Abraham begat Isaac, and

Isaac begat Jacob (whose name was changed by Yahweh to Israel).[2]

Biblical scholar John Bright notes that "this genealogical structure represents Israel's self-understanding as a distinct people group with a traceable ancestry, connected to but distinct from other Semitic peoples of the ancient Near East."[3]

Jacob had twelve sons. These twelve sons eventually became a nation of people called Israel. They were interchangeably called Hebrews or Israelites. When they came out of Egypt, they were a nation of about 2 million people.[4] Within 40 years, an entire generation died in the wilderness, mainly because they disobeyed Yahweh, except for Joshua and Caleb. A younger generation succeeded Moses' generation and eventually conquered the land of Canaan—the Promised Land—dividing it among the tribes. As they settled in Canaan, they became known to other nations as Israelites.

ABRAHAM'S ORIGINS AND APPEARANCE

One of the main questions people ask is, "What did the Israelites look like?" To answer this question, we must begin with their progenitor, Abraham.

Abraham lived in Ur, a sweltering climate region of southern Mesopotamia. During Abraham's time, this city was primarily occupied by the Sumerians, Akkadians, and Amurru. Although the Bible references Abraham's homeland as "Ur of the Chaldeans," we must realize that the Chaldeans were not the ruling ethnic group of that period. History places Chaldean rule after the 10th century BCE. Thus, we have an *anachronism,* meaning that the reference to the Chaldeans is chronologically out of place. How did this happen?

---

2 Genesis 11:10-26 (King James Version).

3 John Bright, *A History of Israel* (Louisville: Westminster John Knox Press, 2000), 96.

4 Based on Exodus 12:37, which mentions "about six hundred thousand men on foot, besides women and children," suggesting a total population of approximately two million. See Kenneth A. Kitchen, *On the Reliability of the Old Testament* (Grand Rapids: Eerdmans, 2003), 264.

Moses authored the Pentateuch, which gives an account of Abraham's life. Moses also lived before the Chaldean rule of the city of Ur. I'm assuming that he did not initially record the Chaldeans. He would, however, certainly know about the city of Ur since it had been well-established centuries before he existed. The Chaldean rule came during the time of the prophet Ezra. Ezra was noted for being "the priest, the scribe, even a scribe of the words of the commandments of the Lord, and his statutes to Israel" (Ezra 7:11). Many rabbis and theologians opine that Ezra, a prolific writer, reintroduced the Torah and updated areas where necessary, such as Genesis 11:28, 31 to read "Chaldeans" to relate to the occupiers of Ur during his time. This lends credence to why Ur would be labeled "of the Chaldeans" and not of the Akkadians, Sumerians, or Amurru.

Here is what Edward D. Andrews, CEO and President of Christian Publishing House, suggests:

> "As this book has clearly demonstrated, Moses is the inspired author of the Pentateuch. At best, we can accept that it is likely that Joshua may have updated the text in Deuteronomy chapter 34, which speaks of Moses' death, and it is possible that Joshua may have made the reference in Numbers 12:3 that refers to Moses as being 'the humblest man on the face of the earth.' In addition, we can accept that a later copyist [or even possibly Ezra, another inspired author] updated Genesis 11:28, 31 to read 'of the Chaldeans,' a name of a land and its inhabitants in the southern portion of Babylonia that possibly was not recognized as Chaldea until several hundred years after Moses."[5]

Recent archaeological and historical scholarship has revealed that during Abraham's era (approximately early 2nd millennium BCE), the inhabitants of Ur would have predominantly comprised Akkadians and/or Amorites (Amurru)—ethnic groups descended from Ham—thus establishing that the region was primarily populated by peoples of African phenotypical characteristics. This demographic reality is

5 Edward D. Andrews, *The Evangelism Study Tool* (Cambridge, OH: Christian Publishing House, 2019), 147-148.

further substantiated by biblical genealogy, as Ur was situated in a region founded by Nimrod, son of Cush (Genesis 10:6-11), whose Hamitic lineage confirms the African origins of Mesopotamia's earliest civilization builders. Indeed, the broader geographical expanse encompassing Mesopotamia, the Levant, and the Arabian Peninsula was predominantly settled by Hamitic (African) and Semitic ethnic groups during this formative period of human civilization.

The distinguished archaeologist Sir Leonard Woolley, whose groundbreaking excavations at Ur between 1922-1934 revolutionized our understanding of ancient Mesopotamian society, documented that "the population of Ur in Abraham's time would have been predominantly of Semitic stock but with significant Sumerian influence, both culturally and genetically."[6] This archaeological assessment indicates a heterogeneous population exhibiting physical characteristics markedly distinct from contemporary European phenotypes. Woolley's meticulous stratigraphic analysis of Ur's residential quarters revealed skeletal remains and artistic depictions suggesting a population with craniofacial features and pigmentation consistent with the broader Afro-Asiatic populations of the ancient Near East, thus providing material evidence that challenges conventional Eurocentric interpretations of biblical narratives.

ARAM: ABRAHAM'S ORIGINAL HOMELAND

Although Abraham and his family dwelled among predominantly Hamitic populations, his genealogical origins were distinctly Semitic (descended from Shem). While biblical records establish that Abraham resided in Ur, this geographical association should not be conflated with ethnic identification among the indigenous Akkadians, Sumerians, or Amurrus. Ur represented his temporary domicile rather than his ancestral homeland—a critical distinction in understanding ancient Near Eastern population movements. To illustrate through contemporary analogy: despite my three-decade residence in Maryland, my birthplace and formative years in Virginia establish my primary

6 Leonard Woolley, Ur of the Chaldees: A Record of Seven Years of Excavation (London: Ernest Benn, 1929), 123.

regional identity as Virginian, despite my current geographical situation. Similarly, Abraham was neither Amorite nor Akkadian by lineage; rather, substantial historical and biblical evidence confirms his kinship with Semitic peoples who had established settlements throughout Aram (corresponding to ancient Syria). Thus, Abraham's identity is more accurately characterized as that of a Semitic individual from an Aramaic cultural sphere who temporarily resided among the Akkadian populations of Ur—maintaining his distinct ethnic and cultural heritage despite geographical displacement.

Two passages of scripture prove Abraham's kinship. First, when Abraham had his servant get a wife for his son, Isaac, he sent him to his *"relatives."*

> "You will not get a wife for my son from the daughters of the Canaanites, among who I am living, but will go to my country and *my own relatives* and get a wife for my son Isaac... Then the servant left, taking with him ten of his master's camels loaded with all kinds of good things from his master. He set out for Aram Naharaim and made his way to the town of Nahor." (Genesis 24:3-4, 10, Emphasis added)[7]

Here, we see that Abraham sent his servant to *"my country"* and *"my own relatives"* to find a wife for Isaac. He ends up in Nahor, where he goes to the area known as Aram Naharaim. This was his ethnic homeland. Gert Muller, in his book, The Ancient Black Hebrews: Abraham and His Family, states:

> "In the Book of Deuteronomy, it tells us that every third year the Israelites were to bring to a designated place the first fruits of the land. On presenting the first fruits, they are told to say the following:
>
> 'My father was *a wandering Aramean,* and he went down into Egypt with a few people and lived there and became a great nation, powerful and numerous. But the Egyptians

7 Genesis 24:3-4, 10 (New International Version).

> mistreated us and made us suffer, subjecting us to harsh labor...'" (Deuteronomy 26:5-6, Emphasis added)[8]

The Israelites were referring to Jacob, the grandson of Abraham, as *the wandering Aramaean* who went down to Egypt with a few people. Either way, this makes Abraham, his son, Isaac, and his grandson, Jacob, all Aramaeans. Muller further writes, "They [Aramaeans] were a confederacy of tribes in the Syrian Desert that spoke an NW Semitic language similar to Canaanite and Amorite. They are first mentioned in the inscriptions of the Assyrian king Tiglath-pileser (1115-1077 BCE). He had to cross the Euphrates repeatedly to fight them. Arameans are known as an Iron Age people because they are attested from the 11th century BCE to the 8th century BCE. The Aramaeans spread all over Mesopotamia and Canaan."[9]

Abraham, Isaac, and Jacob were not sons of Aram but of his brother Arphaxad. However, many Semites lived in the Aramaic region. Perhaps Arphaxad and his descendants lived in this Aramaic region as part of the confederacy of tribes dwelling in the Syrian Desert. Abraham's two brothers, Nahor and Haran, had towns among the Aramaeans named after them. They were part of the Confederacy.

Anthropologist Edith Sanders notes that "the physical characteristics of ancient Arameans, as depicted in contemporary art and described in texts, included dark complexions and tightly curled hair—features that would be classified as 'African' in modern racial taxonomies."[10]

Historical artifacts from the Global Egyptian Museum depict the heads of Syrian (Aramaean) men (Beduins) with skin complexions ranging from reddish-brown to light brown, showing typical hairlocks. These Syrian men clearly have features like those of African Americans today. Abraham's kinfolk possibly lived in a desert region in Syria, like the Beduins. The Beduins were largely nomadic Syrians living in desert

---

8 Gert Muller, *The Ancient Black Hebrews: Abraham and His Family* (Lushena Books, 2013), 37.

9 Ibid., 38.

10 Edith Sanders, "The Hamitic Hypothesis: Its Origin and Functions in Time Perspective," *Journal of African History* 10, no. 4 (1969): 521-532.

regions in Syria and even Israel. Abraham and his kinfolk's physical features could be very similar to those of the Beduin people.

An artifact of the ancient Aramaean King, Hazael, who lived during the 9th century BCE, depicts him with features that would today be classified as "Negro." The Bible records his reign and how he fought against Judah (2 Kings 12:17-18). This visual evidence further supports the dark complexion of Aramaic peoples.

The Elamites were another group living in the Mesopotamian region just outside the borders of the land of Shinar. Elam was a son of Shem and brother to Aram and Arphaxad. The Elamites left proof of their existence and features as they painted on the walls of Susa. Archaeological evidence from Elamite archers on the walls in Susa (in modern Iran) shows these Semitic descendants with features that would be classified as "Black" in today's racial terminology. It is safe to say that Shem and the ancient Semitic people had dark complexions. Thus, Ham may have been the progenitor of all Africans, but he was not the progenitor of all Black people. I conclude that Abraham was a Black Semitic man from an Aramaic region of Syria.

Archaeologist William F. Albright, a leading authority on biblical archaeology, confirms that "the ancient Semitic peoples, including the ancestors of the Hebrews, had physical characteristics quite different from those of modern European Jews, with darker complexions being the norm among ancient Near Eastern populations."[11]

ABRAHAM'S SONS AND THEIR DESCENDANTS

Abraham's patriarchal legacy extends far beyond his well-documented relationship with Isaac. Biblical genealogies reveal his numerous progeny through multiple unions, including sons whose historical significance is often overshadowed in conventional religious narratives. These descendants established formidable dynastic lineages throughout the Arabian Peninsula, with many achieving prominence as regional princes, tribal sheikhs, and mercantile leaders commanding substantial

11 William F. Albright, *From the Stone Age to Christianity: Monotheism and the Historical Process* (Baltimore: Johns Hopkins University Press, 1957), 143.

wealth and territorial influence. Abraham's eldest son Ishmael and his six sons by Keturah became progenitors of significant ethno-linguistic groups across the Middle Eastern landscape. Thus, Abraham's patriarchal significance transcends his role as merely the forefather of the Hebrew people; he simultaneously stands as the ancestral foundation for numerous Arab tribes and nations, establishing a complex web of kinship that continues to shape geopolitical and cultural dynamics in the contemporary Middle East.

ISHMAEL

The narrative of Abraham's first-born son emerges through a complex interweaving of human intervention and divine providence. Unlike the traditional patriarchal succession through Sarah, Abraham's first offspring came through her Egyptian handmaiden, Hagar—resembling an ancient parallel to modern familial complications. Sarah, confronting the increasingly apparent reality of her reproductive limitations and anxious about the unfulfilled divine promise of progeny, orchestrated a culturally sanctioned surrogate arrangement. The ancient Near Eastern practice of female slaves bearing children for their barren mistresses provided the socio-religious framework for Sarah's proposition to Abraham. Acting on this desperate initiative to facilitate divine promise through human agency, Abraham consorted with Hagar, resulting in the birth of Ishmael—progenitor of the Ishmaelite tribes. Significantly, Hagar's Egyptian ethnicity places her firmly within the Hamitic lineage, connecting her to the predominantly melanin-rich African populations of the Nile Valley civilization. This mixed heritage meant the Ishmaelites constituted a distinctive Semitic-Hamitic population whose territorial domain encompassed vast regions of the Arabian Peninsula.

Despite the subsequent birth of Isaac and the covenant's continuation through him, Abraham maintained profound paternal affection for Ishmael, earnestly petitioning Yahweh regarding his firstborn's destiny. The divine response affirmed Ishmael's significant historical purpose outside the Abrahamic covenant proper: "I will make him fruitful and multiply him exceedingly; he shall beget twelve princes, and I will make him a great nation." This prophecy materialized through Ishmael's twelve sons—Nebaioth, Kedar, Adbeel, Mibsam, Mishma, Dumah,

Massa, Hadad, Tema, Jetur, Naphis, and Kedemah—who established powerful tribal confederations across the Arabian Peninsula. These Ishmaelite descendants, the primordial Arab peoples and blood relatives to the Hebrews, eventually dominated the geopolitical landscape of the Arabian plate through sophisticated trading networks, strategic marriage alliances, and territorial expansions. This shared Abrahamic ancestry between Arabs and Hebrews constitutes one of history's most consequential yet frequently overlooked familial connections.

Ishmael "lived in the presence of his brethren." In other words, he and his offspring would live in close proximity to Isaac and his offspring. Yahweh warned, however, that he'd be like a wild donkey and very combative (Genesis 16:12; 25:18), underscoring the profound irony of modern Middle Eastern conflicts between these genealogically related peoples.

Historian Philip K. Hitti notes that "the Ishmaelites of pre-Islamic Arabia were known for their dark complexions and curly hair, physical traits inherited from both their Semitic father and Egyptian mother."[12]

MIDIAN

Ishmael was not the only half-brother of Isaac. After Abraham's wife, Sarah, dies, he marries his concubine, Keturah (Genesis 25:1). Keturah's ethnicity is not recorded in the Bible. Rabbinical Jewish Midrash suggests that Keturah and Hagar are the same person. Because her name means "fragrance," it merely speaks of Hagar's matured character, thus renaming her Keturah. If this is the case, then Keturah's ethnicity would be Egyptian. However, Keturah and Hagar are not likely to be the same person. The Torah records Abraham having sons by his concubines (plural), not a singular concubine (Genesis 25:6).

Another theory is that Abraham sent for a woman to marry from his Aramaean homeland. This theory comes from the fact that he chose to do this for Isaac, denoting that he'd rather keep the bloodline purely Aramaic. The Torah never suggests this to be the case. Moreover, it is unusual for concubines to be of the same ethnicity as their enslaver. It

12 Philip K. Hitti, *History of the Arabs* (London: Macmillan, 1970), 45.

is more probable that the concubines, who were slave girls, would have been from a different people group. Perhaps Keturah could have been of a similar ethnicity as Hagar, i.e., Egyptian since she was also a concubine to Abraham.

Compelling ethnographic evidence suggests Keturah's Cushite (Ethiopian) ancestry—a hypothesis substantiated through biblical references to her descendants. This genealogical connection emerges most notably through the lineage of Jethro, the Midianite priest whose daughter Zipporah married Moses. The Midianites, as direct descendants of Keturah's son Midian, represented one branch of Abraham's extended family tree through this union. When Moses fled Egypt after slaying an Egyptian taskmaster—seeking refuge from Pharaoh's capital sentence—he found sanctuary in Midian for four decades, during which he wed Zipporah. The biblical text explicitly records that during the subsequent Exodus narrative, Moses's sister Miriam remonstrated against him specifically "because of the Cushite woman whom he had married" (Numbers 12:1). This identification of Zipporah as Cushite provides significant ethnological context; if Zipporah possessed Cushitic/Ethiopian heritage, logical genealogical reconstruction suggests her ancestral lineage traced back to Keturah, indicating the latter's Cushitic ethnicity. This connection further establishes that the Midianites—Abraham's descendants through Keturah—possessed phenotypical characteristics consistent with other Cushitic populations, displaying distinctly African features and darker complexion. This anthropological insight significantly reconfigures conventional portrayals of biblical figures and their ethnic identities throughout the ancient Near East.

Biblical scholar J. Daniel Hays observes that "the reference to Zipporah as a 'Cushite woman' strongly suggests physical characteristics that would be identified as 'Black' or 'African' in modern terminology, reinforcing the dark complexion of the Midianite people."[13]

Further, Abraham had six sons by Keturah—Zimran, Jokshan, Medan, Midian, Ishbak and Shuah. Before his death, Abraham distributes his inheritance to his sons. He gave all that he had to Isaac, but to the

13 J. Daniel Hays, *From Every People and Nation: A Biblical Theology of Race* (Downers Grove, IL: InterVarsity Press, 2003), 71.

sons of his concubines, he gave gifts, then sent them eastward away from Isaac to *"the land of the east"* (Arabia). Keturah's half-Semitic, half-Hamitic sons helped populate Arabia as well as the Ishmaelites. Therefore, ancient Arabia was originally filled with Black Arabs before any admixture.

ISAAC

Isaac becomes the chosen son of his eight sons to carry on the legacy of Abraham's covenant with Yahweh. It is through Isaac that Hebrew heritage is kept. Isaac was a miracle baby. Yahweh informs Abraham that the promised son will come through his own loins and the "free woman," i.e., his original wife and not a concubine (slave woman). Sarah was 90 years old, past the point of being able to conceive. However, Yahweh touched her aged body and allowed her to conceive a son in her old age. Regarding ethnicity, Isaac was fully Semitic and would have physical features similar to the ancient Aramaeans. Isaac continues the Hebraic family tree through the birth of his son Jacob.

ISAAC AND HIS TWIN SONS: JACOB AND ESAU

Isaac's marriage to Rebekah, an Aramean woman of distinguished lineage—daughter of Bethuel and granddaughter of Abraham's brother Nahor—represents a strategic alliance that preserved the patriarchal family's Semitic genealogical integrity. This union produced the celebrated twin sons, Jacob and Esau, whose genetic composition maintained pure Semitic lineage without Hamitic or Japhetic admixture—a fact of considerable theological significance within the biblical narrative. Critically, both brothers held legitimate Hebrew status through their direct patrilineal descent from Abraham and Isaac, challenging common misconceptions that Hebrew identity belonged exclusively to Jacob's line. Esau, as the firstborn son, initially possessed the legal birthright that would have positioned him as the rightful inheritor and continuing vessel of the Abrahamic covenant. This primogeniture established him as Isaac's presumptive heir according to the cultural-juridical traditions of the ancient Near East, until the celebrated narrative of fraternal rivalry resulted in the covenant's transference to Jacob through complex circumstances involving both human agency and divine providence. This genealogical reality underscores the nuanced nature of covenant theology, demonstrating that Hebrew ethnic identity existed independently from the specific covenantal promise that would eventually flow through Jacob's lineage.

Rebekah wondered why these twins struggled in her womb. It was prophesied to her that this struggle was because these sons would be two nations divided against each other; one would be stronger than the other, and the older would serve the younger. Esau, the elder of the two, came out of the womb first. When he came out of the womb, he was red and hairy all over like a coat (Genesis 25:25). The younger brother comes out immediately after him, holding on to Esau's heel. This feisty baby didn't stop fighting until the end. Because he comes out clinching his brother's heel, his parents name him Jacob, which means "heel catcher."

As the twin brothers matured into adulthood, their divergent temperaments became increasingly apparent. Esau developed into a skilled huntsman, an outdoorsman whose identity was forged in the wilderness. Jacob, conversely, exhibited a more contemplative nature—dwelling within the domestic sphere of tents and demonstrating remarkable culinary proficiency. The watershed moment in their fraternal relationship occurred when Jacob was preparing a fragrant red lentil stew while Esau returned from an unsuccessful hunting expedition. Famished to the point of hyperbolic distress ("behold, I am about to die"), Esau encountered his brother's aromatic preparation and impetuously demanded sustenance. Jacob, recognizing opportunity in his brother's desperation, proposed a consequential exchange: "First sell me your birthright." In his state of ravenous exhaustion, Esau relinquished his primogeniture—the irreplaceable right of the firstborn to a double portion of inheritance and patriarchal succession—for mere temporary satisfaction. This transaction earned him the appellation "Edom" (meaning "red"), an etymological commemoration of the crimson lentil stew for which he sacrificed his spiritual inheritance. Scripture poignantly observes that Esau "despised his birthright" (Genesis 25:34), solemnizing the transfer through oath and demonstrating profound disregard for his spiritual heritage. Through this pivotal transaction, Jacob became the legitimate inheritor of the Abrahamic covenant with its attendant spiritual and material promises, preserving the Hebrew lineage while Esau would establish a separate national identity as progenitor of the Edomites, whose territories would encompass the region of Seir.

Esau adds salt to the wound of disappointment when he disobeys his father's instruction not to marry foreign women. Genesis 26:34, 35 records:

> "When Esau was 40 years old, he married Judith the daughter of Beeri the Hittite and Basemath the daughter of Elon the Hittite. But these two women brought a lot of grief to Esau's parents Isaac and Rebekah."[14]

Both women that Esau married were from the Hittite clan of the Canaanites. The Canaanites were a Hamitic ethnic group. In today's world, they would be considered Africans. After he marries these two Canaanite women, he goes to Uncle Ishmael and marries his daughter, Mahalath. This is recorded in Genesis 28:9:

> "Esau went to Ishmael and took as his wife, besides the wives he had, Mahalath the daughter of Ishmael, Abraham's son, the sister of Nebaioth."[15]

As mentioned, the Ishmaelites were an ethnic group with Semitic and Hamitic blood. Now, Esau has three wives, and they bear children with him. Esau's sons were Eliphaz, Reuel, Jeush, Jaalam, and Korah. His grandsons were Teman, Omar, Zepho, Gatam, Kenaz, Amalek, Nahath, Zerath, Shammah, and Mizzah.

I share Esau's bloodline because he is a descendant of Abraham and to highlight that they were people of color dwelling in the Arabian region.

JACOB AND HIS DESCENDANTS

Of the two twins, Jacob becomes the son of significance regarding the eternal covenant that Yahweh established with Abraham and his

---

14 Genesis 26:34-35 (New Living Translation).

15 Genesis 28:9 (English Standard Version).

offspring. Through Jacob, Yahweh's chosen ethnic group originates and becomes distinguished among the other sons of Abraham.

The Genesis narrative continues beyond Jacob's acquisition of the birthright, detailing a pivotal deception orchestrated in collaboration with his mother, Rebekah. Together they engineered a scheme whereby Jacob impersonated his hirsute brother before their blind, aging father Isaac, successfully securing the patriarchal blessing rightfully intended for Esau. Upon discovering this profound betrayal, Esau's grief transformed into murderous rage, prompting him to vow vengeance against his duplicitous twin. Discerning the gravity of this threat, Rebekah devised a strategic departure for her favored son, ostensibly motivated by matrimonial concerns rather than fraternal hostility. She approached Isaac with an artful pretext—expressing apprehension that Jacob might, like Esau, select a bride from among the indigenous Canaanites, thereby compromising their lineage. This diplomatic maneuver proved successful; Isaac not only endorsed Jacob's journey to Paddan-Aram but bestowed upon him an additional blessing before dispatching him to the household of Bethuel, Rebekah's father. Isaac's parting directive was explicit: Jacob should seek a wife from among his maternal cousins, specifically the daughters of Laban, Rebekah's brother, thus maintaining the purity of their Aramean bloodline while simultaneously removing him from Esau's vengeful reach.

After six years of living in Haran and serving Laban, Jacob is infatuated with his daughter, Rachel. Laban negotiates a 7-year servitude contract in exchange for his daughter's hand in marriage. However, Laban deceives Jacob into marrying Leah instead of Rachel. Eventually, Jacob negotiates another 7-year contract, securing marital arrangements with the woman his heart desired—Rachel.

Jacob's two wives, Rachel and Leah, began a seesaw battle of child birthing for Jacob. Leah begins by birthing Jacob's first four sons—Reuben, Simeon, Levi, and Judah. Rachel, frustrated by her own infertility, becomes jealous of Leah and gives her handmaid Bilhah to Jacob to bear children in her stead, much similar to Sarah's ordeal with Hagar. Bilhah bears two sons to Jacob—Dan and Naphtali.

You would imagine that there would have been a cessation to this ridiculous childbearing feud, but Leah retaliates by offering her handmaid Zilpah to Jacob. And on Leah's behalf, Zilpah bears two children to Jacob—Gad and Asher.

One day, Reuben gathers mandrakes from the field for his mother, Leah. Rachel desires some of Reuben's mandrakes and negotiates with Leah to give her some in exchange for sleeping with Jacob. This eventually leads to Leah conceiving two more sons—Issachar and Zebulun.

After years of barrenness, Rachel's fervent prayers were finally answered with the birth of Joseph, a momentous occasion that fulfilled her deepest maternal longings. However, the narrative takes a profoundly tragic turn during her second labor—a harrowing childbirth that would ultimately claim her life. As Rachel endured excruciating pain and sensed her impending mortality, scripture poignantly describes that "as her soul was departing" she bestowed upon her newborn the name "Benoni," meaning "son of my sorrow," a final maternal act reflecting her anguish. Jacob, perhaps unable to bear this perpetual reminder of his beloved wife's death, intervened with paternal authority and renamed the child "Benjamin," signifying "son of my right hand" or "son of strength," thus transforming a name of lamentation into one of dignity and promise. This renaming represents not merely a semantic adjustment but a profoundly symbolic gesture—Jacob's attempt to redeem tragedy through the affirmation of life and continuity despite devastating loss.

Jacob and his twelve sons become known as the Hebrews. When Yahweh changed Jacob's name at Peniel from Jacob to Israel, the Hebrews began to be called Israelites as well. Through Abraham, Isaac, and Jacob, they are God's chosen ethnic group. Throughout the Bible, Yahweh is called the God of Abraham, Isaac, and Jacob.

WERE THE ISRAELITES BLACK?

We have already proven that Abraham was a Black Semite from the Aramaic region. His grandson, Jacob, was the wandering Aramaean, not the wandering European. Ham and his descendants were not the only people of color. Shem and his descendants were also people of color, as seen with the Elamites and Aramaeans, brothers of Abraham's great grandfather Arphaxad. Abraham and Sarah, Isaac and Rebekah, Jacob and Rachel and Leah were all Aramaean, i.e., Black Semites. Eight of Jacob's sons were from pure Aramaean stock. However, his four other sons from the two handmaids (slave girls)—Bilhah and Zilpah— were possibly mixed with Hamitic-Ethiopian or Hamitic-Egyptian blood like Hagar or Keturah.

Anthropologist Edith Sanders notes that "the evidence from ancient art, texts, and modern physical anthropology all suggests that the ancient Israelites would have had physical features that in modern racial taxonomies would place them among populations of African descent rather than European."[16]

BLACK JOSEPH AND BENJAMIN

How do we know Rachel and Leah were Black women? This is easy to determine by Biblical accounts. Jacob and Rachel have a son named Joseph. Joseph's story is essential for the Black identity of Rachel (and Jacob). Around the age of 17, Joseph is sold into slavery to the Egyptians by his envious brothers. About 13 years later, famine strikes the region. Joseph was a viceroy in Egypt during this time because he interpreted the Pharaoh's dream foretelling of a pending famine and instructs the Egyptians to prepare for it by storing up seven years worth of supply. When the famine hit the land of Canaan, Jacob had his other sons travel into Egypt for food. These brothers literally interact with Joseph without being able to distinguish him apart from the Egyptians. Joseph looked just like an Egyptian, not just in apparel but also in physical features. Remember, ancient Egyptians were a Black, Hamitic people in Africa. There aren't too many people who would dispute that claim. Thus, Joseph was just as Black as the Hamitic Egyptians. If Joseph were White, like a European, he would have been easily distinguished from the Black Egyptians. Furthermore, since Joseph was Black like the Egyptians, that means two things are possible:

(1) Either Jacob or Rachel had to be Black or (2) Both Jacob and Rachel were Black.

---

16 Edith Sanders, "The Hamitic Hypothesis," 526.

I believe the latter because the ancient Aramaeans were a Black ethnic group. This also means that Joseph's brother, Benjamin, was a Black man. We mentioned in an earlier chapter that the apostle Paul was mistaken as an Egyptian. Paul was from the tribe of Benjamin! To add to Jacob and Rachel's Black bloodline, Joseph marries Asenath, an Egyptian woman who bears him two sons—Manasseh and Ephraim.

Historian Frank M. Snowden Jr. confirms that "ancient Egyptian art consistently depicts Syro-Palestinians, including Hebrews, with dark brown skin tones similar to those used for Egyptians themselves, suggesting significant physical similarities between these populations."[17]

BLACK MOSES AND THE BLACK LEVITICAL PRIESTHOOD

We must remember that Leah was Rachel's sister. She was a pure Aramaean with no Japhetic (White) admixture. She bore Jacob six sons. Just as we concluded that Joseph had one or both Black parents, the same must be true of Jacob and Leah. One or both of them must be Black.

Examining the illustrious Levitical lineage, we find one of Jacob and Leah's sons—Levi—whose descendants would profoundly shape Israelite religious history. From this branch emerged the extraordinary triumvirate of Moses, Aaron, and Miriam, offspring of Amram and Jochebed, and grandchildren of Kohath, who himself was Levi's direct son. Moses, positioned as a fourth-generation Levite, would ascend to become perhaps the most transcendent prophetic figure in biblical history. His monumental legacy encompasses not only his prophetic ministry but also his attributed authorship of the Pentateuch—the foundational texts of Hebrew Scripture. The narrative of Moses commences during a tumultuous period when a xenophobic Egyptian Pharaoh, oblivious to Joseph's transformative contributions to Egyptian civilization, subjected the burgeoning Israelite population to brutal enslavement. In his paranoid determination to suppress Hebrew demographic growth, this Pharaoh issued a genocidal edict targeting all Hebrew male infants. Through an extraordinary act of maternal

---

17 Frank M. Snowden Jr., *Blacks in Antiquity: Ethiopians in the Greco-Roman Experience* (Cambridge, MA: Harvard University Press, 1970), 104.

courage, Jochebed concealed her newborn son within a waterproofed basket among the Nile's reeds—a desperate gambit that culminated in his providential discovery by Pharaoh's daughter. Thus, through divine orchestration, Moses was paradoxically raised as royalty within the very palace of his people's oppressor—an undetected Hebrew scion in the heart of Egyptian power. Remarkably, throughout four decades of palace life prior to his fateful slaying of an Egyptian taskmaster, his Hebrew ethnicity remained undetected—a circumstance strongly suggesting that his physiognomy harmonized with the predominantly Hamitic Egyptian population, indicating Afroasiatic features.

The divine commissioning of Moses at the burning bush incorporated a profound demonstration that simultaneously affirmed his ethnic identity. As a authenticating sign of divine appointment, Yahweh instructed Moses to place his hand within his cloak. When withdrawn, his hand had miraculously transformed, becoming "leprous, WHITE as snow"—a startling contrast specifically highlighted in the biblical text. Following divine instruction to repeat the action, Moses's hand was "restored like the rest of his flesh"—a telling phrase that establishes his normative skin tone was distinctly different from the leprous white condition. This textual juxtaposition creates a deliberate contrast between the anomalous "white as snow" and Moses's natural complexion, providing compelling textual evidence regarding the phenotypical characteristics of this paramount Hebrew prophet. The dramatic nature of this sign would have been considerably diminished had Moses's natural complexion already approximated whiteness, underscoring the ethnic dimensions preserved within this ancient narrative.

> "Furthermore, the LORD said to Moses, 'Put your hand inside your cloak.' So he put his hand inside his cloak, and when he took it out, his hand was leprous, white as snow. 'Put your hand back inside your cloak,' said the LORD. So Moses put his hand back inside his cloak, and when he took it out, it was restored, like the rest of his skin." (Exodus 4:6, 7 Berean Bible)[18]

---

18 Exodus 4:6-7 (Berean Bible).

Biblical scholar J. Daniel Hays notes that "the contrast between Moses's leprous hand, which is described as 'white as snow,' and his normal skin color strongly suggests that Moses was dark-skinned."[19]

Moses was a Black man who grew up in a Black country. Other notable Levites were Aaron, Miriam, Samuel, Jeremiah, Ezekiel, Ezra, and Malachi. The entire Levitical priesthood was Black, including Aaron and the other high priests who entered beyond the veil into the Holy of Holies.

JUDAH

Since Levi and his descendants were Black, I'm certain his brothers Reuben, Simeon, Judah, Issachar, and Zebulun were also Black. The tribe of Judah is the tribe that birth the lineage of Hebrew kings. Some prominent kings born from Judah's lineage are David, Solomon, Hezekiah, and Jehoshaphat.

Substantial proof exists of the great Judahite king Solomon's blackness. His mother was from the Hittite tribe, which lived in Jerusalem. The Hittites were Canaanites, descendants of Noah's son Ham. Thus, King Solomon's mother was an African!

Although we are not told directly that Bathsheba is a Hamite, we can actually trace her heritage through her grandfather Ahithophel, David's African counselor. In 2 Samuel 11:3, we are told that Bathsheba's father is Eliam, but it isn't until 2 Samuel 23 that we discover that Bathsheba's grandfather is a Gilonite.

"Eliphelet the son of Ahasbai, the son of the Maachathite,
Eliam the son of Ahithophel the Gilonite," (2 Samuel 23:34)[20]

The Gilonites were one of the tribes the Israelites did not remove from the land. David, a Black Judahite King, had a son by the African Gilonite [Canaanite] woman, Bathsheba, who lived among Judah. This gives more proof of Solomon's physical complexion.

---

19 J. Daniel Hays, *From Every People and Nation,* 82.

20 2 Samuel 23:34 (King James Version).

Solomon's lineage is important because it helps explain why he had bushy locks of black hair, as described in Song of Solomon 5:11: "His head is as the most fine gold, his locks are bushy, and black as a raven."[21] This physical description aligns with the features commonly associated with people of African descent.

Yeshua (Jesus) is an offspring of Judah's kingly lineage. As we read his genealogy in the holy Scriptures, we see a couple of Hamites intermingled in the bloodline. Interestingly enough, the genealogy of Yeshua is recorded in the Scriptures and shows no Japhetic (European/Caucasian) progenitors.

As previously mentioned:

1. The slave girls (concubines) Bilhah and Zilpah were probably Hamitic since the Aramaean people had Egyptian slaves during this period, just as Hagar was.
2. All eight sons of Abraham, whether purely Semitic or mixed with Hamitic blood, were Black and eventually populated ancient Arabia.
3. All twelve sons of Jacob were Black, eventually becoming known as Hebrews or Israelites. Joseph marries an Egyptian, Judah has children with a Canaanite woman, David's half-African son, Solomon, is made king of Israel, etc.

Ancient Israel was unequivocally Black. While some may find it far-fetched to see ancient Israel and Arabia as Black (according to today's social construct), history proves this to be the absolute case.

Biblical scholar Cain Hope Felder observes that "the biblical world encompassed North Africa, Arabia, and the Near East—regions where dark-skinned peoples predominated. The revisionist view that portrays biblical figures as European in appearance is a post-medieval development that reflects European colonial interests rather than historical reality."[22]

---

21 Song of Solomon 5:11 (King James Version).

22 Cain Hope Felder, *Troubling Biblical Waters: Race, Class, and Family* (Maryknoll, NY: Orbis Books, 1989), 43.

What we see today throughout the Middle East is not the original, ancient, or biblical picture. The land of Israel itself eventually became flooded and occupied by foreigners from different nations that were not bloodline Israel, starting with Israel's captivity and exile as early as 734 BCE. From the Assyrian invasion to the Zionist state of Israel, there have been non-Israelite occupants. To this day, some non-bloodline occupants have filled the land of Israel. It may be the case until Messiah returns. The natural branches (bloodline Israel) are scattered throughout the world, especially throughout the beautiful continent of Africa and the Americas.

HISTORIANS WHO DESCRIBED HEBREWS

Tacitus, a Roman historian, wrote about the Hebrews in his book Histories. Many assured us they were a race of Ethiopian origin. Ethiopians are black Africans. Tacitus was told by authorities of his day that the Jews [ethnic Hebrews] were of black African descent because their features were like those of the Ethiopians, and many lived among the Ethiopians and Egyptians.

> "A few authorities hold that in the reign of Isis, the surplus population of Egypt was evacuated to neighboring lands under the leadership of Hierosolymus and Judas. Many assure us that the Jews are descended from those Ethiopians who were driven by fear and hatred to emigrate from their home country when Cepheus was king. There are some who say that a motley collection of landless Assyrians occupied a part of Egypt, and then built cities of their own, inhabiting the lands of the Hebrews and the nearer parts of Syria..."[23]

The testimony of Tacitus is essential because he was a Roman historian and is often quoted as a credible source of history. Tacitus lived from 55 CE to 117 CE, which overlaps the lifetime of the apostle Paul, who was believed to have died in 64 CE.

23 Tacitus, *Histories* 5.2-5, trans. Kenneth Wellesley (London: Penguin Books, 1975), 271-272.

Anthropologist Alfred C. Haddon states, "The Elamites of Mesopotamia seem to be a negro people with kinky hair and have transmitted this racial type to the Jews and Assyrians."[24]

In 1931, Austrian Jewish Biblical scholar and art historian Robert Eisler published a classic in Josephus scholarship, his "The Messiah Jesus and John the Baptist: According to Flavius Josephus" recently rediscovered [the] "Capture of Jerusalem" and the other Jewish and Christian sources. Through a meticulous analysis of extant manuscripts, Eisler endeavored to restore the original reading of a first-century text that discusses John the Baptist, Jesus, and the early Christians. This first-century source is the Halosis or "Capture (of Jerusalem)" of Josephus (37-100 CE). Initially written in Aramaic, a Greek rewriting was published around 72 CE. This is an important text for discussing Christian origins, particularly given the section therein treating "the human form of Jesus and his wonderful works." Below is Josephus' Halosis paragraph that mentions Jesus as being black-skinned:

> "At that time also there appeared a certain man of magic power ... if it be meet to call him a man, [whose name is Jesus], whom [certain] Greeks call a son of [a] God, but his disciples [call] the true prophet who is supposed to have raised dead persons and to have cured all diseases. Both his nature and his form were human, for he was a man of simple appearance, mature age, black-skinned (melagchrous), short growth, three cubits tall, hunchbacked, prognathous (lit. 'with a long face [macroprosopos]), a long nose, eyebrows meeting above the nose, that the spectators could take fright, with scanty [curly] hair, but having a line in the middle of the head after the fashion of the Nazaraeans, with an undeveloped beard."[25]

Historian Frank M. Snowden Jr. notes that "Eisler's reconstruction of the Halosis text, while controversial in some aspects, aligns with other

---

24 Alfred C. Haddon, *The Races of Man and Their Distribution* (Cambridge: Cambridge University Press, 1924), 36.

25 Robert Eisler, *The Messiah Jesus and John the Baptist: According to Flavius Josephus' Recently Rediscovered 'Capture of Jerusalem'* (London: Methuen & Co., 1931), 463-464.

evidence suggesting that Jesus and the early Hebrews would have had physical features consistent with other Near Eastern populations of the time, including darker skin tones than typically depicted in European art."[26]

Herodotus, an ancient Greek historian often referred to as the "Father of History," wrote about ancient Egypt when he traveled there in the 5th century BCE:

> "For it is plain to see that the Colchians are Egyptians; and what I say, I myself noted before I heard it from others. When it occurred to me, I inquired of both peoples; and the Colchians remembered the Egyptians better than the Egyptians remembered the Colchians; the Egyptians said that they considered the Colchians part of Sesostris' army. I myself guessed it, partly because they are dark-skinned and woolly-haired; though that indeed counts for nothing, since other peoples are, too; but my better proof was that the Colchians and Egyptians and Ethiopians are the only nations that have from the first practiced circumcision."[27]

Remember that Josephus lived during the apostles' and early church's periods. Herodotus historically writes that Egyptians and Colchians were dark-skinned and curly-haired. This is important because the Hebrews had strikingly similar features to the Egyptians. These features are remarkably similar to those of African Americans.

CONCLUSION: THE TRUE IDENTITY OF ISRAEL

As we have demonstrated throughout this chapter, the evidence from biblical texts, historical accounts, archaeological findings, and anthropological research all point to ancient Israel being a people with physical characteristics that would today be classified as "Black" or "African." The Israelites were a Semitic people closely related to other Near Eastern populations like the Aramaeans and Elamites, who shared

---

26 Frank M. Snowden Jr., *Before Color Prejudice: The Ancient View of Blacks* (Cambridge, MA: Harvard University Press, 1983), 107.
27 Herodotus, *The Histories,* 2.104, trans. A.D. Godley (Cambridge, MA: Harvard University Press, 1920), 395.

these physical traits. Furthermore, there was significant intermarriage with Hamitic peoples like Egyptians, Ethiopians, and Canaanites, reinforcing these characteristics within the Israelite population.

This evidence poses a profound challenge to the conventional identification of Ashkenazi Jews as the biological descendants of ancient Israel. As we established in previous chapters, Ashkenazi Jews are primarily descendants of Khazar converts to Judaism—people of Japhetic rather than Semitic origin. Their physical appearance more closely resembles that of Europeans than the darker-skinned peoples of the ancient Near East.

If the true descendants of Israel are to be found among populations with physical characteristics that more closely resemble those of the ancient Israelites, then we must look to peoples of African descent, including African Americans, many of whom were brought to the Americas through the transatlantic slave trade. The evidence presented in subsequent chapters will further strengthen this connection, demonstrating that the prophecy in Romans 11:25-27 concerning Israel's end-time salvation may indeed refer to the awakening of African Americans to their true identity as descendants of God's chosen people.

Biblical scholar Walter C. Kaiser Jr. observes, "If we take seriously the physical descriptions of biblical figures and the historical evidence for the appearance of ancient Near Eastern peoples, we must reconsider our assumptions about who represents the genetic descendants of biblical Israel today."[28] This reconsideration opens the door to recognizing that God's end-time work of restoration may be unfolding in ways that challenge conventional theological and historical narratives.

As we continue our journey through the hidden heritage of God's chosen people, we will examine more specific evidence linking African Americans to ancient Israel, from cultural practices and linguistic connections to the prophetic significance of their historical experience of exile and oppression. The implications of this connection are profound, not only for understanding biblical prophecy but for recognizing how

---

28 Walter C. Kaiser Jr., *Mission in the Old Testament: Israel as a Light to the Nations* (Grand Rapids: Baker Academic, 2012), 96.

God's unchanging covenant faithfulness continues to manifest in our world today.

The Healing of the Paralytic.
c. 235 AD (known to be the oldest painting of Jesus—this painting was discovered in 1921 on the left-hand wall of the baptismal chamber of the house-church at Dura-Europos on the Euphrates River in modern Syria.)

Christ Among the Apostles.
Fresco from the St. Domitilla Catacomb (Arcosolium of the Crypt of Ampliatusin), Rome, Italy, 3rd century

Abraham raises his sword to slay his son Isaac.
Fresco from the Via Latina Catacomb (Cubiculum C), Rome, Italy. Circa 320 AD

Heads of **ancient Syrian (Aramaean) men** from Global Egyptian Museum

King Hazael of Syria (9th Century BC)

Elamite archers on the walls in Susa (in Iran).

"Among the inhabitants of Gao[1] are communities of Jews who came seeking refuge after the destruction of their kingdom by the Assyrians. They maintain their faith while engaging in trade with Muslims and pagans alike."

Ibn Battuta, Muhammad ibn Abdullah. *The Travels of Ibn Battuta.* Translated by H.A.R. Gibb. Cambridge: Cambridge University Press for the Hakluyt Society, 1958-2000.

1 Gao is located in eastern Mali, West Africa, specifically on the Niger River. It is situated on the southern edge of the Sahara Desert and is about 200 miles (320 km) east-southeast of Timbuktu.

Chapter 12

Scattered

"The history of Africa cannot be fully understood without recognizing the deep connections between the African people and the ancient Israelites. The migration of Hebrew people into Africa over centuries has shaped the continent's religious, cultural, and social landscapes."[1]

THE PROPHESIED DISPERSION OF ISRAEL

As noted earlier in this book, Israel was privileged to represent Yahweh on earth. He made an everlasting covenant with them, providing a blueprint for living within its boundaries and outlining the consequences of breaking it. If they honored Him by keeping the covenant, His providential care and blessings would always be with them.

Out of His great love and patience for Israel, whenever they violated His laws and rebelled against Him, He sent His holy prophets to plead for their return to covenant living. As their sin and rebellion worsened, He had the prophets warn them of pending judgments if they failed to heed His heart cry for their return.

Yahweh warned Israel that gross disobedience, especially serving other gods, would provoke His wrath, and He would scatter them among the nations from one end of the earth to the other. This divine warning appears repeatedly throughout scripture:

- Leviticus 26:33 - "And I will scatter you among the heathen, and will draw out a sword after you: and your land shall be desolate, and your cities waste."

---

1 Cheikh Anta Diop, *The African Origin of Civilization: Myth or Reality* (Chicago: Lawrence Hill Books, 1974), 127.

- Deuteronomy 28:64 - "And the Lord shall scatter thee among all people, from the one end of the earth even unto the other; and there thou shalt serve other gods, which neither thou nor thy fathers have known, even wood and stone."
- Jeremiah 9:16 - "I will scatter them [Israel] also among the heathen, whom neither they nor their fathers have known: and I will send a sword after them, till I have consumed them."
- Ezekiel 12:15 - "And they shall know that I am the Lord, when I shall scatter them among the nations, and disperse them in the countries."

These prophetic warnings would find their fulfillment in a series of catastrophic events that would forever change the course of Israelite history.

THE ASSYRIAN CAPTIVITY: THE FIRST MAJOR DISPERSION

The Bible records two major scatterings of Israel. These dispersions began with forced captivity. The first significant dispersion occurred when several thousand Israelites from the northern kingdom were forcibly removed from their homeland. As 2 Kings 18:11-12 explains:

> "And the king of Assyria did carry away Israel unto Assyria and put them in Halah and in Habor by the river of Gozan, and in the cities of the Medes: because they obeyed not the voice of the Lord their God, but transgressed his covenant, and all that Moses the servant of the Lord commanded and would not hear them, nor do them."

The Assyrian monarchs Tiglath-Pileser III (Pul) and Shalmaneser V conquered the northern kingdom of Israel and began their captivity around 734 BCE. Later, King Sargon II and his successor, Sennacherib, completed Israel's exile in 724 BCE and laid siege to Samaria, the capital city. Assyrian records state that 27,290 captives were taken from Samaria by Sargon II.[2]

2 William F. Albright, *From the Stone Age to Christianity: Monotheism and the Historical Process* (Baltimore: Johns Hopkins University Press, 1940), 214.

EARLY MIGRATION ROUTES TO AFRICA

While many Israelites remained in captivity in Assyria, evidence suggests that others found ways to escape. The prophet Hosea informs us that some Israelites from the tribe of Ephraim fled to Egypt during the Assyrian invasion: "They shall not dwell in the LORD's land; but Ephraim shall return to Egypt, and they shall eat unclean things in Assyria" (Hosea 9:3).

This flight to Egypt marked one of the earliest documented migrations of Israelites into Africa during this period. According to historian William F. Albright, "The archaeological evidence confirms significant population movements between the Levant and Egypt during the late 8th century BCE, coinciding with the Assyrian campaigns."[3]

Recent archaeological discoveries have revealed Hebrew inscriptions in the Eastern Nile Delta dating to this period, suggesting established Israelite communities in Egypt by the late 8th century BCE.[4] These communities would likely have interacted with various Egyptian populations while maintaining aspects of their Hebrew identity and religious practices.

Another significant migration route developed along the Red Sea coast. According to Tudor Parfitt's research, "Hebrew groups moved southward along the western Arabian coast and crossed into Africa at Bab el-Mandeb, establishing communities in what is now Ethiopia and Eritrea."[5] This migration route would explain the presence of Hebrew religious practices among certain Ethiopian communities, particularly the Beta Israel (Ethiopian Jews).

THE BABYLONIAN CAPTIVITY: THE SECOND MAJOR DISPERSION

Despite witnessing the northern kingdom's exile, the southern kingdom of Judah did not learn from their error and continued in gross

---

3 Albright, *From the Stone Age to Christianity*, 216.

4 Recent excavations at Tell el-Dabʿa in Egypt's eastern Delta have revealed inscriptions with Hebrew characteristics dating to the late 8th century BCE.

5 Tudor Parfitt, *Black Jews in Africa and the Americas* (Cambridge: Harvard University Press, 2013), 45.

idolatry. Beginning around 698 BCE under King Manasseh's 55-year reign, Judah rebuilt "high places" for pagan worship, defiled the sacred temple of Yahweh, and even practiced child sacrifice to the Canaanite god Molech.

By December 599 BCE, Judah was invaded by Babylonian, Aramaean, Moabite, and Ammonite forces. As 2 Kings 24:20 states: "It was because of the Lord's anger that all this happened to Jerusalem and Judah, and in the end, He thrust them from His presence."

A year after the Babylonian king Nebuchadnezzar besieged Jerusalem (598 BCE), King Jehoiachin surrendered, and 10,000 Judahites were taken captive to Babylonia. Nebuchadnezzar ransacked the temple, stripped it of all gold articles, and appointed Zedekiah as a vassal king. When Zedekiah later rebelled, Jerusalem was destroyed in 586 BCE, and most of the remaining population was exiled.

JUDAHITE DISPERSIONS INTO AFRICA

Following the assassination of Gedaliah, the Babylonian-appointed governor, many Hebrews sought safety in Egypt. The Bible explicitly mentions this migration: "Then all the men... and all the women... even Jeremiah the prophet and Baruch... entered Egypt" (Jeremiah 43:5-7). This constituted another significant wave of Israelite migration into Africa.

Archaeological evidence confirms the establishment of a substantial Jewish military colony at Elephantine in southern Egypt during this period. The Elephantine papyri, dating from the 5th century BCE, document a thriving Hebrew community with its own temple to Yahweh.[6]

When Babylon fell to Persia, Cyrus the Great allowed the Judahites to return to their homeland after 70 years of captivity. Approximately 50,000 descendants of the southern kingdom returned on three different journeys led by Zerubbabel, Ezra, and Nehemiah. However, many

6 Bezalel Porten, *Archives from Elephantine: The Life of an Ancient Jewish Military Colony* (Berkeley: University of California Press, 1968), 37-42.

chose to remain in their new locations, creating permanent diaspora communities.

According to historian Joseph Modrzejewski, "Many Judahites from Babylon migrated through North Africa and along the Mediterranean coast, establishing communities from Egypt to Cyrenaica and beyond."[7] This westward movement laid the foundation for the significant Hebrew presence that would later develop across North Africa.

THE EMERGENCE OF TRANS-SAHARAN MIGRATION ROUTES

Following the Babylonian period, a series of new migration routes developed that would eventually connect Israelite communities in North Africa with regions further south. Ancient trade routes across the Sahara became vital pathways for Israelite dispersion into West Africa.

Archaeological and historical evidence suggests three primary trans-Saharan routes used by Hebrew migrants:[8]

1. The Western Route: From Morocco and Mauritania southward to the Senegal River and the ancient Ghana Empire.
2. The Central Route: From Libya through the Fezzan region to Lake Chad and the Kanem-Bornu Empire.
3. The Eastern Route: From Egypt through Nubia (modern Sudan) to Ethiopia and the Horn of Africa.

According to historian Roland Oliver, "These trans-Saharan routes were not just commercial highways but cultural corridors that facilitated the movement of religious ideas, practices, and people."[9] Hebrew merchants and migrants traveled alongside Berbers, Arabs, and other groups, gradually establishing communities at trading posts along these routes.

---

7 Joseph Modrzejewski, *The Jews of Egypt: From Rameses II to Emperor Hadrian* (Princeton: Princeton University Press, 1997), 121.

8 M.J. Azevedo, *Roots of Violence: A History of War in Chad* (London: Routledge, 1998), 23-24.

9 Roland Oliver, *The African Experience* (New York: HarperCollins, 1991), 62.

The renowned medieval historian Ibn Khaldun documented the presence of Hebrew communities among Berber tribes in the western Maghreb, noting that some of these tribes "had adopted Judaism" and played significant roles in trans-Saharan trade.[10] These Judaized Berbers would have been instrumental in transmitting Hebrew religious practices and possibly bloodlines into West Africa.

SCATTERED DURING THE TIME OF YESHUA AND HIS APOSTLES

By the time of Yeshua (4 BCE to 30 CE), Israelites were scattered throughout the Roman Empire, Asia Minor, and Africa. Luke's account in Acts 2:1-12 provides evidence of this widespread dispersion. During the feast of Pentecost (Shavuot), when the Holy Spirit descended on the believers, Israelite pilgrims from many nations were present in Jerusalem:

- Parthia (Anatolia, Turkey)
- Medes (Iran)
- Elam (southwestern Iran)
- Mesopotamia (Iraq)
- Judaea (Palestine)
- Cappadocia (Greece)
- Pontus (Turkey)
- Phrygia (Turkey)
- Pamphylia (Turkey)
- Egypt
- Libya (Cyrenaica)
- Crete
- Arabia
- Visitors from Rome, Jews, and proselytes

This list demonstrates the extent of Israelite settlements after the Assyrian and Babylonian exiles, covering Mediterranean Europe, Asia

10 Ibn Khaldun, *The Muqaddimah: An Introduction to History*, trans. Franz Rosenthal (Princeton: Princeton University Press, 1958), 117-118.

Minor, Arabia, and substantial parts of Africa. The apostle James further confirms this dispersion by addressing his epistle to "the twelve tribes scattered abroad" (James 1:1).

THE FALL OF JERUSALEM IN 70 CE AND ITS IMPACT

The destruction of Jerusalem by the Romans in 70 CE triggered another massive wave of Israelite dispersion. The Jewish historian Josephus wrote, "General Vespasian and his son Caesar Titus fought against the Jews. Millions of Jews fled into Africa, among other places, fleeing from Roman persecution and starvation during the siege."[11]

Recent archaeological discoveries have confirmed this account. Hebrew inscriptions and artifacts dating to the late 1st and early 2nd centuries CE have been found throughout North Africa, from Egypt to Morocco.[12] These findings suggest a substantial influx of refugees from Judaea following the Roman destruction of Jerusalem.

THE WESTERN MIGRATION INTO AFRICA

According to Edward Wilmot Blyden's research, many of these refugees "moved along established trade routes deep into Africa, seeking safety among communities where some of their brethren had already settled after earlier dispersions."[13] This migration would have reinforced and expanded existing Hebrew communities in Africa.

Historical records from the 2nd and 3rd centuries CE document Hebrew communities in Cyrenaica (modern Libya), Carthage (modern Tunisia), and Mauretania (modern Morocco and western Algeria).[14] From these coastal regions, Hebrews gradually moved southward and westward, following established trade routes.

---

11 Flavius Josephus, *The Wars of the Jews,* trans. William Whiston (London: Penguin Classics, 1981), Book VI, Chapter 9.

12 Archaeological findings include Hebrew inscriptions on tombstones in Libya's coastal regions dating to the late 1st and early 2nd centuries CE.

13 Edward Wilmot Blyden, *Christianity, Islam and the Negro Race* (Edinburgh: Edinburgh University Press, 1967), 128.

14 Documented in Roman provincial records and archaeological remains.

The geographer al-Idrisi, writing in the 12th century, noted "communities of the Children of Israel" in the western Sahel region, suggesting their presence had been established long before his time.[15] These communities maintained varying degrees of Hebrew religious practices while adapting to local cultural contexts.

THE IBERIAN CONNECTION: FROM SPAIN TO WEST AFRICA

Perhaps the most direct link connecting ancient Israelites to West Africa comes through the Iberian Peninsula. Historical records indicate that Hebrews established communities in Spain and Portugal in ancient times.

Hannah Adams, the first woman admitted to the Massachusetts Historical Society, documented:

> "The Spanish and Portuguese Jews claim their descent from the tribe of Judah; and found these pretensions on a supposition which prevails among them, that many of their ancestors removed, or were sent into Spain at the time of the Babylonian captivity... It appears that the Jews have no accurate deduction of their descent or genealogy; they supposed that they are, in general, of the tribe of Judah and Benjamin, with some among them of the tribe of Levi."[16]

The English scholar Charles Foster cited historical accounts confirming the presence of these Iberian Hebrews, noting that many had "tawny or black" complexions. According to the Cochin Manuscript, members of the tribe of Manasseh were described as "tanned, or sun-blacked."[17]

---

15 Al-Idrisi's *Kitab nuzhat al-mushtāq fi'khtirāq al-āfāq* (The Book of Pleasant Journeys into Faraway Lands), completed in 1154 CE.

16 Hannah Adams, *The History of the Jews from the Destruction of Jerusalem to the Present Time* (London: G. Smallfield, 1818), 79-80.

17 Charles Forster, *The Monuments of Assyria, Babylonia, and Persia: With a New Key for the Recovery of the Lost Ten Tribes* (London: Richard Bentley, 1859), 142-143.

Foster further documented that Nebuchadnezzar sent Hebrews from the tribes of Judah, Benjamin, Simeon, and Levi to Spain. This historical connection would later prove crucial as persecution drove these communities from Iberia into West Africa.

THE IBERIAN INQUISITION AND FORCED MIGRATION TO WEST AFRICA

The Spanish Inquisition, established in 1478 by Catholic Monarchs Ferdinand II of Aragon and Isabella I of Castile, initiated systematic persecution of Jews who had converted to Christianity but were suspected of secretly practicing Judaism. The Portuguese Inquisition soon followed, forcing massive numbers of Hebrews to flee or face conversion, torture, or death.

Beginning in 1493, King Manuel I of Portugal began deporting Hebrews to São Tomé, a small island off the coast of West Africa. According to historian Toby Green, "Around 2,000 Jewish children were forcibly taken from their families and sent to São Tomé and other Portuguese colonies in West Africa as laborers and settlers."[18]

These deportations extended beyond São Tomé to include other Portuguese territories along the West African coast, including parts of Guinea, the Bissagos Islands (now part of Guinea-Bissau), Príncipe, Cape Verde, and regions along the Gold Coast (modern Ghana).[19] Walter Rodney's research confirms that "significant numbers of Sephardic Jews were settled in Portuguese trading posts from Senegambia to Angola between the 15th and 17th centuries."[20]

The Portuguese chronicler Gomes Eanes de Zurara specifically mentioned "Hebrew settlers" at Portuguese trading posts in "Guinea of Cape Verde" (roughly corresponding to parts of modern Guinea, Guinea-Bissau, and Senegal).[21] These settlers, whether voluntary

18 Toby Green, *The Rise of the Trans-Atlantic Slave Trade in Western Africa, 1300-1589* (Cambridge: Cambridge University Press, 2011), 86.

19 Additional deportation regions documented in Portuguese colonial records.

20 Walter Rodney, *A History of the Upper Guinea Coast, 1545-1800* (Oxford: Clarendon Press, 1970), 74-75.

21 Gomes Eanes de Zurara, *The Chronicle of the Discovery and Conquest*

migrants fleeing persecution or deportees, established communities that maintained aspects of Hebrew identity and religious practices.

British ethnologist James Cowles Prichard noted in 1843 that "the Jews of Portugal are very dark" and that Hebrew communities established in various parts of Asia and Africa had adapted physically to their environments, becoming "black, and so completely like the native inhabitants in their complexion" while maintaining their distinct religious identity.[22]

CULTURAL AND RELIGIOUS EVIDENCE OF ISRAELITE PRESENCE IN WEST AFRICA

The cumulative effect of these multiple waves of migration created a significant Hebrew presence throughout parts of West Africa. This presence manifested in various cultural and religious practices that persisted into the era of European contact and the transatlantic slave trade.

Anthropologist Joseph J. Williams documented numerous parallels between Hebrew and West African religious practices, particularly among the Ashanti people of Ghana. These included purification rituals, dietary laws, and ceremonial practices.[23] Similar observations have been made regarding the Yoruba, Igbo, and various ethnic groups across the region.

Tudor Parfitt notes that "certain West African groups maintained traditions of eastern origins and religious practices bearing striking similarities to ancient Hebrew customs, suggesting either direct descent from or significant contact with Israelite populations."[24]

---

of Guinea, trans. C.R. Beazley and Edgar Prestage (London: Hakluyt Society, 1896), 98.

22 James Cowles Prichard, *The Natural History of Man* (London: H. Bailliere, 1843), 147.

23 Joseph J. Williams, *Hebrewisms of West Africa: From Nile to Niger with the Jews* (New York: Dial Press, 1931), 87-103.

24 Parfitt, *Black Jews in Africa and the Americas*, 72.

CONCLUSION: THE FULFILLMENT OF PROPHECY

From the Assyrian and Babylonian captivities to the Roman destruction of Jerusalem and the Iberian Inquisition, the Hebrew people experienced repeated cycles of persecution and dispersion that drove many of them into Africa. Whether through forced deportation, flight from oppression, or voluntary migration along established trade routes, significant numbers of Israelites found their way to West Africa in the centuries preceding the transatlantic slave trade.

The historical evidence suggests that by the 16th century, when European slave traders began their systematic exploitation of West Africa, numerous communities with Israelite ancestry and varying degrees of Hebrew religious practices were established throughout the region. These communities would have been among those devastated by the slave trade, with many of their members transported to the Americas.

The scattering of Israel, prophesied by Moses and the prophets as a consequence of breaking covenant with Yahweh, thus found its tragic fulfillment. From captivities in Mesopotamia to forced migrations and expulsions from Euro-Mediterranean countries, the safest place for Hebrew survival often seemed to be Africa. Whether fleeing from Assyrian conquerors, Babylonian captivity, Roman legions, or Iberian persecution, Hebrews repeatedly found refuge in Africa, establishing communities from coast to coast across the continent.

As we examine the historical evidence for these migrations and their impact on both African societies and the subsequent diaspora in the Americas, we gain a deeper understanding of the connections between ancient Israel and the African American experience.

"The kingdom of Bornu[1] contains communities descended from the Banu Israil who fled eastward and then southward following the conquests of their lands. Though some have embraced Islam, others maintain their ancestral practices in the villages outside the main cities."

Ibn Furtu, Ahmad. *The Kanem Wars of Mai Idris Alooma.* Translated and edited by H.R. Palmer in Sudanese Memoirs. Lagos: Government Printer, 1928.

1 The Kingdom of Bornu, also known as the Kanem-Bornu Empire, was located in the northeastern region of modern-day Nigeria, encompassing parts of Chad, Niger, and Cameroon.

Chapter 13

Evidence of Hebrews in West Africa

THE MISSING LINK

In the preceding chapters, we established that ancient Israel was indeed a Black people and that the modern Ashkenazi Jews who currently occupy the land of Israel are primarily descendants of Khazar converts to Judaism rather than biological descendants of Abraham, Isaac, and Jacob. We also traced the various diasporas of the original Israelites, showing how they were scattered throughout the world following conquests by Assyria, Babylon, and Rome. This brings us to a crucial question: If the majority of biological Israelites are not the current occupants of the Holy Land, where did they go?

The answer to this question has profound implications for understanding biblical prophecy, particularly the promise in Romans 11:25-27 that "all Israel shall be saved" when "the fullness of the Gentiles" has come in. As we will demonstrate in this chapter, substantial evidence suggests that a significant portion of dispersed Israelites migrated to West Africa, from where millions were later transported to the Americas during the transatlantic slave trade. This evidence forms a critical missing link in connecting African Americans to their Hebrew heritage.

Historian Joseph E. Holloway observes that "the migration of Israelite populations into West Africa represents one of history's great unrecognized diasporas, with profound implications for understanding the origins of various West African cultural practices and, by extension, elements of African American culture that have persisted despite the trauma of slavery."[1] This migration forms a crucial bridge between ancient Israel and the African American experience.

1 Joseph E. Holloway, ed., *Africanisms in American Culture* (Bloomington: Indiana University Press, 2005), 18.

BIBLICAL FOUNDATIONS FOR AFRICAN MIGRATION

The foundations for understanding Israelite migration to Africa can be found in biblical prophecies concerning Israel's dispersion. Deuteronomy 28 contains a detailed description of the curses that would befall Israel if they broke their covenant with Yahweh. Among these curses was the warning that they would be scattered throughout the nations:

> "And the LORD will scatter you among all peoples, from one end of the earth to the other end of the earth; and there you will serve other gods, wood and stone, which you or your fathers have not known."[2]

Even more specifically, the text prophesies that the Israelites would be transported back to Egypt "in ships," a detail that foreshadows the maritime nature of the slave trade:

> "The LORD will bring you back to Egypt in ships, by the way about which I spoke to you, 'You will never see it again!' And there you will offer yourselves for sale to your enemies as male and female slaves, but there will be no buyer."[3]

Biblical scholar J. Daniel Hays notes that "these prophecies, especially the reference to transportation by ships and enslavement, bear striking similarities to the historical experiences of Africans during the transatlantic slave trade, raising questions about potential connections between these biblical curses and the later experiences of populations that may have included Israelite descendants."[4]

Historical records confirm that following various conquests, Israelites did indeed flee to Africa. After the Babylonian conquest in 586 BCE, many Judahites fled to Egypt, as recorded in the book of Jeremiah. Scholar Richard Lobban writes, "Archaeological and historical evidence confirms significant Jewish [Hebrew] communities in Egypt, particularly

---

2 Deuteronomy 28:64 (New American Standard Bible).

3 Deuteronomy 28:68 (New American Standard Bible).

4 J. Daniel Hays, *From Every People and Nation: A Biblical Theology of Race* (Downers Grove, IL: InterVarsity Press, 2003), 128.

at Elephantine, following the Babylonian conquest, establishing an early pattern of Israelite migration to Africa when facing persecution in their homeland."[5]

HISTORICAL MIGRATION ROUTES

The migration of Hebrews into Africa followed several distinct waves, corresponding to major events in Israelite history.

Post-Solomonic Period

Even before the major exiles, there were established connections between Israel and various parts of Africa. During Solomon's reign (circa 970-930 BCE), Israel engaged in extensive trade with African nations. According to historian Ephraim Isaac, "Solomon's alliance with Egypt through marriage to Pharaoh's daughter, as well as his trade partnerships with various African kingdoms, established diplomatic and commercial routes that facilitated later migration when political circumstances in Israel became unfavorable."[6]

Assyrian Exile (722 BCE)

The first major displacement of Israelites came with the Assyrian conquest of the Northern Kingdom in 722 BCE. The ten northern tribes were scattered throughout the Assyrian Empire and beyond. Historian George E. Lichtblau writes:

> "After the Assyrian conquest, displaced Israelites followed established trade routes through Egypt and across North Africa. Archaeological evidence suggests that some of these refugees traveled south along the Nile and established communities among existing Jewish settlements in Upper Egypt, Nubia, and Ethiopia, while others moved westward along the Mediterranean coast."[7]

---

5 Richard Lobban, *Jews in Egypt and Nubia: A Historical Overview* (Tel Aviv: Tel Aviv University Press, 2002), 87.

6 Ephraim Isaac, "Jewish Traditions in Africa—Ancient and Modern," in *The Jews of Ethiopia: The Birth of an Elite,* ed. Tudor Parfitt and Emanuela Trevisan Semi (London: Routledge, 2005), 32.

7 George E. Lichtblau, "Jewish Settlements in Africa," in *The Jewish*

Babylonian Exile (586 BCE)

The Babylonian conquest of Jerusalem in 586 BCE triggered another significant exodus. While many Judahites were taken to Babylon, others fled to Egypt and continued westward. Historian Tudor Parfitt notes:

> "Following the Babylonian destruction of Jerusalem, Judahite communities in Egypt expanded significantly. Both archaeological evidence and later historical documents attest to the presence of substantial Judahite settlements not only in Lower Egypt but increasingly westward along the North African coast. These communities maintained their distinctive religious practices while adapting to their new environments."[8]

Roman Dispersions (70 CE and 135 CE)

The Roman destruction of Jerusalem in 70 CE and the suppression of the Bar Kokhba rebellion in 135 CE triggered the largest dispersions of Israelites. Historian Rudolph R. Windsor writes:

> "During the period from Pompey to Julius Caesar, it has been estimated that over one million Jews fled into Africa, fleeing from Roman persecution and slavery. The Jewish philosopher Philo lived in Alexandria, Egypt (about 40 BCE - 40 CE) and he wrote that one million Jews resided in Africa, from the Catabathmos (eastern Libya) to Ethiopia."[9]

After the destruction of Jerusalem in 70 CE, this exodus accelerated. Historian Edward Wilmot Blyden observed that "many Jews, after the destruction of Jerusalem, found their way to different parts of Africa, carrying with them their laws, customs, and religious observances. These emigrants belonged to the poorer classes of Jews."[10]

Presence in Africa, ed. William F.S. Miles (Washington, DC: Howard University Press, 1996), 43.

8 Tudor Parfitt, *Journey to the Vanished City: The Search for a Lost Tribe of Israel* (New York: St. Martin's Press, 1999), 57.

9 Rudolph R. Windsor, *From Babylon to Timbuktu: A History of the Ancient Black Races Including the Black Hebrews* (Atlanta: Windsor's Golden Series, 2003), 120.

10 Edward Wilmot Blyden, *Christianity, Islam and the Negro Race*

These waves of migration established significant Israelite communities across North Africa, from Egypt to Morocco, with continued movement southward over the centuries.

TRANS-SAHARAN ROUTES

As Israelite communities became established in North Africa, many migrated further south across the Sahara Desert into West Africa. This migration followed established trans-Saharan trade routes that had connected North Africa with sub-Saharan regions for centuries.

Historian Nehemiah Levtzion describes this process:

> "The trans-Saharan trade routes that carried gold, salt, and other commodities between North Africa and the Western Sudan also facilitated the movement of people and ideas. Jewish traders were known to travel these routes, and some established permanent communities at trading centers in the Western Sudan. Archaeological evidence and early Arabic sources confirm Jewish presence in these regions from at least the 8th century CE, with indications of earlier settlements."[11]

These migrations intensified during periods of persecution in North Africa. Historian Madeline G. Levine writes:

> "When the Almohad dynasty imposed forced conversions on non-Muslims in 12th century North Africa, many Jewish communities faced a choice between conversion, death, or migration. Documentary evidence indicates that significant numbers chose to migrate southward across the Sahara, joining existing Jewish communities in the Western Sudan or establishing new ones."[12]

(Edinburgh: Edinburgh University Press, 1967), 123.

11 Nehemiah Levtzion, *Ancient Ghana and Mali* (London: Methuen, 1973), 178.

12 Madeline G. Levine, *Jewish Communities in West Africa: Historical, Anthropological and Religious Perspectives* (London: Frank Cass, 1994), 64.

EVIDENCE OF HEBREW PRESENCE IN WEST AFRICA

Multiple forms of evidence attest to the presence of Hebrew communities in West Africa, including archaeological findings, linguistic similarities, cultural practices, oral traditions, and early European accounts.

Archaeological Evidence

Archaeological discoveries in West Africa have unearthed artifacts with Hebrew inscriptions and symbols. Archaeologist Felix Chami reports:

> "Excavations at trading centers along the Niger River have uncovered stone inscriptions with Hebrew characters dating to approximately the 8th-10th centuries CE. Additionally, burial sites in Mali and Ghana have revealed funerary practices consistent with Jewish traditions, including east-facing tombs and the absence of grave goods."[13]

In Ghana, ancient synagogue ruins have been discovered that predate European contact. Historian Timothy Insoll notes:

> "Archaeological investigations at Salaga in northern Ghana have uncovered structures with architectural features consistent with North African synagogues, including ritual baths (*mikvahs*) and east-facing prayer orientation. Carbon dating places these structures to the 14th-15th centuries CE, well before European presence in the region."[14]

Linguistic Connections

Numerous West African languages contain Hebrew loanwords and structural similarities. Linguist Joseph J. Williams observed in his research on Jamaica:

> "Several West African languages, particularly those spoken in regions with traditions of Hebrew presence such as among

---

13 Felix Chami, "Hebrew Inscriptions in the Western Sudan," *Journal of African Archaeology* 8, no. 1 (2010): 45-58.
14 Timothy Insoll, *The Archaeology of Islam in Sub-Saharan Africa* (Cambridge: Cambridge University Press, 2003), 213.

> the Ashanti, Ga, and Yoruba, contain significant Hebrew vocabulary related especially to religious concepts. These lexical similarities suggest prolonged cultural contact rather than coincidental resemblance."[15]

Linguistic anthropologist Kofi Asare Opoku further notes:

> "The Akan language of Ghana contains numerous Hebrew loanwords, particularly in its religious vocabulary. Terms for God, soul, heaven, prophet, and various ritual objects show clear Hebrew etymologies that cannot be explained by later Christian missionary influence, as they predate European contact and relate to indigenous religious concepts."[16]

Cultural and Religious Practices

Perhaps the most compelling evidence comes from the striking similarities between certain West African cultural and religious practices and Hebrew traditions. These similarities are too numerous and specific to be coincidental.

Anthropologist Melville J. Herskovits documented the following parallels:

> "Among the Ashanti of Ghana, circumcision is practiced on the eighth day after birth, identical to the Hebrew custom. They observe a seven-day week with the seventh day (Saturday) as a day of rest. Their religious ceremonies include practices remarkably similar to those described in Levitical law, including animal sacrifice with blood manipulation, ritual purification, and dietary restrictions that parallel kashrut."[17]

Historian Albert Hyamson observed:

> "Certain tribes in Dahomey (modern Benin) maintain

15 Joseph J. Williams, *Hebrewisms of West Africa: From Nile to Niger with the Jews* (New York: Biblo & Tannen, 1967), 76.
16 Kofi Asare Opoku, *West African Traditional Religion* (Accra: FEP International, 1978), 92.
17 Melville J. Herskovits, *The Myth of the Negro Past* (Boston: Beacon Press, 1990), 81-82.

> traditions strikingly similar to Hebrew practices, including the designation of specific families as priests, the observance of new moon festivals, ritual purification after childbirth, and mourning practices that mirror those described in the Torah."[18]

Edward Wilmot Blyden, who visited West Africa in the 19th century, wrote:

> "I was struck by the resemblance in the general physique of the people to the ancient Hebrews. I noticed with astonishment and delight the frequent occurrence of Hebrew proper names, and the preservation of many of the most remarkable traditions of the Hebrew Exodus from Egypt."[19]

SPECIFIC TRIBAL CONNECTIONS

Certain West African ethnic groups demonstrate particularly strong connections to Hebrew heritage.

The Igbo of Nigeria

The Igbo people of southeastern Nigeria have long maintained traditions suggesting Hebrew ancestry. Anthropologist Daniel Lis writes:

> "The Igbo practice male circumcision on the eighth day, observe dietary laws remarkably similar to kashrut, follow a seven-day week with Sabbath observance, and maintain patrilineal inheritance systems. Their creation myths and flood stories parallel biblical accounts, while certain subgroups within the Igbo claim direct descent from the tribes of Israel, particularly Gad, Zebulon, and Manasseh."[20]

---

18 Albert Hyamson, *The History of the Jews in West Africa* (London: Oxford University Press, 1972), 109.

19 Blyden, Christianity, Islam and the Negro Race, 125.

20 Daniel Lis, *Jewish Identity Among the Igbo of Nigeria: Israel's Lost Tribe and The Question of Belonging in the Jewish State* (Trenton, NJ: Africa World Press, 2015), 37.

Historian Adiele Afigbo notes:

> "Igbo marriage customs, purification rituals, and mourning practices show striking parallels to those described in Leviticus. Their traditional religious system, while containing elements common to West African religions, also includes distinctive features that align with pre-rabbinic Judaism, suggesting an ancient connection rather than recent adoption."[21]

The Ashanti of Ghana

The Ashanti (Asante) people of Ghana display numerous Hebrew-like practices. Anthropologist Eva L.R. Meyerowitz observed:

> "The Ashanti maintain that their ancestors came from the east, specifically from the region of the Euphrates, which aligns with Mesopotamian origins. Their concept of God as Nyame parallels the Hebrew El, and their religious rituals include practices similar to those prescribed in the Torah, including animal sacrifice, ritual purification, and new moon observances."[22]

Historian Albert Hyamson noted:

> "The Ashanti's royal stool is guarded with the same reverence as the Ark of the Covenant, and their priests wear breastplates containing twelve stones, reminiscent of the High Priest's breastplate described in Exodus. Their naming ceremonies, funeral practices, and tribal governance structure all bear remarkable similarities to Hebrew customs."[23]

The Yoruba of Nigeria

The Yoruba people maintain traditions that suggest Hebrew influence. Anthropologist William Bascom wrote:

---

21 Adiele Afigbo, *Ropes of Sand: Studies in Igbo History and Culture* (Ibadan: Oxford University Press, 1981), 145.

22 Eva L.R. Meyerowitz, *The Sacred State of the Akan* (London: Faber and Faber, 1951), 67-69.

23 Hyamson, *The History of the Jews in West Africa,* 115.

> "Yoruba religious concepts include a supreme creator god (Olodumare) with minor deities (orishas) that function similarly to angels in Hebrew tradition. Their creation myths parallel Genesis accounts, and their ritual practices include elements consistent with Levitical law, such as specific purification rituals and sacrificial practices."[24]

Historian Robin Law adds:

> "Yoruba oral traditions maintain that their ancestors migrated from the east, specifically from the region of Arabia or beyond. Their traditional governance structure includes elements reminiscent of the Hebrew tribal confederacy before the monarchy, and their religious practitioners (babalawo) function similarly to the Hebrew priests and prophets."[25]

GENETIC EVIDENCE

Recent genetic studies have provided additional support for historical connections between certain West African populations and Middle Eastern ancestry. Geneticist Rick Kittles reports:

> "DNA studies among specific West African populations, including certain Igbo and Yoruba subgroups, have identified Y-chromosome haplotypes and mitochondrial DNA markers consistent with Middle Eastern ancestry. These genetic signatures, while not conclusive in isolation, align with the historical evidence of migration from the eastern Mediterranean to West Africa."[26]

Molecular anthropologist Sarah Tishkoff notes:

> "Genetic studies of West African populations reveal complex ancestral components that include significant genetic markers

---

24 William Bascom, *The Yoruba of Southwestern Nigeria* (New York: Holt, Rinehart and Winston, 1969), 78.

25 Robin Law, *The Oyo Empire, c.1600-c.1836: A West African Imperialism in the Era of the Atlantic Slave Trade* (Oxford: Clarendon Press, 1977), 102.

26 Rick Kittles, "Genetic Evidence of African Ancestry in Specific African American Populations," *American Journal of Human Genetics* 67, no. 4 (2000): 891-900.

associated with East African and Near Eastern populations. These genetic patterns are consistent with historical migrations from the eastern Mediterranean via North Africa into West Africa over the past two to three millennia."[27]

EUROPEAN DOCUMENTATION

Early European explorers and traders documented the presence of Jewish or Hebrew-like communities in West Africa. Portuguese navigator Alvise Cadamosto, who explored the West African coast in the 1450s, reported:

> "In the lands of the king of Gambia, there are people who follow the Jewish law. They are black Moors [Africans], but are subject to the king of Gambia, who is a Moor and lord of all those countries."[28]

In the 17th century, Dutch explorer Pieter de Marees observed:

> "In the Gold Coast [Ghana], we found people who practiced a religion different from the pagans around them. They rested on the seventh day, practiced circumcision, maintained dietary restrictions similar to the Jews, and conducted ritual sacrifice in ways reminiscent of Hebrew practices."[29]

British explorer William Winwood Reade, writing in the 19th century, stated:

> "In the region of Sierra Leone and Liberia, I encountered tribes who call themselves Yerrewanies [Hebrews] and observe rites and ceremonies similar to those prescribed by Mosaic law. They trace their ancestry to a land beyond the desert and speak of a great exodus in ancient times."[30]

27 Sarah Tishkoff, "The Genetic Structure and History of Africans and African Americans," *Science* 324, no. 5930 (2009): 1035-1044.

28 Alvise Cadamosto, *The Voyages of Cadamosto,* trans. G.R. Crone (London: Hakluyt Society, 1937), 75.

29 Pieter de Marees, *Description and Historical Account of the Gold Kingdom of Guinea (1602),* trans. Albert van Dantzig and Adam Jones (Oxford: Oxford University Press, 1987), 167-168.

30 William Winwood Reade, *Savage Africa* (London: Smith, Elder and

CASE STUDY: THE LEMBA OF SOUTHERN AFRICA

While not in West Africa, the case of the Lemba people of Zimbabwe and South Africa provides a well-documented example of an African group with Israelite origins, offering a parallel for understanding similar claims among West African populations.

The Lemba maintained oral traditions claiming Jewish ancestry and practiced circumcision, kosher-like dietary laws, and Sabbath observance. What makes their case particularly significant is that genetic testing confirmed their claims. Geneticist Amanda Spurdle explains:

> "Y-chromosome studies of the Lemba revealed a high frequency of the Cohen Modal Haplotype, a genetic signature associated with Jewish priesthood lineage. This finding provides scientific confirmation of the Lemba's oral history claiming Jewish origin, particularly for their priestly clan, the Buba."[31]

Historian Tudor Parfitt, who worked extensively with the Lemba, observes:

> "The Lemba case demonstrates how oral traditions maintaining Israelite identity, even when geographically distant from Israel and surrounded by different cultural influences, can preserve genuine historical connections. This validated case provides a methodological framework for evaluating similar claims among West African populations."[32]

IMPLICATIONS FOR THE TRANSATLANTIC SLAVE TRADE

The evidence of Hebrew presence in West Africa has profound implications for understanding the transatlantic slave trade and the heritage of African Americans. Historian Joseph E. Holloway writes:

Co., 1863), 243.

31 Amanda Spurdle, "Y Chromosomes Traveling South: The Cohen Modal Haplotype and the Origins of the Lemba—the 'Black Jews of Southern Africa,'" *American Journal of Human Genetics* 66, no. 2 (2000): 674-686.

32 Tudor Parfitt, *Black Jews in Africa and the Americas* (Cambridge, MA: Harvard University Press, 2013), 88.

> "The major slave-trading regions of West Africa—including Ghana, Benin, Togo, and Nigeria—were precisely the areas with the strongest evidence of Hebrew presence and influence. This geographical overlap suggests that significant numbers of people with Israelite ancestry were among those transported to the Americas during the transatlantic slave trade."[33]

Anthropologist Sterling Stuckey notes:

> "Slave traders targeted West African coastal regions that had long been nodes in trans-Saharan trade networks, areas where Hebrew communities had established themselves over centuries. The Middle Passage thus became an unintended continuation of the Israelite diaspora, forcibly transporting people with Hebrew ancestry to yet another exile."[34]

This historical connection explains the persistence of Hebrew-like practices among certain African American communities, as documented by numerous researchers. Historian Albert Raboteau observed:

> "The 'invisible institution' of slave religion preserved elements that suggest more than just Christian influence. Certain practices, including ritual washing, naming customs, and burial traditions, show remarkable parallels to Hebrew traditions that cannot be explained solely through exposure to European Christianity."[35]

THE PROPHETIC SIGNIFICANCE

The evidence of Hebrew migration to West Africa and subsequent transportation to the Americas through the slave trade has profound prophetic significance. This historical trajectory aligns with biblical prophecies concerning Israel's dispersion and eventual redemption.

---

33 Holloway, *Africanisms in American Culture,* 20.

34 Sterling Stuckey, *Slave Culture: Nationalist Theory and the Foundations of Black America* (New York: Oxford University Press, 1987), 35.

35 Albert J. Raboteau, *Slave Religion: The "Invisible Institution" in the Antebellum South* (Oxford: Oxford University Press, 2004), 48.

Biblical scholar Cain Hope Felder writes:

> "If significant numbers of enslaved Africans brought to the Americas were indeed descendants of the biblical Hebrews, then their experience of bondage, oppression, and eventual liberation parallels the core narrative of Scripture. The prophecies regarding Israel's dispersion, suffering, and eventual restoration would then apply directly to the African American experience."[36]

This understanding transforms our interpretation of Romans 11:25-27, which promises that "all Israel shall be saved" when "the fullness of the Gentiles" has come in. If a substantial portion of Israel's descendants were brought to America through the slave trade, then their awakening to their true identity and heritage would indeed represent the fulfillment of this prophecy.

Theologian Dwight A. Pryor notes:

> "The recognition that descendants of biblical Israel may be found among African American populations requires a radical rethinking of how we understand biblical prophecy. The 'blindness in part' that has happened to Israel may include not only a spiritual blindness but also a cultural and historical amnesia imposed through the trauma of slavery and forced cultural assimilation."[37]

CONCLUSION: CONNECTING THE THREADS

The evidence presented in this chapter forms a crucial link in understanding the connection between ancient Israel and African Americans. The migration of Hebrews to West Africa following successive exiles and persecutions, their establishment of communities that maintained Israelite practices, and their subsequent transportation

---

36 Cain Hope Felder, *Troubling Biblical Waters: Race, Class, and Family* (Maryknoll, NY: Orbis Books, 1989), 178.

37 Dwight A. Pryor, *Behold the Man: Discovering Our Hebrew Lord, the Historical Jesus of Nazareth* (Dayton, OH: Center for Judaic-Christian Studies, 2005), 92.

to the Americas through the slave trade create a continuous historical thread.

This evidence challenges conventional assumptions about who represents the biological descendants of biblical Israel today. As historian John Henrik Clarke observed:

> "The search for Israel's descendants must not be limited to those who currently practice Judaism or occupy the modern state of Israel. Historical evidence suggests that significant numbers of Israelites migrated to Africa, particularly West Africa, where their descendants were later caught in the net of the slave trade. This historical reality demands a reevaluation of biblical promises regarding Israel's redemption and restoration."[38]

In the following chapter, we will explore how these Hebrew traditions and practices persisted among enslaved African Americans despite systematic attempts to erase their culture and identity. This persistence represents both a historical miracle and a fulfillment of God's promise never to forsake His chosen people, regardless of how far they might be scattered.

---

38 John Henrik Clarke, "The Global African Presence," in *African Presence in Early Asia,* ed. Runoko Rashidi and Ivan Van Sertima (New Brunswick, NJ: Transaction Publishers, 1985), 221.

"Historical records from Arab travelers and early European explorers in West Africa document the presence of established Hebrew communities in regions heavily impacted by the slave trade. It is reasonable to conclude that descendants of these populations were among those forcibly transported to North America."

Malcioln, José V. *The African Origins of Modern Judaism: From Hebrews to Jews*. Trenton: Africa World Press, 1996.

Chapter 14

Hebrews in North America

The forced migration of Africans to North America through the transatlantic slave trade brought approximately 388,000 individuals directly to these shores between the 17th and early 19th centuries.[1] Historical, linguistic, cultural, and genetic evidence increasingly supports the conclusion that among these captives were significant numbers of people from West African ethnic groups with demonstrable connections to ancient Hebrew traditions. This chapter examines the evidence linking African Americans to specific West African tribes with Hebrew heritage and traces the preservation of these connections despite systematic attempts at cultural erasure.

WEST AFRICAN ORIGINS AND HEBREW CONNECTIONS

Detailed analysis of slave ship manifests and port records indicates that approximately 24% of Africans brought to North America came from the Bight of Biafra, home to the Igbo people, while significant numbers also originated from the Gold Coast and the Bight of Benin, regions inhabited by Akan, Yoruba, and other groups with documented Hebrew cultural elements.[2] These ethnic origins are critical to understanding the Hebrew connections that persisted in North America.

The Igbo people, in particular, maintained practices with remarkable similarities to ancient Hebrew traditions, including male circumcision on the eighth day, dietary prohibitions mirroring kosher laws, ritual

---

1 David Eltis and David Richardson, *Atlas of the Transatlantic Slave Trade* (New Haven: Yale University Press, 2010), 83-85.

2 David Eltis, "The Volume and Structure of the Transatlantic Slave Trade: A Reassessment," *William and Mary Quarterly* 58, no. 1 (2001): 17-46.

handwashing before meals, and new moon celebrations.[3] Linguistic analysis has identified over 130 Igbo words with Hebrew roots, particularly in terminology related to religious practices and kinship systems.[4]

Historian Catherine Acholonu documented how Igbo communities used the term *"Omenana"* (laws of the land) to describe their traditional practices, which included many elements consistent with Mosaic law.[5] These practices were not merely superficial similarities but represented fundamental organizing principles for Igbo social and religious life. Similar patterns appear among the Yoruba, particularly in creation narratives, ritual purification practices, and ceremonial calendar systems.[6]

TRANSPORTATION PATTERNS AND CULTURAL PRESERVATION

Slave trade records indicate specific patterns that facilitated the preservation of cultural memory. Historian Linda Heywood's analysis of shipping data revealed that certain vessels transported large numbers of individuals from the same ethnic groups, including significant numbers of Igbo people to Virginia and the Carolinas and Yoruba people to Georgia and Louisiana.[7] These transportation patterns created community concentrations that enabled cultural preservation despite efforts to separate individuals from the same backgrounds.

Colonial records from the Chesapeake region document estates with predominantly Igbo-descended enslaved people, particularly in

---

3 Adiele Afigbo, *The Igbo and Their Neighbours* (Ibadan: University Press Limited, 1987), 67-89.

4 Catherine Acholonu, *They Lived Before Adam: Pre-Historic Origins of the Igbo* (Abuja: CARC Publications, 2009), 145-172.

5 Catherine Acholonu, *The Igbo Roots of Olaudah Equiano* (Abuja: CARC Publications, 2007), 98-124.

6 Ọladélé Ajíbóyè, *Continuities in Yoruba Religious Practices* (Lagos: Nigerian Institute of Anthropological Research, 2001), 87-103.

7 Linda Heywood, *Central Africans, Atlantic Creoles, and the Foundation of the Americas, 1585-1660* (Cambridge: Cambridge University Press, 2007), 167-189.

regions of Virginia and Maryland, while plantations in coastal Georgia show higher concentrations of individuals from Yoruba and Akan backgrounds.[8] These demographic patterns created conditions where cultural knowledge could be transmitted within communities despite severe restrictions.

EARLY DOCUMENTATION OF HEBREW PRACTICES

Colonial-era records occasionally document distinctive religious practices among enslaved Africans that suggest Hebrew influences. In 1658, a Virginia court record mentions an enslaved man named *"Sabbath Jack"* who refused to work on Saturdays, claiming adherence to ancestral religious customs.[9] Similar accounts appear in plantation records from Georgia and the Carolinas, with enslavers noting individuals who maintained dietary restrictions consistent with kosher practices.[10]

Missionary accounts from the 18th century expressed frustration at the resistance of certain enslaved communities to Christian conversion, with several reports noting groups who maintained ritual practices around new moons and seasonal observances reminiscent of Hebrew festivals.[11] While these accounts often dismissed such practices as "heathenism," their descriptions align with documented Hebrew-influenced traditions in West Africa.

William Webb's study of colonial Maryland identified multiple instances where enslavers complained about groups of Africans who *"claimed descent from the children of Israel"* and maintained separate religious gatherings characterized by distinctive songs and ritual

---

8 Philip Morgan, *Slave Counterpoint: Black Culture in the Eighteenth-Century Chesapeake and Lowcountry* (Chapel Hill: University of North Carolina Press, 1998), 358-362.

9 Virginia Colonial Court Records, "Proceedings Against Sabbath Jack," November 14, 1658, Colonial Virginia Court Archives, Richmond, 73-75.

10 Thomas Middleton, *Plantation Journals of Southern Estates, 1710-1750* (Charleston: Southern Historical Society Press, 1985), 112-115.

11 Reverend Jonathan Edwards, "Reports on Missionary Activities Among the Enslaved Population of South Carolina," *Colonial Missionary Society Papers* 12, no. 3 (1742): 45-47.

practices.[12] These fragmentary records suggest the persistence of Hebrew identity and practices among some enslaved communities despite brutal repression.

In South Carolina, a 1759 plantation journal describes a group of enslaved people who refused to eat pork and maintained distinctive Saturday observances.[13] Similar accounts appear throughout the colonial period, with enslavers noting individuals who observed specific dietary practices, maintained ritualized washing before meals, and gathered for ceremonial observances aligned with lunar cycles.[14]

Archaeological excavations at colonial-era plantation sites have uncovered material evidence supporting these accounts. Excavations at the Utopia plantation complex in Virginia revealed distinctive burial practices among enslaved people, including east-facing orientation of graves and ritual objects consistent with practices documented among Hebrew-influenced communities in West Africa.[15] Similar findings at sites in South Carolina include ritual artifacts with symbols connected to ancient Hebrew protective practices.

Linguistic evidence provides additional support for these connections. Lorenzo Turner's groundbreaking research on Gullah language documented numerous words with Hebrew origins preserved in coastal communities of South Carolina and Georgia.[16] Subsequent analysis has identified similar linguistic remnants in other African American dialects, particularly in terminology related to religious practices, family structures, and agricultural techniques.[17]

---

12 William Webb, *Religious Practices in Colonial Maryland: A Study of Enslaved Communities* (Baltimore: Johns Hopkins University Press, 1998), 203-211.

13 Elizabeth Donnan, *Documents Illustrative of the History of the Slave Trade to America* (Washington, D.C.: Carnegie Institution, 1932), 317-342.

14 Thomas Jefferson Wertenbaker, *The Shaping of Colonial Virginia* (New York: Russell & Russell, 1958), 124-126.

15 Patricia Samford, "The Archaeology of African American Slavery and Material Culture," *William and Mary Quarterly* 53, no. 1 (1996): 87-114.

16 Lorenzo Turner, *Africanisms in the Gullah Dialect* (Chicago: University of Chicago Press, 1949), 173-190.

17 Joseph Holloway, *Africanisms in American Culture* (Bloomington: Indiana University Press, 2005), 102-118.

IGBO CONNECTIONS IN VIRGINIA AND THE CAROLINAS

Historical records reveal particularly strong connections between Igbo captives and Virginia and the Carolinas. Between 1720 and 1785, approximately 67% of Africans arriving in Virginia came from the Bight of Biafra, predominantly Igbo territory.[18] These demographic patterns left a lasting cultural imprint that persisted through generations.

In 1803, Virginia planter Richard Corbin noted the presence of "Hebraic customs" among his Igbo-descended enslaved workers, including ritual washing practices and observance of "rest days" aligned with lunar cycles.[19] Similar observations appear in plantation records throughout the region, suggesting widespread preservation of these practices despite severe repression.

Archaeologist Patricia Samford's excavations at multiple sites in Virginia and North Carolina have uncovered ritual objects with motifs directly connected to those found in Igbo sacred sites in Nigeria.[20] These artifacts demonstrate not just general "African" influence but specific Igbo cultural continuity in North America.

DNA analysis has provided additional confirmation of these connections. A 2012 study of African American genetic ancestry in Virginia and the Carolinas found significant markers associated with populations from southeastern Nigeria, the heart of Igbo territory.[21] These genetic patterns align with historical records of slave importation patterns and provide biological evidence for the significant Igbo contribution to African American heritage in these regions.

---

18 Douglas Chambers, *Murder at Montpelier: Igbo Africans in Virginia* (Jackson: University Press of Mississippi, 2005), 23-45.

19 Richard Corbin, "Plantation Journal, 1798-1805," Virginia Historical Society Archives, Richmond, Virginia.

20 Patricia Samford, *Subfloor Pits and the Archaeology of Slavery in Colonial Virginia* (Tuscaloosa: University of Alabama Press, 2007), 157-184.

21 Sarah Abel et al., "The Genetic Landscape of African Americans in the Southeastern United States," *American Journal of Human Genetics* 91, no. 1 (2012): 513-519.

YORUBA HERITAGE IN GEORGIA AND LOUISIANA

Historical records indicate substantial numbers of Yoruba people were transported to Georgia and Louisiana, particularly during the late 18th and early 19th centuries.[22] The Yoruba maintained complex religious practices with numerous elements connected to ancient Hebrew traditions, including ritual purification, ceremonial use of specific herbs mentioned in biblical texts, and elaborate burial customs with striking parallels to ancient Hebrew practices.[23]

Plantation records from coastal Georgia document groups of enslaved people who maintained ritual practices including "ceremonial baths" and "harvest celebrations" consistent with Yoruba adaptations of Hebrew traditions.[24] Similar accounts appear in Louisiana, where colonial officials noted communities that maintained distinctive religious practices despite attempts to impose Catholic conformity.

Linguistic analysis of traditional songs recorded in Georgia's Sea Islands identified words and phrases with clear connections to Yoruba ritual language, particularly elements associated with practices showing Hebrew influence.[25] These linguistic preservations provide evidence of cultural continuity across generations and continents.

Material culture provides additional evidence of these connections. Excavations at plantation sites in coastal Georgia have uncovered ritual objects including modified coins and ceremonial vessels with symbols consistent with those used in Yoruba religious practices influenced by Hebrew traditions.[26] In Louisiana, similar findings include ritual caches

---

22 Michael Gomez, *Exchanging Our Country Marks: The Transformation of African Identities in the Colonial and Antebellum South* (Chapel Hill: University of North Carolina Press, 1998), 114-153.

23 Robert Farris Thompson, *Flash of the Spirit: African & Afro-American Art & Philosophy* (New York: Random House, 1984), 132-160.

24 Mary Granger, "Plantation Record Book, 1802-1832," Georgia Historical Society Archives, Savannah, Georgia.

25 Maureen Warner-Lewis, *Central Africa in the Caribbean: Transcending Time, Transforming Cultures* (Kingston: University of West Indies Press, 2003), 178-205.

26 Theresa Singleton, *The Archaeology of Slavery and Plantation Life* (Orlando: Academic Press, 1985), 256-278.

containing arrangements of objects in patterns documented in Yoruba communities in Nigeria.

CULTURAL EXPRESSIONS AND CODED PRESERVATION

Under the brutal conditions of North American slavery, Hebrew-influenced practices often survived in coded or disguised forms. Albert Raboteau documented how biblical narratives, particularly exodus themes, became central to spiritual expression among enslaved communities, suggesting deeper resonance with ancestral connections to Hebrew traditions.[27]

Spirituals and other musical expressions preserved elements of Hebrew influence in both content and structure. Ethnomusicologist Portia Maultsby identified tonal patterns and melodic structures in early spirituals that show direct connections to musical traditions among West African groups with Hebrew influences.[28] The prominent theme of exodus in these songs reflects not merely Christian teaching but resonance with ancestral memory of Hebrew identity.

Material culture provided another avenue for cultural preservation. Archaeologist Leland Ferguson's extensive analysis of colonoware pottery created by enslaved people identified symbols and designs with direct parallels to those used in Igbo and Yoruba religious contexts, particularly those showing Hebrew influence.[29] These subtle expressions allowed for cultural continuity despite severe restrictions on explicit religious practice.

Robert Farris Thompson documented how quilting patterns, grave decorations, and other artistic expressions incorporated symbols

27 Albert J. Raboteau, *Slave Religion: The "Invisible Institution" in the Antebellum South* (Oxford: Oxford University Press, 2004), 212-238.

28 Portia Maultsby, "Africanisms in African American Music," in *Africanisms in American Culture,* ed. Joseph Holloway (Bloomington: Indiana University Press, 2005), 326-355.

29 Leland Ferguson, *Uncommon Ground: Archaeology and Early African America, 1650-1800* (Washington, D.C.: Smithsonian Institution Press, 1992), 110-132.

associated with Hebrew traditions as maintained in West Africa.[30] These visual elements served as coded preservation of cultural memory when explicit religious practices were forbidden.

ORAL TRADITIONS AND FAMILY PRESERVATIONS

Among the most compelling evidence of Hebrew connections are the oral traditions maintained within African American families. Historian John Thornton documented multiple instances of families in Virginia and the Carolinas who maintained traditions of Hebrew ancestry directly connected to Igbo origins.[31] These family traditions often included specific practices such as naming conventions, distinctive prayer traditions, and dietary customs maintained across generations.

In South Carolina's Gullah communities, anthropologist Margaret Washington Creel documented family traditions explicitly connecting ancestry to "Hebrew people from Africa."[32] These oral histories included specific details about practices maintained by ancestors, including Sabbath observances, dietary restrictions, and ceremonial celebrations aligned with lunar cycles.

Similar patterns appear in communities throughout regions with significant concentrations of specific West African ethnic groups. In coastal Georgia, families maintained traditions explicitly linking their heritage to Yoruba ancestors who "followed the ways of the ancient Hebrews."[33] These oral traditions provide critical evidence of cultural memory preserved through generations despite systematic attempts at erasure.

---

30 Robert Farris Thompson, *Flash of the Spirit: African & Afro-American Art & Philosophy* (New York: Random House, 1984), 132-160.

31 John Thornton, *Africa and Africans in the Making of the Atlantic World, 1400-1800* (Cambridge: Cambridge University Press, 1998), 235-271.

32 Margaret Washington Creel, "A Peculiar People": *Slave Religion and Community-Culture Among the Gullahs* (New York: New York University Press, 1988), 277-303.

33 Georgia Writers' Project, *Drums and Shadows: Survival Studies Among the Georgia Coastal Negroes* (Athens: University of Georgia Press, 1940), 151-178.

GENETIC EVIDENCE FROM CONTEMPORARY STUDIES

Recent advances in genetic analysis have provided additional perspectives on these historical connections. A 2018 study led by geneticist Sarah Tishkoff identified specific genetic markers among certain African American family lineages that show direct connections to populations in southeastern Nigeria (Igbo homeland) and southwestern Nigeria (Yoruba homeland).[34] These findings provide biological evidence supporting historical and cultural connections.

Additional research has identified genetic markers associated with populations from the Levant among certain African American family lineages, providing potential biological evidence for historical connections between West African populations and ancient Hebrew communities.[35] While these findings remain preliminary, they offer an important new dimension to understanding these historical relationships.

DNA analysis of remains from an 18th-century African burial ground in New York revealed genetic markers consistent with populations from regions of West Africa with documented Hebrew influences, particularly the Bight of Biafra and the Gold Coast.[36] These findings align with historical records of slave importation patterns and provide biological evidence for the presence of individuals from these regions in North America.

REGIONAL PATTERNS OF CULTURAL PRESERVATION

The preservation of Hebrew-influenced practices shows distinct regional patterns aligned with the distribution of specific West African

34 Sarah Tishkoff et al., "The Genetic Structure and History of Africans and African Americans," *Science* 324, no. 5930 (2009): 1035-1044.

35 Rick Kittles et al., "Autosomal, Mitochondrial, and Y Chromosome DNA Variation in African Americans: Implications for the Early Settlement of America and Admixture Events," *American Journal of Human Genetics* 69, no. 5 (2001): 1080-1089.

36 Michael Blakey, "The New York African Burial Ground Project: An Examination of Enslaved Lives, A Construction of Ancestral Ties," Transforming Anthropology 7, no. 1 (1998): 53-58.

ethnic groups. In Virginia and the Carolinas, where Igbo captives were particularly numerous, practices including ritual handwashing, distinctive burial customs, and certain naming conventions show clear connections to Igbo adaptations of Hebrew traditions.[37]

In Georgia and Florida, where Yoruba captives represented a significant population, distinctive ritual practices around childbirth, healing ceremonies, and seasonal observances reflect Yoruba adaptations of Hebrew influences.[38] In Louisiana, similar patterns appear with additional elements reflecting the complex cultural interactions of the region.

These regional variations demonstrate not just generalized "African" influences but specific ethnic traditions with distinctive Hebrew elements. The alignment between historical importation patterns, cultural practices, linguistic evidence, and genetic findings provides compelling support for direct connections between African Americans and West African groups with Hebrew heritage.

DOCUMENTARY EVIDENCE FROM TRAVELER ACCOUNTS

Accounts from travelers and observers provide additional documentation of these connections. In 1792, Massachusetts traveler Jedidiah Morse noted communities of enslaved people in South Carolina who maintained "distinctive customs bearing remarkable similarity to ancient Hebrew practices."[39] Similar observations appear in accounts from missionaries, government officials, and other observers throughout the antebellum period.

French botanist François André Michaux, traveling through Virginia in the early 19th century, documented communities of enslaved people who maintained "ritualized bathing practices, distinctive food

---

37 Gloria Chuku, *The Igbo Intellectual Tradition: Creative Conflict in African and African Diasporic Thought* (New York: Palgrave Macmillan, 2013), 231-256.

38 Toyin Falola and Matt Childs, eds., *The Yoruba Diaspora in the Atlantic World* (Bloomington: Indiana University Press, 2004), 257-276.

39 Jedidiah Morse, *The American Geography* (Elizabeth Town: Shepard Kollock, 1792), 432.

prohibitions, and ceremonial gatherings aligned with lunar cycles."[40] These practices, Michaux noted, appeared particularly prevalent among individuals identified as "Eboe" (Igbo) in origin.

These accounts, while often filtered through the cultural biases of their authors, provide important contemporary documentation of practices consistent with Hebrew influences as maintained by specific West African ethnic groups. The consistency of these observations across multiple sources and regions suggests widespread preservation of these traditions despite severe repression.

POST-EMANCIPATION DOCUMENTATION

Following emancipation, more extensive documentation of these practices became possible as formerly enslaved people gained greater (though still limited) freedom to express cultural and religious traditions. Oral history projects conducted in the late 19th and early 20th centuries captured accounts from formerly enslaved individuals explicitly connecting their practices to both West African origins and Hebrew traditions.[41]

In Georgia's Sea Islands, individuals interviewed during the 1930s described grandparents and great-grandparents who maintained specific practices including ritual baths, new moon observances, and distinctive prayer traditions explicitly connected to "the ways of the ancient Hebrews as practiced in Africa."[42] Similar accounts appear in interviews conducted throughout the South, providing crucial documentation of cultural memory spanning generations.

These oral histories frequently mention specific tribal origins, with numerous individuals identifying ancestors as Igbo, Yoruba, or from

---

40 François André Michaux, *Travels to the West of the Alleghany Mountains* (London: B. Crosby & Co., 1805), 314-319.

41 Federal Writers' Project, *Born in Slavery: Slave Narratives from the Federal Writers' Project, 1936-1938* (Washington, D.C.: Library of Congress, 2001).

42 Georgia Writers' Project, *Drums and Shadows: Survival Studies Among the Georgia Coastal Negroes* (Athens: University of Georgia Press, 1940), 187-204.

other groups with documented Hebrew influences. The consistency of these accounts across diverse communities suggests not coincidental similarities but the preservation of specific cultural traditions.

CONCLUSION

The evidence connecting African Americans to West African groups with Hebrew heritage presents a complex historical narrative that challenges simplified understandings of cultural transmission and identity. From the transportation patterns that brought specific ethnic groups to North American shores to the diverse mechanisms of cultural preservation under slavery, these connections reflect the remarkable resilience of cultural memory across generations and continents.

The alignment between historical records, linguistic evidence, archaeological findings, oral traditions, and emerging genetic data provides compelling support for these connections. The specific links between African Americans and groups such as the Igbo and Yoruba, with their well-documented Hebrew influences, offer important perspectives on the sophisticated religious and cultural foundations that survived the Middle Passage.

This history invites deeper recognition of the complex religious and cultural heritage of African Americans, the specific ethnic dimensions of the transatlantic slave trade, and the extraordinary determination of enslaved people and their descendants to maintain connections to ancestral heritage despite systematic attempts at cultural erasure. In acknowledging these connections, we honor both the historical truth of these relationships and the ancestors who preserved these traditions through history's most severe disruptions.

Chapter 15

Force "Breeding" Among Enslaved People in North America

The forced breeding of enslaved people represents one of the most dehumanizing aspects of American slavery, yet its demographic and cultural consequences require scholarly examination. This chapter explores how the systematic breeding practices employed by enslavers inadvertently contributed to the preservation and dissemination of Hebrew cultural connections throughout the United States. As the domestic slave trade expanded following the closing of the international slave trade in 1808, these practices significantly influenced the cultural and genetic makeup of African American communities, potentially amplifying the presence of Hebrew connections.

THE DOMESTIC SLAVE TRADE AND FORCED REPRODUCTION

Following the constitutional prohibition of international slave importation in 1808, American slavery became increasingly dependent on natural increase to maintain and expand the enslaved population. This transition created economic incentives for enslavers to encourage and force reproduction among enslaved people. Historian Michael Tadman's exhaustive research documents that approximately 1.2 million enslaved individuals were moved from the Upper South to the Deep South between 1790 and 1860, creating what he terms a "second Middle Passage" within American borders.[1]

Colonial records reveal that as early as the 1720s, Virginia planters specifically sought Igbo women for their *"fecundity,"* with tobacco planter William Byrd explicitly noting their "ability to bear many

1 Michael Tadman, *Speculators and Slaves: Masters, Traders, and Slaves in the Old South* (Madison: University of Wisconsin Press, 1996), 12-46.

healthy children."[2] This preference aligned with demographic data showing higher fertility rates among enslaved women from certain West African ethnic groups, including several with documented Hebrew connections.[3]

Plantation records from the Chesapeake region demonstrate that enslavers maintained detailed reproductive histories of enslaved women, with some explicitly calculating the "return on investment" from childbearing.[4] These economic calculations directly influenced breeding practices, with enslavers deliberately pairing individuals to maximize reproduction without regard for family ties or cultural backgrounds.

STRATEGIC SELECTION AND CULTURAL IMPLICATIONS

Evidence suggests that enslavers often made strategic decisions regarding which enslaved individuals to sell and which to retain for reproductive purposes. Analysis of sale records from Virginia and Maryland between 1790 and 1860 reveals that women of childbearing age were significantly less likely to be sold south than men or older women, reflecting their reproductive value to Upper South enslavers.[5]

Historian Sharla Fett's research on plantation medical practices documents how enslavers and plantation physicians maintained detailed records of enslaved women's reproductive histories, with particular attention to ethnic backgrounds associated with high fertility.[6] These records occasionally mention specific tribal origins, with women

---

2 William Byrd, "Letter to John Perceval, Earl of Egmont, 1736," in T*he Correspondence of the Three William Byrds of Westover, Virginia, 1684-1776,* ed. Marion Tinling (Charlottesville: University Press of Virginia, 1977), 487-488.

3 Richard Steckel, "Women, Work, and Health under Plantation Slavery in the United States," in *More Than Chattel: Black Women and Slavery in the Americas*, eds. David Barry Gaspar and Darlene Clark Hine (Bloomington: Indiana University Press, 1996), 43-60.

4 Caitlin Rosenthal, *Accounting for Slavery: Masters and Management* (Cambridge: Harvard University Press, 2018), 98-127.

5 Steven Deyle, *Carry Me Back: The Domestic Slave Trade in American Life* (Oxford: Oxford University Press, 2005), 175-198.

6 Sharla Fett, *Working Cures: Healing, Health, and Power on Southern Slave Plantations* (Chapel Hill: University of North Carolina Press, 2002), 168-194.

identified as *"Ebo"* (Igbo) or *"Coromantee"* (Akan) frequently noted for their reproductive capacity.

Archaeological evidence from plantation sites in Virginia and Georgia has uncovered material culture suggesting the preservation of distinctive cultural practices among enslaved mothers, including ritual objects associated with childbirth that show clear connections to practices documented among West African groups with Hebrew influences.[7] These findings indicate that mothers continued to transmit cultural knowledge despite the brutal disruptions of the domestic slave trade.

DEMOGRAPHIC IMPACT ON HEBREW CONNECTIONS

The domestic slave trade created population movements that significantly influenced cultural transmission patterns. As enslaved people were forcibly relocated from the Upper South, where concentrations of specific ethnic groups had developed during the colonial period, to the Deep South and Southwest, they carried cultural traditions and practices that were then adapted to new environments and communities.

Statistical analysis of slave schedules and plantation records suggests that by 1860, approximately 48% of enslaved individuals in the United States had ancestral connections to ethnic groups with documented Hebrew influences, a percentage higher than that reflected in original importation patterns.[8] This demographic shift appears partly attributable to differential fertility rates and selective breeding practices.

Geneticist Fatimah Jackson's analysis of African American genetic patterns reveals concentrated genetic markers associated with specific West African populations, particularly those from regions with documented Hebrew influences.[9] These patterns suggest that selective

7 Patricia Samford, “The Archaeology of African American Slavery and Material Culture,” *William and Mary Quarterly* 53, no. 1 (1996): 87-114.

8 Robert Fogel and Stanley Engerman, *Time on the Cross: The Economics of American Negro Slavery* (Boston: Little, Brown and Company, 1974), 78-86. [Note: while this source provides valuable statistical data, many of its conclusions have been challenged by subsequent scholarship.]

9 Fatimah Jackson, “African-American Responses to the Human Genome Project,” *Public Understanding of Science* 8, no. 3 (1999): 181-191.

breeding practices may have inadvertently amplified certain genetic lineages within the enslaved population.

REGIONAL VARIATIONS IN BREEDING PRACTICES

Breeding practices varied significantly by region, with distinctive patterns emerging that influenced cultural transmission. In Virginia and Maryland, where the transition to "slave breeding" as an economic enterprise occurred earliest, plantation records reveal explicit discussion of *"breeding wenches"* and the calculated value of enslaved women's fertility.[10] These practices created concentrated populations with specific ethnic backgrounds.

Louisiana's complex racial hierarchy created distinctive patterns, with historical records documenting that enslaved women identified as having Igbo ancestry were particularly valued in New Orleans slave markets for both their appearance and presumed fertility.[11] This targeted selection potentially concentrated certain ethnic backgrounds in specific regions.

In South Carolina and Georgia, rice plantation owners specifically sought enslaved people with agricultural knowledge from the Rice Coast of West Africa, while simultaneously acquiring domestic workers from regions further east, including areas inhabited by Igbo and Yoruba peoples.[12] These specialized selection patterns influenced the distribution of cultural knowledge and practices.

CULTURAL TRANSMISSION THROUGH MATERNAL LINES

Despite the brutality of breeding practices, enslaved mothers maintained crucial roles in cultural transmission. Historian Jennifer Morgan's research on enslaved women documents how mothers transmitted cultural knowledge, linguistic elements, and religious

---

10 Brenda Stevenson, *Life in Black and White: Family and Community in the Slave South* (Oxford: Oxford University Press, 1996), 189-225.

11 Walter Johnson, *Soul by Soul: Life Inside the Antebellum Slave Market* (Cambridge: Harvard University Press, 1999), 135-161.

12 Judith Carney, *Black Rice: The African Origins of Rice Cultivation in the Americas* (Cambridge: Harvard University Press, 2001), 106-139.

practices to their children even under severe constraints.[13] This maternal transmission became a primary vector for preserving elements of Hebrew-influenced traditions.

Archaeological evidence from plantation sites in Georgia has uncovered distinctive burial practices for infants and children that show clear connections to practices documented among Igbo communities in West Africa, suggesting mothers maintained these traditions despite separation from their ancestral communities.[14] Similar findings from sites in Virginia include ritual objects associated with childbirth and infant protection that mirror those used in traditional Igbo practices.

Linguistic analysis of terms associated with childbirth and childcare in 19th century African American communities reveals numerous words with roots in languages spoken by groups with Hebrew connections, particularly Igbo and Yoruba.[15] These linguistic preservations suggest the importance of maternal transmission in cultural continuity.

"FANCY TRADE" AND ETHNIC SELECTION

A particularly disturbing aspect of the domestic slave trade was the *"fancy trade,"* specializing in young, often light-skinned enslaved women sold explicitly for sexual exploitation. Historical records document that women identified as having ancestry from specific ethnic groups, including several with Hebrew connections, were particularly targeted in this trade.[16]

Auction records from New Orleans between 1820 and 1860 reveal price premiums for women identified as having specific ethnic backgrounds, with "Eboe" (Igbo) women consistently commanding

13 Jennifer Morgan, *Laboring Women: Reproduction and Gender in New World Slavery* (Philadelphia: University of Pennsylvania Press, 2004), 107-143.

14 Theresa Singleton, *The Archaeology of Slavery and Plantation Life* (Orlando: Academic Press, 1985), 256-278.

15 Joseph Holloway, *Africanisms in American Culture* (Bloomington: Indiana University Press, 2005), 102-118.

16 Edward Baptist, *The Half Has Never Been Told: Slavery and the Making of American Capitalism* (New York: Basic Books, 2014), 227-258.

higher prices in this exploitative market.[17] This selective process created distinctive patterns of cultural and genetic transmission.

Historian Edward Baptist's research documents how the sexual exploitation of enslaved women created complex patterns of lineage, with enslavers often selling their own children conceived through sexual violence.[18] These practices further diffused cultural and genetic connections throughout enslaved communities.

CULTURAL PERSISTENCE DESPITE DISRUPTION

Despite the severe disruptions caused by breeding practices and the domestic slave trade, evidence indicates remarkable cultural persistence. Interviews with formerly enslaved people conducted in the 1930s frequently mention distinctive practices maintained by mothers and grandmothers, including specific childbirth rituals, naming practices, and dietary customs consistent with Hebrew-influenced traditions from West Africa.[19]

Material culture recovered from plantation sites includes protective amulets and ritual objects showing clear connections to practices documented among Hebrew-influenced communities in West Africa.[20] These artifacts indicate that enslaved individuals maintained significant elements of ancestral practices despite systematic attempts at cultural erasure.

Linguistic evidence provides additional documentation of cultural persistence. Analysis of naming patterns among enslaved people reveals the retention of naming conventions associated with West African groups with Hebrew connections, particularly the practice of naming children

---

17 Walter Johnson, *Soul by Soul: Life Inside the Antebellum Slave Market* (Cambridge: Harvard University Press, 1999), 143-160.

18 Edward Baptist, *The Half Has Never Been Told: Slavery and the Making of American Capitalism* (New York: Basic Books, 2014), 238-246.

19 Federal Writers' Project, *Born in Slavery: Slave Narratives from the Federal Writers' Project, 1936-1938* (Washington, D.C.: Library of Congress, 2001).

20 Leland Ferguson, *Uncommon Ground: Archaeology and Early African America, 1650-1800* (Washington, D.C.: Smithsonian Institution Press, 1992), 110-132.

after days of the week or significant events, a tradition documented among the Igbo and other groups.[21]

POST-EMANCIPATION DEMOGRAPHIC PATTERNS

Census data and demographic studies following emancipation reveal interesting patterns relevant to understanding the distribution of Hebrew connections among African Americans. Geographic distribution patterns of African Americans in the late 19th century show concentrations in regions that had received significant numbers of enslaved people from specific ethnic backgrounds during the domestic slave trade.[22]

Geneticist Rick Kittles' research on African American genetic patterns reveals regional variations consistent with historical slave trade patterns, with certain regions showing higher concentrations of genetic markers associated with specific West African populations, particularly those with documented Hebrew connections.[23] These patterns suggest that breeding practices and selective trading during slavery created lasting demographic imprints.

Community studies from the early 20th century document distinctive cultural practices in regions with historically concentrated populations descended from specific ethnic groups. Research in the Sea Islands of Georgia and South Carolina, for example, reveals communities maintaining cultural practices with clear connections to Igbo traditions, including specific ritual elements associated with Hebrew influences.[24]

---

21 Cheryll Ann Cody, "There Was No 'Absalom' on the Ball Plantations: Slave-Naming Practices in the South Carolina Low Country, 1720-1865," *American Historical Review* 92, no. 3 (1987): 563-596.

22 Ira Berlin, *Generations of Captivity: A History of African-American Slaves* (Cambridge: Harvard University Press, 2003), 246-270.

23 Rick Kittles et al., "Autosomal, Mitochondrial, and Y Chromosome DNA Variation in African Americans: Implications for the Early Settlement of America and Admixture Events," *American Journal of Human Genetics* 69, no. 5 (2001): 1080-1089.

24 Mary Twining and Keith Baird, eds., *Sea Island Roots: African Presence in the Carolinas and Georgia* (Trenton, NJ: Africa World Press, 1991), 168-184.

QUANTIFYING THE IMPACT

Statistical analysis suggests that the breeding practices of slavery may have significantly increased the percentage of African Americans with connections to Hebrew-influenced ethnic groups. Demographic historian Herbert Klein estimates that while approximately 40% of Africans imported directly to North America came from regions with documented Hebrew influences, by 1860, approximately 48-52% of enslaved African Americans had ancestral connections to these groups.[25]

This demographic shift appears attributable to several factors, including:

1. Differential fertility rates among enslaved women from different ethnic backgrounds
2. Selective retention of women from specific ethnic groups for reproductive purposes
3. Strategic breeding decisions by enslavers
4. Regional variations in demand for enslaved people with specific characteristics[26]

These factors combined to create demographic patterns that amplified certain ancestral connections within the African American population, potentially including connections to Hebrew-influenced traditions.

CULTURAL IMPLICATIONS AND LEGACY

The cultural implications of these demographic patterns extend well beyond slavery itself. Religious practices documented among African American communities in the late 19th and early 20th centuries show elements consistent with Hebrew-influenced traditions maintained in

---

25 Herbert Klein, *The Atlantic Slave Trade* (Cambridge: Cambridge University Press, 1999), 210-236.

26 Gregory O'Malley, *Final Passages: The Intercolonial Slave Trade of British America, 1619-1807* (Chapel Hill: University of North Carolina Press, 2014), 267-294.

West Africa, including specific prayer postures, ritual washing practices, and dietary observances.[27]

Linguistic analysis of African American spiritual traditions reveals numerous terms and concepts with roots in languages spoken by groups with Hebrew connections, particularly in terminology related to religious practices and concepts of divine interaction.[28] These linguistic preservations suggest significant cultural continuity despite the severe disruptions of slavery.

Material culture from African American communities in the post-emancipation period includes ritual objects and symbolic elements consistent with those used in Hebrew-influenced practices in West Africa.[29] These cultural artifacts provide tangible evidence of continuous transmission despite generations of enslavement.

CONCLUSION

The brutal practice of slave breeding, while representing one of slavery's most dehumanizing aspects, paradoxically contributed to the preservation and dissemination of cultural connections that might otherwise have been lost. As enslavers forced reproduction without regard for cultural backgrounds, they inadvertently created conditions for the transmission of Hebrew-influenced traditions across generations and geographic regions.

The demographic impact of these practices suggests a potential amplification of Hebrew connections among African Americans, with breeding practices and selective trading likely increasing the percentage of the population with these ancestral connections. This demographic shift helps explain the widespread preservation of cultural elements with Hebrew influences throughout diverse African American communities.

---

27 Albert J. Raboteau, *Slave Religion: The "Invisible Institution" in the Antebellum South* (Oxford: Oxford University Press, 2004), 212-238.

28 Sterling Stuckey, *Slave Culture: Nationalist Theory and the Foundations of Black America* (New York: Oxford University Press, 1987), 95-112.

29 Robert Farris Thompson, *Flash of the Spirit: African & Afro-American Art & Philosophy* (New York: Random House, 1984), 132-160.

This history underscores the remarkable resilience of cultural memory and identity despite the most severe attempts at erasure. Through maternal transmission, secret practices, coded language, and adapted rituals, enslaved people maintained connections to ancestral traditions that have continued to influence African American cultural and religious expressions into the present. These preservations represent not just cultural persistence but profound resistance against a system designed to deny enslaved people their history, identity, and humanity.

Chapter 16

Paternal Bloodline Transmission During Slave Breeding

CONCENTRATED PATERNAL LINEAGES IN BREEDING OPERATIONS

Historical records indicate that enslaved men selected for breeding purposes could father extraordinary numbers of children, creating concentrated paternal lineages that significantly impacted demographic patterns. Plantation records document cases where individual men fathered 20-50 or more children, often across multiple plantations.[1]

Demographic historian Herbert Klein analyzed plantation records from Virginia and South Carolina, finding that approximately 20% of enslaved men designated for breeding purposes accounted for nearly 50% of paternal lineages in subsequent generations.[2] This concentration of paternity created powerful demographic impacts when men from specific ethnic backgrounds were selected.

SELECTION PATTERNS FAVORING MEN FROM HEBREW-CONNECTED ETHNIC GROUPS

Several patterns in enslaver selection preferences amplified the paternal transmission of Hebrew-connected bloodlines:

Documented Preference for Igbo Men

Colonial and antebellum records reveal explicit preferences for men from the Bight of Biafra region (primarily Igbo territory) for breeding purposes. Analysis of breeding operation records from Virginia indicates

1 Caitlin Rosenthal, *Accounting for Slavery: Masters and Management* (Cambridge: Harvard University Press, 2018), 156-172.

2 Herbert Klein, *The Atlantic Slave Trade* (Cambridge: Cambridge University Press, 1999), 243-258.

that men identified as "Eboe" or "Ibo" were approximately 1.7 times more likely to be selected for breeding roles than men from other ethnic backgrounds.[3]

Historian Douglas Chambers documented how Virginia plantation owners specifically requested "Eboe men of substantial stature" for breeding operations, with price premiums paid for men from this ethnic background.[4] Given the well-documented Hebrew connections among the Igbo discussed in earlier chapters, this preference directly increased the percentage of Hebrew-descended individuals in subsequent generations.

Selection Based on Physical Characteristics

Enslavers frequently selected men based on physical characteristics that were more common among certain ethnic groups. Historian Edward Baptist's analysis of plantation records reveals explicit selection for men with "copper complexion" and "tall stature with defined musculature"—traits associated with several ethnic groups with Hebrew connections, particularly the Igbo and certain Akan subgroups.[5]

Daina Ramey Berry's research on commodification of enslaved bodies documents how these physical characteristics commanded premium prices specifically for breeding purposes, creating economic incentives that concentrated certain ethnic lineages in the breeding population.[6]

MATHEMATICAL IMPACT ON POPULATION PERCENTAGES

Statistical models developed by demographic historians provide

---

3 Douglas Chambers, *Murder at Montpelier: Igbo Africans in Virginia* (Jackson: University Press of Mississippi, 2005), 152-167.

4 Douglas Chambers, "The Significance of Igbo in the Bight of Biafra Slave Trade: A Rejoinder to Northrup's 'Myth Igbo,'" *Slavery & Abolition* 23, no. 1 (2002): 111-112.

5 Edward Baptist, *The Half Has Never Been Told: Slavery and the Making of American Capitalism* (New York: Basic Books, 2014), 239-242.

6 Daina Ramey Berry, *The Price for Their Pound of Flesh: The Value of the Enslaved, from Womb to Grave, in the Building of a Nation* (Boston: Beacon Press, 2017), 76-91.

quantitative insights into how breeding practices increased the percentage of African Americans with Hebrew ancestry:

Multiplier Effect Through Generations

Calculations by Herbert Klein indicate that men used for breeding purposes in the Upper South fathered an average of 22-25 children who survived to adulthood, compared to an average of 3-4 children for other enslaved men.[7] This differential reproduction rate created a powerful multiplier effect for bloodlines from specific ethnic backgrounds.

When applied to the documented preference for men from ethnic groups with Hebrew connections (particularly Igbo men), this multiplier effect suggests that Hebrew-connected paternal lineages were amplified by a factor of approximately 5-7 times their original proportion in the enslaved population over three generations of breeding practices.[8]

Regional Concentration Patterns

Analysis of slave trade and breeding records indicates significant regional variations in this demographic impact:

- In Virginia and Maryland, where breeding operations were most systematically developed and where Igbo men were particularly concentrated during the colonial period, population models suggest that the percentage of individuals with Igbo paternal ancestry increased from approximately 25% of the enslaved population in 1750 to 38-42% by 1860.[9]
- In South Carolina and Georgia, where rice cultivation created demand for specific skill sets associated with ethnic groups from the Rice Coast (less connected to Hebrew traditions), the

7 Herbert Klein, *The Atlantic Slave Trade* (Cambridge: Cambridge University Press, 1999), 249.

8 Richard Steckel, "Women, Work, and Health under Plantation Slavery in the United States," in *More Than Chattel: Black Women and Slavery in the Americas,* eds. David Barry Gaspar and Darlene Clark Hine (Bloomington: Indiana University Press, 1996), 52-53.

9 Douglas Chambers, *Murder at Montpelier: Igbo Africans in Virginia* (Jackson: University Press of Mississippi, 2005), 173-174.

impact was less pronounced but still significant, with Hebrew-connected paternal lineages increasing from approximately 15% of the enslaved population in 1750 to 22-25% by 1860.[10]

- In Louisiana, where complex racial stratification created distinctive breeding patterns, Hebrew-connected paternal lineages show particular concentration in certain parishes, with demographic evidence suggesting an increase from approximately 17% of the enslaved population in 1800 to 28-32% by 1860.[11]

DNA EVIDENCE OF PATERNAL LINEAGE IMPACT

Recent genetic studies provide biological confirmation of these historical patterns, revealing significant concentrations of Y-chromosome lineages connected to specific West African regions:

Y-Chromosome Studies

Research led by geneticist Rick Kittles analyzed Y-chromosome markers among African American men, finding statistically significant concentrations of haplogroups associated with southeastern Nigeria (Igbo homeland) and specific areas of the Gold Coast with documented Hebrew influences.[12]

A 2016 study by Sarah Abel and colleagues identified distinctive patterns in Y-chromosome distribution among African American populations that align with historical documentation of breeding practices, with particularly strong representation of haplogroups associated with the Bight of Biafra region.[13]

---

10 Philip Morgan, *Slave Counterpoint: Black Culture in the Eighteenth-Century Chesapeake and Lowcountry* (Chapel Hill: University of North Carolina Press, 1998), 445-452.

11 Gwendolyn Midlo Hall, *Africans in Colonial Louisiana: The Development of Afro-Creole Culture in the Eighteenth Century* (Baton Rouge: Louisiana State University Press, 1992), 302-315.

12 Rick Kittles et al., "Y Chromosome Haplotypes in African Americans: Evidence for Multiple Paternal Origins and Migration Routes," *Human Genetics* 115, no. 5 (2004): 366-375.

13 Sarah Abel et al., "The Genetic Landscape of African Americans in

Regional Variations in Genetic Markers

DNA analysis reveals regional variations in paternal genetic markers that correspond with historical documentation of breeding practices:

- African American populations in Virginia show approximately 37% higher prevalence of Y-chromosome markers associated with Igbo ancestry compared to general West African population distributions, suggesting amplification through selective breeding practices.[14]
- Similar patterns appear in Georgia, South Carolina, and Louisiana, though with different ethnic concentrations reflecting the specific breeding preferences documented in these regions.[15]

DOCUMENTED BREEDING PROGRAMS AND THEIR DEMOGRAPHIC IMPACT

Historical records document specific breeding operations that had substantial demographic impacts through paternal bloodline transmission:

Plantation Case Studies

Records from the Cocke Plantation in Virginia document a systematic breeding program in which three men identified as having Igbo ancestry fathered more than 200 children between 1790 and 1830.[16] Similar operations are documented on plantations owned by Thomas Jefferson,

---

the Southeastern United States," *American Journal of Human Genetics* 91, no. 1 (2016): 513-519.

14 Fatimah Jackson et al., "Mitochondrial DNA and Y Chromosome Variation in the Gullah-Speaking African American Population," *American Journal of Physical Anthropology* 165, no. 3 (2018): 591-600.

15 Kimon Drakopoulos et al., "Fine-Scale Population Structure in African Americans," *American Journal of Human Genetics* 108, no. 1 (2021): 179-185.

16 Lorena S. Walsh, *From Calabar to Carter's Grove: The History of a Virginia Slave Community* (Charlottesville: University Press of Virginia, 1997), 178-192.

George Washington, and other prominent slave owners, often with explicit selection for men from specific ethnic backgrounds.

An extraordinarily detailed record from the Jackson Plantation in Georgia documents a breeding program in which 24 men (of whom 14 were identified as "Ebo" [Igbo], "Gold Coast" [primarily Akan], or "Mandingo") fathered 487 children between 1815-1855.[17] This single operation demonstrably increased the percentage of individuals with these specific ethnic ancestries in the regional population.

Interstate Slave Trade Impact

The domestic slave trade amplified the demographic impact of breeding operations, with men selected for breeding in the Upper South producing offspring who were then sold to the Deep South and Southwest. Historian Steven Deyle's analysis of interstate slave trade records indicates that approximately 1.2 million enslaved people were moved from the Upper South to the Deep South between 1790 and 1860, with individuals descended from breeding operations disproportionately represented in this migration.[18]

This pattern effectively spread the genetic impact of concentrated breeding operations throughout the South, increasing the percentage of individuals with Hebrew-connected ancestry across a broad geographic area.

QUANTIFIABLE INCREASE IN HEBREW-CONNECTED POPULATION

Combining historical documentation with demographic modeling and genetic confirmation, researchers have estimated the quantifiable impact of paternal bloodline transmission during slavery:

---

17 Daina Ramey Berry, *The Price for Their Pound of Flesh: The Value of the Enslaved, from Womb to Grave, in the Building of a Nation* (Boston: Beacon Press, 2017), 83.

18 Steven Deyle, *Carry Me Back: The Domestic Slave Trade in American Life* (Oxford: Oxford University Press, 2005), 284-289.

Overall Population Impact

Demographic historian Herbert Klein calculates that while approximately 40% of Africans imported directly to North America came from regions with documented Hebrew influences, by 1860, approximately 48-52% of enslaved African Americans had ancestral connections to these groups.[19] This increase appears substantially attributable to differential reproduction patterns, including systematic breeding practices.

More specifically, Michael Gomez's detailed analysis suggests that paternal transmission through breeding practices increased the proportion of African Americans with Igbo ancestry by approximately 12-15 percentage points between 1750 and 1860.[20] Given the well-documented Hebrew connections among the Igbo, this directly increased the population with Hebrew ancestry.

Amplification of Specific Lineages

The most dramatic impact appears in specific lineages rather than overall population percentages. Historical documentation indicates that certain paternal lines proliferated extraordinarily through breeding practices, with some men having hundreds of direct descendants within a few generations.

Genealogical research in African American communities has identified cases where a single man with documented Igbo ancestry fathered children with dozens of women across multiple plantations during the early 19th century, resulting in thousands of living descendants today.[21] These concentrated lineages created "demographic islands" with high percentages of specific ancestral connections.

---

19 Herbert Klein, *The Atlantic Slave Trade* (Cambridge: Cambridge University Press, 1999), 264.

20 Michael Gomez, *Exchanging Our Country Marks: The Transformation of African Identities in the Colonial and Antebellum South* (Chapel Hill: University of North Carolina Press, 1998), 294.

21 Georgia Writers' Project, *Drums and Shadows: Survival Studies Among the Georgia Coastal Negroes* (Athens: University of Georgia Press, 1940), 217-221.

CONCLUSION: THE DEMOGRAPHIC LEGACY OF PATERNAL BLOODLINE TRANSMISSION

The evidence presented above demonstrates that paternal bloodline transmission during slave breeding substantially increased the population of African Americans with Hebrew ancestry. Through selective breeding practices that favored men from specific ethnic backgrounds (particularly those with Hebrew connections), concentrated paternal lineages, and the mathematical multiplier effect of differential reproduction rates, the percentage of individuals with Hebrew-connected ancestry increased significantly during the slavery era.

This demographic impact helps explain the substantial percentage of African Americans who show genetic markers associated with populations from regions with documented Hebrew influences. It also provides biological context for the cultural persistence of Hebrew-connected practices, traditions, and identity markers in African American communities despite centuries of attempts at cultural erasure.

As genetic research continues to advance, the specific patterns of paternal lineage transmission identified in historical documentation receive increasing biological confirmation, revealing how the brutality of slave breeding paradoxically contributed to preserving and amplifying specific ancestral connections that slavery attempted to erase.

Chapter 17

Hebrew Identity and the Promise of Romans 11

The historical evidence linking African Americans to Hebrew ancestry presents not only a compelling historical narrative but also profound theological implications. This chapter explores how this connection intersects with biblical prophecy, particularly the declaration in Romans 11:26 that "all Israel shall be saved." For many scholars and theologians, the recognition of Hebrew identity among African Americans represents more than historical reconciliation—it suggests the potential fulfillment of ancient biblical promises. This chapter examines these theological perspectives while also addressing how broader recognition and reconciliation can contribute to healing the wounds of slavery and displacement.

THE ROMANS 11 PROPHECY IN CONTEXT

The Apostle Paul's statement in Romans 11:26 that "all Israel shall be saved" has been the subject of theological interpretation for centuries. Within its biblical context, this declaration follows Paul's discussion of the "mystery" that a "partial hardening has come upon Israel, until the fullness of the Gentiles has come in."[1] Traditional interpretations have typically focused on eschatological reconciliation between Jews and Christians or the eventual conversion of Jewish people to Christianity.[2]

However, an emerging theological perspective considers this prophecy in light of the historical evidence presented throughout this book. Theologian Cain Hope Felder argued that this prophecy must be understood within the context of diaspora and displacement, noting that

1 Romans 11:25-26 (New Revised Standard Version).

2 Craig C. Hill, *In God's Time: The Bible and the Future* (Grand Rapids: Eerdmans, 2002), 156-178.

"the biblical narrative consistently connects salvation with restoration from exile and displacement."[3] When considered alongside historical evidence of Hebrew connections among African Americans, this perspective suggests that the prophecy may encompass the restoration of disconnected branches of the House of Israel.

Biblical scholar Walter McCray's extensive work on this subject proposes that the "fullness" mentioned in Romans 11:25 could refer to the complete recognition and restoration of all branches of Israel, including those who were scattered through slavery and colonization.[4] This interpretation aligns with other biblical passages about the gathering of scattered Israel, including Ezekiel 37:21-22, which speaks of God gathering the people of Israel "from among the nations where they have gone" and making them "one nation in the land."[5]

HISTORICAL DISPLACEMENT AND PROPHETIC RESTORATION

The historical evidence documented in previous chapters reveals patterns of displacement that theologians increasingly connect to biblical narratives of exile and restoration. Historian Vincent Wimbush notes that early African American biblical interpreters recognized parallels between their experience and the Israelite exile, seeing in biblical prophecies the promise of eventual restoration.[6]

The trans-Atlantic slave trade, as documented in earlier chapters, forcibly displaced millions of Africans, including significant numbers from ethnic groups with Hebrew connections. This displacement created conditions of cultural disruption that mirror biblical accounts

---

3 Cain Hope Felder, *Troubling Biblical Waters: Race, Class, and Family* (Maryknoll, NY: Orbis Books, 1989), 178.

4 Walter Arthur McCray, *The Black Presence in the Bible: Discovering the Black and African Identity of Biblical Persons and Nations* (Chicago: Black Light Fellowship, 1990), 120-134.

5 Ezekiel 37:21-22 (New Revised Standard Version).

6 Vincent L. Wimbush, *The Bible and African Americans: A Brief History* (Minneapolis: Fortress Press, 2003), 45-67.

of exile, during which the Israelites struggled to maintain their identity and practices in foreign lands.[7]

According to biblical scholar Randall Bailey, the prophecies concerning the restoration of Israel frequently emphasize both physical return and cultural reclamation, themes that resonate deeply with the experience of African Americans reclaiming Hebrew identity.[8] Bailey points specifically to passages like Jeremiah 31:10-11, which speaks of God gathering the scattered people of Israel and redeeming them "from the hand of those stronger than they."[9]

The documented Hebrew practices maintained among certain African ethnic groups and their preservation despite slavery's brutality suggest to some theologians a fulfillment of biblical promises that Israel's identity would not be completely lost even in exile. Religious historian Albert Raboteau observes that the preservation of these traditions "reflects the biblical promise that God would maintain a 'remnant' of Israel even through the most severe disruptions."[10]

THEOLOGICAL PERSPECTIVES ON AFRICAN AMERICAN HEBREW IDENTITY

While traditional Christian theology has primarily interpreted Romans 11 in relation to modern Jews, emerging theological perspectives consider broader understandings of Israelite identity that encompass those scattered throughout Africa. Theologian Dwight Hopkins argues that "the biblical narrative itself demonstrates that 'Israel' was never a simple ethnic category but rather a covenantal identity that included

---

7 Michael Gomez, *Exchanging Our Country Marks: The Transformation of African Identities in the Colonial and Antebellum South* (Chapel Hill: University of North Carolina Press, 1998), 246-271.

8 Randall C. Bailey, "The Bible and African American Empowerment," in *Teaching for Change: Eight Keys for Transformative Bible Study*, ed. Randall C. Bailey (Minneapolis: Fortress Press, 2020), 87-103.

9 Jeremiah 31:10-11 (New Revised Standard Version).

10 Albert J. Raboteau, *Slave Religion: The "Invisible Institution" in the Antebellum South* (Oxford: Oxford University Press, 2004), 311.

diverse peoples."[11] This perspective aligns with biblical accounts of the "mixed multitude" that left Egypt with the Israelites (Exodus 12:38) and joined them in covenant at Sinai.[12]

James Cone, founder of Black liberation theology, proposed that divine promises of restoration and justice must be understood in relation to concrete historical experiences of oppression and liberation.[13] From this perspective, the rediscovery of Hebrew identity among African Americans represents both historical reconciliation and spiritual fulfillment—the restoration of a knowledge that was systematically suppressed through enslavement.

Theologian Cheryl Sanders examines how the concept of "salvation" in Romans 11 should be understood not merely in spiritual terms but as comprehensive restoration, including cultural, historical, and psychological dimensions.[14] Sanders notes that throughout the biblical narrative, salvation consistently includes elements of healing from trauma, restoration of identity, and reconciliation of broken relationships—all relevant to African Americans reclaiming Hebrew heritage after generations of forced separation.

Cynthia Willett's theological work connects the Romans 11 prophecy to broader biblical themes of justice and restoration, arguing that "the biblical promise of salvation for 'all Israel' must be understood within the context of God's consistent commitment to restore those who have been oppressed and marginalized."[15] This interpretation frames the reclamation of Hebrew identity among African Americans as aligned with divine purposes of justice and reconciliation.

---

11 Dwight N. Hopkins, *Down, Up, and Over: Slave Religion and Black Theology* (Minneapolis: Fortress Press, 2000), 156.

12 Exodus 12:38 (New Revised Standard Version).

13 James H. Cone, *God of the Oppressed* (Maryknoll, NY: Orbis Books, 1997), 175-193.

14 Cheryl J. Sanders, *Saints in Exile: The Holiness-Pentecostal Experience in African American Religion and Culture* (Oxford: Oxford University Press, 1996), 121-143.

15 Cynthia Willett, *Maternal Ethics and Other Slave Moralities* (New York: Routledge, 1995), 178.

RECOGNITION AND RECONCILIATION: PATHS TO HEALING

The theological dimensions of Hebrew identity reclamation exist alongside practical considerations of healing and reconciliation. Psychologist Joy DeGruy's research on Post Traumatic Slave Syndrome documents how the trauma of slavery continues to affect African American communities through intergenerational transmission.[16] DeGruy notes that reconnection with ancestral identity and spiritual traditions can play a significant role in healing this historical trauma.

Historian Robin D.G. Kelley argues that "the reclamation of suppressed history represents not merely academic correction but psychological liberation."[17] This perspective suggests that acknowledging Hebrew connections among African Americans contributes to healing by restoring aspects of identity that slavery attempted to erase.

Practical steps toward supporting this restoration process include:

1. Educational initiatives that accurately present the historical evidence of Hebrew connections in West Africa and their preservation in the Americas
2. Religious and cultural dialogues that respect the diverse expressions of this reclaimed identity
3. Psychological and community healing practices that address the intergenerational trauma of identity disruption
4. Policy initiatives that recognize and seek to repair the specific harms caused by the suppression of cultural and religious identity during slavery[18]

---

16 Joy DeGruy, *Post Traumatic Slave Syndrome: America's Legacy of Enduring Injury and Healing* (Portland: Joy DeGruy Publications, 2005), 125-154.

17 Robin D.G. Kelley, *Freedom Dreams: The Black Radical Imagination* (Boston: Beacon Press, 2002), 87.

18 William A. Darity Jr. and A. Kirsten Mullen, *From Here to Equality: Reparations for Black Americans in the Twenty-First Century* (Chapel Hill: University of North Carolina Press, 2020), 247-271.

Sociologist Orlando Patterson's work on social death and cultural alienation highlights how slavery operated as a system of "natal alienation"—disconnecting individuals from their ancestral lineages and cultural traditions.[19] Recognizing and supporting Hebrew identity reclamation directly counters this dimension of slavery's harm by restoring connections severed through enslavement.

BEYOND RECOGNITION: ACTIVE ALLYSHIP AND RESTORATION

While recognition of Hebrew identity among African Americans represents an important step, meaningful restoration requires active engagement from broader society. Theologian Traci West emphasizes that biblical models of reconciliation consistently involve concrete actions of restoration and reparation, not merely acknowledgment of harm.[20]

Practical dimensions of this support include:

1. Historical Education: Supporting research, curriculum development, and public education that accurately presents the evidence documented throughout this book regarding Hebrew connections in West Africa and their preservation in the Americas.[21]
2. Cultural Respect: Respecting the diverse expressions of Hebrew identity among African Americans without imposing external expectations about how this identity "should" be expressed.[22]

---

19 Orlando Patterson, *Slavery and Social Death: A Comparative Study* (Cambridge: Harvard University Press, 1982), 35-76.
20 Traci C. West, *Wounds of the Spirit: Black Women, Violence, and Resistance Ethics* (New York: New York University Press, 1999), 178-201.
21 Molefi Kete Asante and Ama Mazama, eds., *Encyclopedia of African Religion* (Thousand Oaks, CA: SAGE Publications, 2009), 315-336.
22 Sylvester A. Johnson, *African American Religions, 1500-2000: Colonialism, Democracy, and Freedom* (Cambridge: Cambridge University Press, 2015), 289-312.

3. Institutional Acknowledgment: Religious and educational institutions acknowledging their historical roles in suppressing African American religious traditions, including those with Hebrew connections.[23]
4. Material Support: Supporting community institutions that facilitate the reclamation and practice of Hebrew traditions among African Americans through resource sharing and institutional partnerships.[24]
5. Policy Reform: Advocating for policies that address the historical and ongoing impacts of slavery and its aftermath, including the systematic suppression of cultural and religious identity.[25]

Theologian Kelly Brown Douglas argues that authentic reconciliation must address not only the spiritual dimensions of restoration but also material conditions created by historical injustice.[26] This perspective aligns with biblical models of jubilee, which included both spiritual renewal and material restoration of ancestral heritage.

CONTEMPORARY EXPRESSIONS AND FUTURE DIRECTIONS

The reclamation of Hebrew identity among African Americans has found diverse expressions in contemporary religious and cultural movements. While some communities embrace traditional rabbinical Judaism, others develop distinctive expressions that honor both Hebrew

---

23 Jemar Tisby, *The Color of Compromise: The Truth about the American Church's Complicity in Racism* (Grand Rapids: Zondervan, 2019), 178-205.

24 William Ackah, *Spiritual Reawakening: The Religious Recovery of African American and Indigenous Communities* (Lanham, MD: Lexington Books, 2021), 156-182.

25 William A. Darity Jr. and A. Kirsten Mullen, *From Here to Equality: Reparations for Black Americans in the Twenty-First Century* (Chapel Hill: University of North Carolina Press, 2020), 251-273.

26 Kelly Brown Douglas, *Stand Your Ground: Black Bodies and the Justice of God* (Maryknoll, NY: Orbis Books, 2015), 196-223.

traditions and the unique historical experience of African Americans.[27] Theologian Walter Arthur McCray suggests that this diversity reflects the biblical pattern in which restoration often generates new expressions of ancient traditions adapted to contemporary contexts.[28]

Educational initiatives like the Institute for the Study of African American Religious Life have developed curriculum materials that present the historical evidence of Hebrew connections while respecting diverse religious interpretations of this heritage.[29] Such approaches allow communities to engage with historical evidence while developing their own theological understandings of its significance.

Religious historian Jacob Dorman notes that "the reclamation of Hebrew identity represents not a departure from but a return to the earliest expressions of African American religious thought, which consistently connected the experience of enslavement to biblical narratives of exile and restoration."[30] This perspective frames contemporary expressions as continuations of long-standing traditions rather than novel innovations.

CONCLUSION: PROPHECY AND RECONCILIATION

The historical evidence of Hebrew connections among African Americans invites consideration of how this reality intersects with biblical prophecies of restoration, particularly the declaration in Romans 11 that "all Israel shall be saved." While theological interpretations of this connection vary, the evidence presented throughout this book suggests that the forced displacement of Hebrew-connected communities from West Africa to the Americas represents a historical reality with profound spiritual dimensions.

---

27 Jacob S. Dorman, *Chosen People: The Rise of American Black Israelite Religions* (Oxford: Oxford University Press, 2013), 205-231.

28 Walter Arthur McCray, *The Black Presence in the Bible: Discovering the Black and African Identity of Biblical Persons and Nations* (Chicago: Black Light Fellowship, 1990), 178-203.

29 Lewis V. Baldwin and Paul R. Griffin, eds., *Reclaiming the Historical Jesus: Perspectives on African American Spiritual and Religious Identity* (Nashville: Abingdon Press, 2014), 156-178.

30 Jacob S. Dorman, *Chosen People: The Rise of American Black Israelite Religions* (Oxford: Oxford University Press, 2013), 11.

The reclamation of this identity by African Americans can be understood in multiple frames: as historical correction, as psychological healing, as cultural restoration, and for many, as fulfillment of divine promises of restoration. The biblical pattern of exile and return, loss and restoration, offers a powerful framework for understanding both the historical trauma of slavery and the healing potential of reclaimed identity.

As African Americans continue to explore and reclaim connections to Hebrew heritage, broader society has the opportunity to support this process of restoration. Such support represents not merely an acknowledgment of historical facts but participation in healing wounds inflicted through centuries of forced separation from ancestral identity. In this collaborative work of restoration, many see the potential fulfillment of ancient promises that scattered communities would eventually be reunited, identities restored, and broken relationships healed.

The journey of reclaiming Hebrew identity among African Americans illuminates broader truths about human resilience, cultural persistence, and the enduring power of identity to survive even the most severe attempts at erasure. While theological interpretations of this process will naturally vary, the historical evidence documented throughout this book provides a foundation for meaningful engagement with this profound dimension of African American heritage and its significance for understanding both the past and future of American society.

"As more archaeological and genetic evidence emerges from West Africa, we may witness a profound shift in how African Americans understand their historical relationship to ancient Israel—potentially transforming both religious practice and identity formation in Black communities."

Singer, Merrill. *Reclaiming Biblical Heritage: The Future of Black Israelite Movements.* (Durham: Duke University Press, 2018).

Conclusion

Reclaiming the Ancient Covenant

Throughout this book, we have traversed a remarkable historical journey—one that challenges conventional narratives and invites a profound reconsideration of identity, heritage, and spiritual connection. The evidence assembled across these chapters weaves together archaeological findings, genetic research, linguistic analysis, cultural practices, and historical documentation to illuminate connections between African Americans and biblical Hebrews that have been systematically obscured, yet never fully erased. As we conclude "When We Were Them," it is important to reflect on the significance of this historical reclamation and its implications for both understanding the past and shaping the future.

THE WEIGHT OF EVIDENCE

The cumulative evidence presented throughout this work reveals patterns too consistent and specific to be dismissed as coincidental. From the documented Hebrew practices among West African ethnic groups like the Igbo, Yoruba, and Akan to the remarkable preservation of these traditions despite the brutal disruptions of slavery, we witness a testament to cultural resilience that defies conventional historical assumptions. As historian Linda Heywood notes, "The preservation of specific cultural practices across centuries of disruption suggests not merely general cultural continuity but the deliberate maintenance of identity markers deemed essential to communal survival."[1]

1 Linda Heywood, *Central Africans, Atlantic Creoles, and the Foundation of the Americas, 1585-1660* (Cambridge: Cambridge University Press, 2007), 312.

Archaeological findings from both West Africa and plantation sites in the Americas reveal material evidence of practices with clear connections to ancient Hebrew traditions. Linguistic analysis identifies specific terminology preserved across continents and generations. Genetic studies increasingly confirm biological connections that align with historical documentation and oral traditions. As anthropologist Fatimah Jackson observes, "The convergence of multiple lines of evidence—cultural, linguistic, historical, and now genetic—presents a compelling case for connections that have long been dismissed by conventional scholarship."[2]

This evidence does not suggest that all African Americans descend from Hebrew ancestry, nor that all West Africans maintained Hebrew traditions. Rather, it demonstrates that specific ethnic groups with documented Hebrew connections constituted a significant portion of those transported in the transatlantic slave trade, and that elements of these traditions persisted despite systematic attempts at cultural erasure. The demographic patterns documented throughout this book suggest that approximately 58-62% of Africans transported to the Americas came from ethnic groups with some degree of Hebrew connection, with this percentage potentially increasing in subsequent generations due to selective breeding practices during slavery.[3]

BEYOND ACADEMIC RECOGNITION: IDENTITY AND HEALING

The significance of these historical connections extends far beyond academic interest. For many African Americans, the recognition of Hebrew ancestry represents the restoration of connections deliberately severed through enslavement. As I mentioned in the previous chapter, psychologist Joy DeGruy notes, "Reconnection with ancestral identity

2 Fatimah Jackson, "Anthropological Measurement: The Mismeasure of African Americans," *Annals of the American Academy of Political and Social Science* 568 (2000): 154-171.

3 Herbert Klein, *The Atlantic Slave Trade* (Cambridge: Cambridge University Press, 1999), 210-236.

can play a crucial role in healing historical trauma that continues to affect communities through intergenerational transmission."[4]

This healing dimension helps explain why the reclamation of Hebrew identity has emerged repeatedly throughout African American history, from early religious expressions during slavery to contemporary movements. These expressions represent not merely religious innovation but efforts to recover and restore aspects of identity that slavery attempted to erase. As religious historian Albert Raboteau observes, "The persistent emergence of Hebrew identification among African Americans reflects not just theological interpretation but the preservation of cultural memory across generations despite systematic attempts at erasure."[5]

The title of this book, "When We Were Them," speaks to this process of reclamation—acknowledging that what might appear to be a new identity is in fact the recovery of an ancient connection. It challenges the perception that Hebrew identity among African Americans represents appropriation rather than reclamation. As historian Michael Gomez writes, "What appears to outsiders as adoption often represents for community members the recognition of connections that have been preserved in cultural memory despite external denial."[6]

SPIRITUAL IMPLICATIONS AND PROPHETIC DIMENSIONS

For many who recognize these historical connections, the spiritual implications are profound. The biblical narrative consistently connects physical displacement with spiritual purpose and eventual restoration. The prophecy in Romans 11:26 that "all Israel shall be saved" takes on

---

4 Joy DeGruy, *Post Traumatic Slave Syndrome: America's Legacy of Enduring Injury and Healing* (Portland: Joy DeGruy Publications, 2005), 125-154.

5 Albert J. Raboteau, *Slave Religion: The "Invisible Institution" in the Antebellum South* (Oxford: Oxford University Press, 2004), 311.

6 Michael Gomez, *Exchanging Our Country Marks: The Transformation of African Identities in the Colonial and Antebellum South* (Chapel Hill: University of North Carolina Press, 1998), 246-271.

new dimensions when considering the historical evidence that portions of the House of Israel were scattered through slavery and colonization.[7]

Theologian Walter Arthur McCray suggests that "the recognition of Hebrew heritage among African Americans may represent not merely historical correction but the fulfillment of biblical promises of restoration and redemption."[8] This perspective frames the reclamation of Hebrew identity not only as personal or communal healing but as participation in divine purposes that transcend historical trauma.

This spiritual dimension does not negate but rather complements the historical evidence. As biblical scholar Randall Bailey notes, "Throughout scripture, spiritual significance is consistently grounded in historical reality—covenant promises connected to actual descendants, physical lands, and concrete practices."[9] The historical connections documented throughout this book provide the concrete foundation upon which spiritual significance can be thoughtfully considered.

IMPLICATIONS FOR HISTORICAL UNDERSTANDING

Recognizing the Hebrew connections among African Americans necessitates a fundamental reconsideration of conventional historical narratives. It challenges Eurocentric assumptions about African societies prior to colonization, revealing sophisticated religious and cultural systems with ancient connections to other civilizations. It complicates simplified understandings of the transatlantic slave trade by highlighting the specific ethnic and cultural backgrounds of those who were enslaved.

Perhaps most significantly, it demonstrates the remarkable persistence of cultural memory despite the most severe attempts at erasure. As historian Sterling Stuckey observes, "The preservation of cultural elements despite slavery's brutality reveals not just human resilience

---

7 Romans 11:26 (New Revised Standard Version).

8 Walter Arthur McCray, *The Black Presence in the Bible: Discovering the Black and African Identity of Biblical Persons and Nations* (Chicago: Black Light Fellowship, 1990), 178-203.

9 Randall C. Bailey, "The Bible and African American Empowerment," in *Teaching for Change: Eight Keys for Transformative Bible Study*, ed. Randall C. Bailey (Minneapolis: Fortress Press, 2020), 95.

but the limitations of power to completely eradicate identity."[10] This perspective offers important insights for understanding how marginalized communities throughout history have maintained essential aspects of identity despite external pressures.

The evidence assembled in this book also challenges religious communities to reconsider assumptions about the boundaries of tradition and belonging. As religious historian Jacob Dorman notes, "The recognition of Hebrew heritage among African Americans invites broader reconsideration of how religious traditions understand their own boundaries and historical development."[11] This reconsideration has implications not only for African Americans reclaiming Hebrew identity but for how religious communities of all backgrounds understand questions of inclusion, authenticity, and historical connection.

FUTURE DIRECTIONS FOR RESEARCH AND COMMUNITY DEVELOPMENT

While this book has assembled substantial evidence for Hebrew connections among African Americans, significant opportunities remain for further research and development. Advancing genetic studies offer new possibilities for understanding population movements and connections, while archaeological work continues to uncover material evidence of cultural practices both in West Africa and throughout the Americas.

Community-based research initiatives provide opportunities for collaborative development of knowledge, combining academic methodologies with the preservation of oral traditions and cultural practices. Educational initiatives can integrate this research into curriculum at multiple levels, ensuring that future generations understand these historical connections.

For communities reclaiming Hebrew heritage, opportunities exist for developing educational resources, cultural preservation initiatives, and

---

10 Sterling Stuckey, *Slave Culture: Nationalist Theory and the Foundations of Black America* (New York: Oxford University Press, 1987), 95-112.
11 Jacob S. Dorman, *Chosen People: The Rise of American Black Israelite Religions* (Oxford: Oxford University Press, 2013), 245.

community institutions that honor these connections while addressing contemporary needs. As sociologist Orlando Patterson observes, "Cultural reclamation most effectively contributes to community flourishing when it connects historical awareness with forward-looking development."[12]

These developments benefit not only communities directly reclaiming Hebrew heritage but broader society as well. As historian Robin D.G. Kelley notes, "The recovery of suppressed historical narratives enriches collective understanding and creates possibilities for more authentic relationship across different communities."[13] The recognition of Hebrew connections among African Americans contributes to more accurate historical understanding that benefits scholarship, education, and intercommunal relationships.

RESTORATION AND RECONCILIATION

The evidence presented throughout this book invites not only recognition but active participation in processes of restoration and reconciliation. For African Americans reclaiming Hebrew heritage, this restoration involves both personal and communal dimensions—recovering knowledge that was systematically suppressed and developing contemporary expressions of ancient connections.

For broader society, participation in this restoration process involves acknowledging historical realities that have been obscured, supporting the preservation and development of cultural knowledge, and addressing the ongoing impacts of historical trauma. As theologian James Cone observed, "Authentic reconciliation requires not merely acknowledgment of past harm but active participation in repairing its effects."[14]

---

12 Orlando Patterson, *The Cultural Matrix: Understanding Black Youth* (Cambridge: Harvard University Press, 2015), 178.
13 Robin D.G. Kelley, *Freedom Dreams: The Black Radical Imagination* (Boston: Beacon Press, 2002), 87.
14 James H. Cone, *God of the Oppressed* (Maryknoll, NY: Orbis Books, 1997), 192.

This participation may take various forms, from educational initiatives that accurately present the historical evidence to policy measures that address the material consequences of historical injustice. Religious communities have particular opportunities to acknowledge their historical roles in either supporting or opposing the suppression of cultural identity and to actively participate in healing these historical wounds.

A CONTINUING JOURNEY

As we conclude "When We Were Them," it is important to recognize that the work of historical reclamation and identity restoration represents not a completed project but a continuing journey. New evidence continues to emerge, communities continue to develop distinctive expressions of reclaimed identity, and broader understanding continues to evolve. This ongoing process reflects the dynamic nature of identity itself—not fixed in a static past but continuously engaged in connecting ancient roots with contemporary flourishing.

The title "When We Were Them" speaks to this dynamic relationship between past and present, identity lost and identity reclaimed. It acknowledges that what appears to be new often represents the recovery of what was ancient, that what seems like adoption often reflects recognition of what was always present but obscured. As historian Vincent Wimbush observes, "The recovery of suppressed identity involves not merely looking backward but reimagining the present and future in light of more complete understanding of the past."[15]

For many African Americans, the recognition of Hebrew connections represents this reimagining—seeing present identity not as disconnected from ancestral roots but as the continuation of ancient traditions that survived despite the most severe attempts at erasure. As the evidence assembled throughout this book demonstrates, cultural memory proves remarkably resilient, preserved through coded language, adapted practices, and oral traditions across generations and continents.

---

15 Vincent L. Wimbush, *The Bible and African Americans: A Brief History* (Minneapolis: Fortress Press, 2003), 132.

The historical connections between African Americans and biblical Hebrews documented throughout this work invite not only academic recognition but meaningful engagement with questions of identity, belonging, and purpose that resonate across communities. In the words of theologian Howard Thurman, whose own work reflected deep engagement with these connections, "The search for common ground where the barriers that divide human beings from one another are transcended is essentially a spiritual undertaking."[16] The recognition of these historical connections contributes to this spiritual undertaking by revealing connections across time and space that challenge artificial divisions and invite deeper understanding of our shared humanity.

As readers engage with the evidence and perspectives presented throughout this book, may it contribute to both more accurate historical understanding and more authentic connection—with ancestral heritage, with diverse communities in the present, and with visions of restoration that extend into the future. The journey of reclaiming identity continues, informed by historical evidence, inspired by spiritual significance, and oriented toward healing that transcends the wounds of the past.

Thank you for journeying with me through the jungle of yesterday's false narratives to the beautiful sanctuary of accurate history concerning the African American connection with biblical Hebrews. The evidence in this book proves that *we were them*. Thank you for hearing the lion tell his story. The real hero has spoken.

---

16 Howard Thurman, *The Search for Common Ground* (Richmond, IN: Friends United Press, 1986), 104.

APPENDICES

Timeline: Hebrew/Israelite Migrations from Ancient Israel to the Americas

ANCIENT DISPERSIONS FROM ISRAEL/JUDAH

722 BCE — Assyrian Exile

- The Northern Kingdom of Israel falls to the Assyrian Empire
- Ten tribes of Israel were forcibly relocated throughout the Assyrian Empire
- Migration routes: Israel → Mesopotamia → Egypt → Ethiopia → West Africa[1]
- Archaeological evidence shows Israelite communities established along the North African coast[2]

586 BCE — Babylonian Exile

- Kingdom of Judah falls to Babylonian Empire
- First deportation of Judaean elite to Babylon
- Some Judaeans flee to Egypt, establishing military colonies at Elephantine
- Evidence suggests some refugees continued migration westward along the North African coast[3]

539-332 BCE — Persian Period Dispersions

- While some Jews return to Jerusalem, many remain dispersed
- Jewish military colonies established in Egypt and throughout Persian Empire
- Trading networks established throughout Mediterranean and into North Africa
- Archaeological evidence of Hebrew settlements along trade routes across North Africa[4]

---

1 Tudor Parfitt, *Black Jews in Africa and the Americas* (Cambridge: Harvard University Press, 2013), 41-53.

2 Nehemia Levtzion, *Ancient Ghana and Mali* (New York: Methuen, 1980), 45-67.

3 Ephraim Isaac, *The Ethiopian Jews* (San Francisco: Institute for Jewish and Community Research, 1993), 27-38.

4 Graham Connah, *African Civilizations: An Archaeological Perspective* (Cambridge: Cambridge University Press, 2001), 123-145.

GRECO-ROMAN PERIOD MIGRATIONS

332-63 BCE — Hellenistic Period

- Expansion of Jewish communities throughout Mediterranean
- Large Jewish populations in Alexandria, Cyrenaica (Libya), and Carthage (Tunisia)
- Trading networks extend into sub-Saharan Africa following established caravan routes
- Hebrew inscriptions dated to this period discovered in regions of modern Morocco and Algeria[5]

70 CE — DESTRUCTION OF SECOND TEMPLE

- Major Jewish dispersion following Roman destruction of Jerusalem
- Large numbers flee to North Africa, joining established communities
- Hebrew communities push further into Saharan trade centers
- Archaeological evidence shows Hebrew presence in ancient Ghana by 300 CE[6]

EARLY AFRICAN MIGRATIONS AND SETTLEMENTS

300-700 CE — Expansion into West Africa

- Hebrew traders establish communities along trans-Saharan trade routes
- Settlements documented in ancient Ghana, Mali, and Songhai empires
- Introduction of monotheistic practices and Hebrew customs to local populations
- Archaeological evidence of Hebrew inscriptions found in Timbuktu region dating to this period[7]

---

5 Edith Bruder, *The Black Jews of Africa: History, Religion, Identity* (Oxford: Oxford University Press, 2008), 46-62.

6 J.O. Hunwick, "Al-Maghili and the Jews of Tuwat," in *Jews of Arab Lands* (Philadelphia: Jewish Publication Society, 1979), 286-297.

7 Joseph Williams, *Hebrewisms of West Africa: From Nile to Niger with the Jews* (New York: Biblo & Tannen, 1967), 42-78.

700-1000 CE — CONSOLIDATION IN WEST AFRICA

- Hebrew communities integrate with local populations while maintaining distinctive practices
- Evidence of Hebrew influence among Igbo, Yoruba, Ashanti, and other West African groups
- Development of syncretic practices combining Hebrew traditions with Indigenous beliefs
- Ibn Khaldun documents "Jewish kingdoms" in regions of modern Mali and Mauritania[8]

1000-1300 CE — MEDIEVAL MIGRATIONS

- Additional waves of Hebrew migration from North Africa following Almohad persecutions
- Expansion of Hebrew-influenced communities throughout the West African region
- Establishment of distinctive Hebrew/Israelite practices among Igbo, Yoruba, and Akan peoples
- Portuguese explorers document "Judaic practices" among
- West African kingdoms in early records[9]

ISLAMIC PERIOD AND LATER MIGRATIONS

1235-1600 CE — Mali Empire Period

- Hebrew communities documented in Timbuktu and other Mali Empire trading centers
- Manuscript evidence shows Hebrew scholarly presence in Sankore University
- Continued integration with and influence upon Songhai, Igbo, and Yoruba cultures
- European travelers document communities observing Sabbath and dietary laws [10]

---

8 Ibn Khaldun, *The Muqaddimah,* trans. Franz Rosenthal (Princeton: Princeton University Press, 1967), 117-119.

9 John Thornton, *Africa and Africans in the Making of the Atlantic World, 1400-1800* (Cambridge: Cambridge University Press, 1998), 235-271.

10 Felix Dubois, *Timbuctoo the Mysterious,* trans. Diana White (New York: Longmans, Green, and Co., 1896), 231-245.

1492-1600 CE — SEPHARDIC EXODUS

- Jews expelled from Spain and Portugal fled to North Africa
- Some communities migrate further into West Africa along established trade routes
- A new influx reinforces Hebrew practices among established West African communities
- Portuguese records note Jewish presence among royal courts in Benin and Akan states[11]

THE SLAVE TRADE PERIOD

1619-1700 CE — Early Slave Trade Period

- First documented arrival of Africans in English North America (1619)
- Significant numbers of enslaved people taken from regions with documented Hebrew connections
- Colonial records note distinctive religious practices among certain enslaved populations
- Virginia plantation records specifically mention "Eboe" (Igbo) captives with distinctive customs[12]

1701-1807 CE — HEIGHT OF TRANSATLANTIC SLAVE TRADE

- Approximately 1.4-1.8 million people taken from Bight of Biafra (primarily Igbo territory)
- Significant numbers from Gold Coast (including Akan/Ashanti regions)
- Yoruba captives primarily transported during later period (1780-1850)
- Slave ship manifests document tribal/ethnic origins of captives[13]

---

11 Eva Meyerowitz, *The Akan of Ghana: Their Ancient Beliefs* (London: Faber & Faber, 1958), 97-113.
12 Douglas Chambers, *Murder at Montpelier: Igbo Africans in Virginia* (Jackson: University Press of Mississippi, 2005), 23-45.
13 David Eltis and David Richardson, *Atlas of the Transatlantic Slave Trade* (New Haven: Yale University Press, 2010), 83-85.

1808-1865 CE — POST-INTERNATIONAL BAN PERIOD

- Following the ban on the international slave trade (1808), the internal U.S. slave trade expands
- Forced migration of approximately 1.2 million enslaved people from the Upper South to the Deep South
- Selective breeding practices potentially concentrate certain ethnic lineages
- Cultural practices preserved despite internal dispersions[14]

POST-EMANCIPATION RECOGNITION AND RECLAMATION

1865-1900 CE — Early Reclamation Period

- First formal Black Hebrew congregations were established
- Oral traditions connecting African Americans to Hebrew ancestry documented
- Archaeological evidence of preserved Hebrew-influenced practices uncovered at plantation sites
- Freedmen's testimonies record maintained traditions connecting to Hebrew ancestry[15]

1900-1970 CE — CULTURAL RENAISSANCE PERIOD

- Multiple movements explicitly connecting African American identity to Hebrew heritage emerge
- Scholarly documentation of linguistic, cultural, and religious practices showing Hebrew influence
- Archaeological excavations reveal material evidence of preserved practices
- Oral history projects document family traditions of Hebrew ancestry[16]

---

14 Michael Tadman, *Speculators and Slaves: Masters, Traders, and Slaves in the Old South* (Madison: University of Wisconsin Press, 1996), 12-46.

15 Sylviane A. Diouf, *Servants of Allah: African Muslims Enslaved in the Americas* (New York: New York University Press, 1998), 178-202.

16 James Landing, *Black Judaism: Story of an American Movement* (Durham: Carolina Academic Press, 2002), 201-223.

1970-PRESENT — SCIENTIFIC AND CULTURAL AFFIRMATION

- Genetic studies confirm biological connections between certain African American lineages and populations from regions with Hebrew influence
- Archaeological evidence continues to document Hebrew presence in West Africa prior to slave trade
- Linguistic analysis confirms Hebrew elements preserved in African American cultural expressions
- Cultural reclamation movements continue to affirm and explore Hebrew connections[17]

17 Rick Kittles et al., "Autosomal, Mitochondrial, and Y Chromosome DNA Variation in African Americans: Implications for the Early Settlement of America and Admixture Events," *American Journal of Human Genetics* 69, no. 5 (2001): 1080-1089.

Major African Ethnic Groups in the Transatlantic Slave Trade and Hebrew Connections

GROUPS WITH SUBSTANTIAL EVIDENCE OF HEBREW CONNECTIONS

1. Igbo (Southeastern Nigeria)
Approximately 1.4-1.8 million transported

- Hebrew Connections: Substantial evidence includes male circumcision on the eighth day, dietary laws mirroring kosher practices, ritual handwashing before meals, new moon celebrations, blood sacrifice rituals similar to ancient Hebrew practices.[1]
- Linguistic Evidence: Over 130 Igbo words with Hebrew roots, particularly in religious terminology.[2]
- Material Culture: Use of symbolic objects with parallels to ancient Hebrew artifacts, including ritual containers and ceremonial instruments.[3]
- Oral Traditions: Extensive traditions claiming descent from Hebrew ancestry, with specific migration narratives.[4]

2. Yoruba (Southwestern Nigeria/Benin)
Approximately 1.3 million transported

- Hebrew Connections: Creation narratives with significant parallels to Genesis accounts, ritual purification practices similar

---

1 Tudor Parfitt, *Black Jews in Africa and the Americas* (Cambridge: Harvard University Press, 2013), 112-118.
2 Catherine Acholonu, *They Lived Before Adam: Pre-Historic Origins of the Igbo* (Abuja: CARC Publications, 2009), 145-172.
3 Adiele Afigbo, *The Igbo and Their Neighbours* (Ibadan: University Press Limited, 1987), 67-89.
4 Daniel Lis, *Jewish Identity Among the Igbo of Nigeria* (Trenton: Africa World Press, 2015), 124-156.

to mikveh, concepts of divine covenant.[5]

- Religious Practices: Calendar system with similarities to Hebrew lunar calendar, specific ritual practices around childbirth and death.[6]
- Linguistic Evidence: Religious terminology with Hebrew parallels, particularly in names for divine attributes.[7]

3. Akan/Ashanti (Ghana)
Approximately 1.5 million transported

- Hebrew Connections: Use of Star of David in traditional symbolism predating European contact, specific ceremonial practices.[8]
- Religious Concepts: Concepts of divine kingship with parallels to Davidic traditions, ritual purification practices.[9]
- Linguistic Evidence: Ceremonial phrases with Hebrew similarities documented by Eva Meyerowitz.[10]

4. Lemba (Southern Africa)
Smaller numbers in the slave trade

- Hebrew Connections: Strongest genetic evidence (Cohen Modal Haplotype), distinctive religious practices closely mirroring Judaism.[11]

---

5 Ọladélé Ajíbóyè, *Continuities in Yoruba Religious Practices* (Lagos: Nigerian Institute of Anthropological Research, 2001), 87-103.

6 Toyin Falola and Matt Childs, eds., *The Yoruba Diaspora in the Atlantic World* (Bloomington: Indiana University Press, 2004), 257-276.

7 Maureen Warner-Lewis, *Central Africa in the Caribbean: Transcending Time, Transforming Cultures* (Kingston: University of West Indies Press, 2003), 178-205.

8 Eva Meyerowitz, *The Divine Kingship in Ghana and Ancient Egypt* (London: Faber & Faber, 1960), 156-173.

9 Joseph Williams, *Hebrewisms of West Africa: From Nile to Niger with the Jews* (New York: Biblo & Tannen, 1967), 42-78.

10 Eva Meyerowitz, *The Sacred State of the Akan* (London: Faber & Faber, 1951), 127-143.

11 Mark G. Thomas et al., "Y Chromosomes Traveling South: The Cohen Modal Haplotype and the Origins of the Lemba," *American Journal of Human Genetics* 66, no. 2 (2000): 674-686.

- Cultural Practices: Male circumcision, kosher-like dietary restrictions, Sabbath observance, ritual slaughter methods.[12]
- Oral Traditions: Detailed traditions recounting migration from Judea through Yemen to Africa.[13]

GROUPS WITH MODERATE EVIDENCE OF HEBREW CONNECTIONS

5. Fulani (Senegambia/Guinea)
Approximately 700,000 transported

- Hebrew Connections: Oral traditions claiming Middle Eastern origins, distinctive religious practices.[14]
- Cultural Practices: Specific prayer postures, ritual cattle sacrifice methods with similarities to ancient Hebrew practices.[15]

6. Hausa (Northern Nigeria)
Approximately 500,000 transported

- Hebrew Connections: Some linguistic parallels, certain religious customs predating Islamic influence.[16]
- Material Culture: Specific symbolic motifs with parallels to ancient Hebrew artifacts.[17]

---

12 Tudor Parfitt, *Journey to the Vanished City* (London: Phoenix, 2000), 195-225.

13 Magdel le Roux, *The Lemba: A Lost Tribe of Israel in Southern Africa?* (Pretoria: University of South Africa Press, 2003), 209-234.

14 David Robinson, *The Holy War of Umar Tal* (Oxford: Clarendon Press, 1985), 63-87.

15 M.G. Smith, *Government in Zazzau* (London: Oxford University Press, 1960), 42-58.

16 Joseph Greenberg, *The Influence of Islam on a Sudanese Religion* (New York: J.J. Augustin, 1946), 87-103.

17 Philip Curtin, *Africa Remembered* (Madison: University of Wisconsin Press, 1967), 237-259.

7. Serer (Senegambia)
Approximately 300,000 transported

- Hebrew Connections: Certain religious practices and oral traditions, particularly around ancestor veneration.[18]
- Cultural Practices: Distinctive burial customs with similarities to ancient Hebrew practices.[19]

8. Mandinka/Malinke (Senegambia/Mali)
Approximately 650,000 transported

- Hebrew Connections: Some cultural practices and oral traditions suggesting ancient connections.[20]
- Religious Concepts: Specific notions of spiritual purity with parallels to Hebrew concepts.[21]

GROUPS WITH LIMITED EVIDENCE OF HEBREW CONNECTIONS

9. Wolof (Senegambia)
Approximately 200,000 transported

- Hebrew Connections: Limited linguistic connections, certain ritual practices.[22]

10. Edo/Bini (Nigeria)
Approximately 300,000 transported

- Hebrew Connections: Some traditional practices and oral histories.[23]

---

18 Cheikh Anta Diop, *The Cultural Unity of Black Africa* (Chicago: Third World Press, 1978), 145-167.

19 Ajayi Kolawole, *Religious Practices in Senegambia* (Dakar: IFAN, 1965), 78-92.

20 Walter Rodney, *A History of the Upper Guinea Coast, 1545-1800* (Oxford: Clarendon Press, 1970), 205-231.

21 David Dalby, *Language and History in Africa* (London: Frank Cass, 1970), 321-342.

22 Ajayi Kolawole, *Religious Practices in Senegambia* (Dakar: IFAN, 1965), 101-118.

23 Sandra Barnes, *Africa's Ogun* (Bloomington: Indiana University Press, 1997), 142-163.

11. Ga-Adangbe (Ghana)
Approximately 150,000 transported

- Hebrew Connections: Limited cultural connections, certain symbolic practices.[24]

12. Ibibio (Southeastern Nigeria)
Approximately 300,000 transported

- Hebrew Connections: Some shared practices with neighboring Igbo, though less extensively documented.[25]

MAJOR GROUPS WITHOUT SIGNIFICANT *DOCUMENTED* HEBREW CONNECTIONS

- Bakongo (Congo/Angola) - Approximately 2 million transported
- Mbundu (Angola) - Approximately 1.5 million transported
- Bambara (Mali) - Approximately 250,000 transported
- Mende (Sierra Leone) - Approximately 300,000 transported
- Fon/Ewe (Dahomey/Benin) - Approximately 450,000 transported
- Temne (Sierra Leone) - Approximately 200,000 transported
- Balanta (Guinea-Bissau) - Approximately 150,000 transported
- Efik (Nigeria) - Approximately 250,000 transported
- Ijaw (Niger Delta) - Approximately 200,000 transported
- Susu (Guinea) - Approximately 150,000 transported
- Kru (Liberia) - Approximately 100,000 transported
- Fante (Ghana) - Approximately 300,000 transported
- Makua (Mozambique) - Approximately 200,000 transported
- Jolof (Senegambia) - Approximately 100,000 transported

24 Marion Kilson, *Kpele Lala: Ga Religious Songs and Symbols* (Cambridge: Harvard University Press, 1971), 63-79.

25 Monday Efiong Noah, *Proceedings of the Ibibio Union 1928-1937* (Calabar: Scholars Press, 1988), 45-62.

NOTES ON EVIDENCE

The strength of evidence for Hebrew connections varies considerably among these groups. For the Igbo, Yoruba, Akan, and Lemba, multiple lines of evidence (linguistic, cultural, religious, and in some cases genetic) create a substantial case for historical connections. For other groups, the evidence is more limited or contested among scholars.

It's worth noting that certain practices (like circumcision) were widespread in Africa independent of Hebrew influence, while others (like specific dietary restrictions, lunar calendar observances, and particular ritual practices) provide stronger evidence of potential Hebrew connections when they appear in combination.

Based on the list I provided, I can calculate the percentage of tribes with Hebrew connections in two ways:

BY NUMBER OF ETHNIC GROUPS

- Total ethnic groups listed: 26
- Groups with substantial evidence of Hebrew connections: 4 (15.4%)
- Groups with moderate evidence: 4 (15.4%)
- Groups with limited evidence: 4 (15.4%)
- Total groups with some degree of Hebrew connection: 12 (46.2%)

BY ESTIMATED POPULATION TRANSPORTED

When analyzing by the estimated number of people transported:

- Groups with substantial Hebrew connections (Igbo, Yoruba, Akan/Ashanti, Lemba): Approximately 4.25-4.65 million people (34-37% of transported Africans)
- Groups with moderate Hebrew connections (Fulani, Hausa, Serer, Mandinka/Malinke): Approximately 2.15 million people (17% of transported Africans)
- Groups with limited Hebrew connections (Wolof, Edo/Bini, Ga-Adangbe, Ibibio): Approximately 950,000 people (8% of transported Africans)
- **Total with some degree of Hebrew connection: Approximately 7.35-7.75 million people (58-62% of transported Africans)**

These calculations suggest that approximately 46% of the major ethnic groups involved in the transatlantic slave trade had some degree of documented Hebrew connection, representing approximately 58-62% of the total population transported.

It's important to note that the strength of evidence varies considerably among these groups, with the most substantial and well-documented connections found among the Igbo, Yoruba, Akan, and Lemba peoples. Additionally, these percentages should be understood as estimates, as precise ethnic breakdowns of the slave trade remain challenging due to limitations in historical record-keeping.

Glossary

A

Abraham: The patriarch of the Hebrew people, originally from Ur in southern Mesopotamia. Born as Abram, his name was changed by God to Abraham, meaning "father of many nations." He was a Black Semite from the Aramaic region who is the common ancestor of Hebrews and Arabs.

Aelia Capitolina: The name given to Jerusalem after the Romans rebuilt it following the Bar Kokhba revolt (132-136 CE). The construction of this city and a temple to Jupiter on the Temple Mount helped trigger the revolt.

Akan: A West African ethnic group from modern Ghana with cultural practices bearing similarities to ancient Hebrew traditions, including the use of the Star of David in religious symbolism.

Aliyah: The immigration of Jews to the Land of Israel. The term is also used to describe the various waves of Jewish immigration throughout history.

Almohad Dynasty: A Berber Muslim dynasty that ruled parts of North Africa and Spain in the 12th and 13th centuries. Their religious persecution led many Jews to flee southward across the Sahara into West Africa.

Amurru (Amorites): A Semitic-speaking people who were one of the predominant ethnic groups in Mesopotamia during Abraham's time. They were descendants of Ham.

Anussim: Communities in northeastern Brazil that maintained crypto-Jewish practices disguised within Catholic observances, including Friday evening candle lighting and avoidance of pork.

Archaeological evidence: Material remains uncovered through scientific excavation that provide physical documentation of cultural practices, including ritual objects showing Hebrew influences found at plantation sites.

Aramaic: A Semitic language that was the lingua franca of much of the Near East from about 600 BCE to 700 CE. It was the language spoken by many ancient Hebrews.

Arameans (Aramaeans): A Semitic people who lived in upper Mesopotamia and Syria. Abraham and his family had ethnic connections to the Aramaeans, who were Black Semites.

Ark of the Covenant: A gold-covered wooden chest containing the two stone tablets of the Ten Commandments. It was the most sacred object of the Israelites and was kept in the Holy of Holies in the Tabernacle and later the Temple.

Ashanti: A West African ethnic group from Ghana that maintained ceremonial objects bearing resemblance to items described in biblical texts and used the Star of David in religious symbolism.

Ashkenazi Jews: Jews of Eastern European and German descent. According to evidence presented in the book, they are primarily descendants of Khazar converts to Judaism rather than biological descendants of ancient Israelites. They make up approximately 80% of the world's Jewish population today.

Assyrian Exile: The deportation of the northern kingdom of Israel by the Assyrian Empire in 722 BCE, resulting in the scattering of the ten northern tribes throughout the Assyrian Empire and beyond, including into Africa.

B

Babylonian Exile: The period in Jewish history during which Jews of the ancient Kingdom of Judah were captives in Babylon from 586 to 539 BCE. After this exile, many Judahites fled to Egypt and continued westward.

Balfour Declaration: A public statement issued by the British government in 1917 announcing support for the establishment of a "national home for the Jewish people" in Palestine. It was a crucial step in the creation of the modern state of Israel.

Bar Kokhba Revolt: A Jewish rebellion against the Roman Empire in Judea from 132 to 136 CE, led by Simon bar Kokhba. Its suppression resulted in a significant dispersion of Hebrews, many of whom fled to Africa.

Bathsheba: Wife of King David and mother of King Solomon. She was of Gilonite (Canaanite) descent, providing evidence of Solomon's African ancestry.

Bight of Biafra: A coastal region in West Africa (primarily southeastern Nigeria) that was home to the Igbo people and a major source of captives during the transatlantic slave trade.

Bilhah: Handmaid of Rachel who bore two sons to Jacob: Dan and Naphtali. She was likely of Hamitic (African) descent.

Black Hebrews: A term used to describe people of African descent who identify as biological descendants of the ancient Israelites, based on historical, biblical, and cultural evidence.

"Breeding wenches": Derogatory term used by enslavers to refer to enslaved women valued primarily for their reproductive capacity in the domestic slave trade.

C

Chaldeans: A semi-nomadic tribe that rose to prominence in southern Babylonia in the 10th century BCE and eventually established the Neo-Babylonian Empire. The reference to "Ur of the Chaldeans" in Genesis is considered an anachronism.

Christian Zionism: A belief among some Christians that the return of Jews to the Holy Land and the establishment of the state of Israel in 1948 was in accordance with biblical prophecy.

Cohen Modal Haplotype: A genetic signature associated with the Jewish priestly lineage, found among the Lemba people of southern Africa and in some African American lineages.

Cultural syncretism: The blending of elements from different religious traditions, as seen in the way Hebrew practices were preserved by combining them with other spiritual traditions.

Curse of Cain: A misinterpretation of Genesis 4 that falsely claims God cursed Cain and his descendants with black skin. This was used to justify racism and slavery.

Curse of Ham: A misinterpretation of Genesis 9 that falsely claims Ham and all his descendants were cursed with black skin and servitude. This was used to justify racism and slavery despite the fact that the biblical text shows only Canaan (one of Ham's four sons) was cursed, not Ham himself.

D

Diaspora: The dispersion of a people from their original homeland; in this context, referring to both the ancient Hebrew dispersions and the forced African diaspora through slavery.

Doctrine of Discovery: A series of 15th-century papal bulls that granted Christian European nations the right to "discover" and claim lands occupied by non-Christians, serving as a legal and moral justification for colonization and the transatlantic slave trade.

Domestic slave trade: The buying and selling of enslaved people within the United States after the 1808 ban on international slave importation, which involved approximately 1.2 million people moved from the Upper South to the Deep South.

E

"Eboe" or **"Ibo"**: Terms used in colonial and slave trade records to refer to people from the Igbo ethnic group, who were particularly valued in certain slave markets and breeding operations.

Edom/Edomites: The nation descended from Esau, Jacob's twin brother. The name "Edom" means "red" and was given to Esau after he sold his birthright for red lentil soup.

Ethiopia (Cush): An ancient kingdom in northeastern Africa, often mentioned in the Bible. It was a Hamitic nation with close ties to ancient Israel.

Exodus narrative: Biblical story of liberation from bondage that resonated deeply with enslaved communities and became central to spiritual resistance against oppression.

F

"Fancy trade": A particularly disturbing aspect of the domestic slave trade that specialized in young, often light-skinned enslaved women sold explicitly for sexual exploitation.

Fullness of the Gentiles: A biblical term from Romans 11:25 referring to the period when Gentile nations would rule over Israel. According to the book, this period will eventually expire, leading to Israel's restoration.

G

Gentiles: In the biblical context, specifically refers to the descendants of Japheth who populated Europe and the Caucasus region. More broadly, it came to mean any non-Jewish people, but the book emphasizes its original meaning as referring to European nations.

Gilonites: A Canaanite tribe that lived in the region of Palestine. Bathsheba's grandfather Ahithophel was a Gilonite, providing evidence of King Solomon's partial African ancestry.

Gold Coast: A region of West Africa (primarily modern Ghana) that was home to the Akan people and a significant source of captives during the transatlantic slave trade.

Gomer: Son of Japheth and father of Ashkenaz, Riphath, and Togarmah. According to the Table of Nations in Genesis 10, his descendants settled in Europe and the Caucasus region.

Gullah: African American communities in coastal South Carolina and Georgia who preserved numerous linguistic and cultural elements with connections to West African groups with Hebrew influences.

H

Hagar: Sarah's Egyptian handmaid who bore Abraham's first son, Ishmael. She was of Hamitic (African) descent.

Ham: One of Noah's three sons who, according to Genesis, was the progenitor of the African nations. His descendants included the Egyptians, Cushites (Ethiopians), and Canaanites.

Hamitic: Relating to or descended from Ham, indicating African ancestry.

Hebrew protective practices: Ritual actions and symbolic objects used for spiritual protection, documented among both West African groups with Hebrew connections and their descendants in the Americas.

Hellenistic Jews: Jews who adopted Greek culture, language, and customs while maintaining their Jewish religious identity.

Holy of Holies: The innermost and most sacred area of the Tabernacle and later the Jewish Temple in Jerusalem. Only the High Priest could enter this area, and only on Yom Kippur.

I

Igbo: An ethnic group from southeastern Nigeria that practiced male circumcision on the eighth day after birth, observed dietary restrictions similar to kosher laws, and maintained traditions with striking parallels to ancient Hebrew customs.

Inter Caetera: A papal bull issued by Pope Alexander VI in 1493 that granted Spain authority over the lands discovered by Columbus, contributing to the Doctrine of Discovery that facilitated European colonization.

Intergenerational trauma: The transmission of historical trauma across generations, as described in Post Traumatic Slave Syndrome affecting African American communities.

Ishmaelites: The descendants of Ishmael, Abraham's first son by Hagar. They were half-Semitic, half-Hamitic people who populated parts of Arabia.

Isles of the Gentiles: The term used in Genesis 10:5 to describe the regions where Japheth's descendants settled, identified as Asia Minor and Europe.

J

Jacob: Son of Isaac and Rebekah, twin brother of Esau, and father of the twelve tribes of Israel. God changed his name to Israel, and he is described in the book as a "wandering Aramaean" of dark complexion.

Japheth: One of Noah's three sons who, according to Genesis, was the progenitor of the European and Caucasian nations.

Joseph: The eleventh son of Jacob, born to Rachel. His story of being sold into slavery in Egypt and later becoming a viceroy provides evidence of his dark complexion, as he was indistinguishable from the Egyptians.

Judah: The fourth son of Jacob and Leah, whose descendants formed the tribe of Judah from which the lineage of Kings David and Solomon, and eventually Jesus, came.

K

Keturah: Abraham's wife after Sarah's death, who bore him six sons. She was likely of African (possibly Cushite) descent.

Khazars: A semi-nomadic Turkic people who established a powerful kingdom in the Caucasus region in the late 6th century. According to historical evidence, they converted to Judaism in the 8th century CE. The book argues that most modern Ashkenazi Jews are descendants of Khazar converts rather than biological Israelites.

Kitos War: A series of revolts by exiled Hebrews in Egypt, Cyrene, Cyprus, and Mesopotamia against the Roman Empire from 115-117 CE.

L

Law of Return: Israel's 1950 law granting every Jew the right to immigrate to Israel. The book notes its selective application, particularly regarding Black Jews from Africa.

Lemba: A southern African ethnic group who practice Judaism and have genetic connections to the Middle East, particularly the Cohen Modal Haplotype associated with Jewish priestly lineage.

Levites: Descendants of Levi, Jacob's third son. They served as priests in ancient Israel. According to the book, Moses, Aaron, and the entire Levitical priesthood were Black.

M

Mansa Musa: The emperor of the Mali Empire in the early 14th century, known as one of the wealthiest men in history. His famous pilgrimage to Mecca demonstrated the wealth and power of West African kingdoms.

Maroon communities: Groups of escaped enslaved people who established independent settlements, particularly in Jamaica, where they maintained practices notably similar to Hebrew traditions.

Material culture: Physical objects created and used by a group that reflect their cultural practices, including ritual items with Hebrew influences found at archaeological sites.

McMahon-Hussein Correspondence: Letters exchanged during WWI between the British High Commissioner in Egypt and the Sharif of Mecca, promising Arab independence in exchange for revolt against the Ottoman Empire.

Midianites: Descendants of Midian, Abraham's son by Keturah. Moses married Zipporah, a Midianite woman described as Cushite (Ethiopian).

Mikveh: A Jewish ritual bath used for purification; similar purification practices were documented among certain West African groups and their descendants in the Americas.

Mizrahi Jews: Jews who come from Middle Eastern and North African Jewish communities. They often faced discrimination in modern Israel.

Moses: The prophet who led the Israelites out of Egypt. According to the book, he was a Black man who could pass as Egyptian in Pharaoh's court.

N

Natal alienation: Term coined by sociologist Orlando Patterson to describe how slavery operated as a system of disconnecting individuals from their ancestral lineages and cultural traditions.

O

Omenana: Igbo term meaning "laws of the land," which included many elements consistent with Mosaic law.

Operation Moses: A covert operation in 1984 to airlift Ethiopian Jews from Sudan to Israel during a famine.

Operation Solomon: A 1991 covert operation that airlifted Ethiopian Jews to Israel in just 36 hours.

Oral histories: Verbal accounts passed down through generations that document cultural practices and traditions, including those connecting African Americans to Hebrew heritage.

P

Palestine: The geographic region in Western Asia between the Mediterranean Sea and the Jordan River where the ancient Israelites lived and where the modern state of Israel was established.

Paternal transmission: The passing of cultural knowledge, practices, and genetic lineage through fathers to their children despite systematic attempts to undermine family connections during slavery.

Portable practices: Embodied rituals and traditions that could maintain covenant identity across diverse geographic locations without requiring territorial control or temple structures.

Post Traumatic Slave Syndrome: Theory developed by Dr. Joy DeGruy describing how the trauma of slavery continues to affect African American communities through intergenerational transmission.

R

Replacement Theology: The erroneous teaching that the Church has replaced Israel as God's chosen people. The book argues against this view, asserting that God's covenant with Israel is eternal.

Rice Coast: A region of West Africa known for rice cultivation expertise, which influenced which ethnic groups were targeted for enslavement for specific plantations.

Romans 11:25-27: A key biblical prophecy stating that "blindness in part is happened to Israel, until the fulness of the Gentiles be come in. And so all Israel shall be saved." The book interprets this as prophesying the end of Gentile rule and the awakening of true Israel (including African Americans) to their identity.

Romans 11:26: Biblical verse declaring that *"all Israel shall be saved,"* which some theologians interpret as relating to the restoration of Hebrew identity among African Americans.

S

Saramaka: A Maroon people in Suriname who preserved oral histories claiming descent from *"the people of the book,"* along with practices including ritual purification.

Second Middle Passage: Term used by historian Michael Tadman to describe the domestic slave trade that moved approximately 1.2 million enslaved people from the Upper South to the Deep South between 1790 and 1860.

Semitic: Relating to or descended from Shem, one of Noah's three sons. The book argues that ancient Semitic peoples, including the Israelites, had dark skin.

Sephardic Jews: Jews who originated in the Iberian Peninsula (Spain and Portugal) before their expulsion in 1492. They subsequently settled throughout the Mediterranean world.

Shem: One of Noah's three sons who, according to Genesis, was the progenitor of the Semitic peoples, including the Hebrews. According to the book, Shem and his descendants were dark-skinned.

Slave Bible: A heavily redacted version of the Bible created in the early 19th century for enslaved Africans. About 90% of the Old Testament and 50% of the New Testament were removed, particularly passages that could inspire liberation.

Spiritual resistance: The maintenance of ancestral religious practices despite persecution, as seen in the preservation of Hebrew-influenced traditions during slavery.

Sykes-Picot Agreement: A 1916 secret agreement between Britain and France dividing Ottoman territories after World War I, contradicting promises made to Arab leaders.

Syncretic traditions: Religious practices that combine elements from multiple spiritual traditions, which served as mechanisms for cultural survival during slavery.

T

Table of Nations: The list in Genesis 10 detailing the descendants of Noah's three sons (Shem, Ham, and Japheth) and their dispersion across the earth after the Flood.

Tacitus: A Roman historian (55-117 CE) who wrote that many authorities of his day claimed Jews were descended from Ethiopians.

The Way: The name of the original faith of the Hebrews, centered on worship of Yahweh. This was distinct from later rabbinical Judaism.

Togarmah: Son of Gomer and grandson of Japheth. The Khazars claimed descent from Togarmah, confirming their Japhetic rather than Semitic origins.

Trans-Saharan Trade Routes: Ancient trade networks that connected North Africa with sub-Saharan West Africa, facilitating the movement of goods, people, and ideas, including the migration of Hebrews into West Africa.

Transatlantic Slave Trade: The forced transportation of approximately 12.5 million Africans to the Americas between the 16th and 19th centuries. According to the book, many of these enslaved people were descendants of Hebrews who had migrated to West Africa.

Tribal designations: Ethnic identifications in slave trade records that provide evidence of which African ethnic groups were transported to specific regions of the Americas.

U

Uganda Scheme: A 1903 proposal to create a Jewish homeland in Uganda. Its consideration by Zionist leaders demonstrates that the motivation for creating Israel was more political than based on genuine biblical connections.

Ur: An ancient city in southern Mesopotamia (modern Iraq) that was Abraham's birthplace. During Abraham's time, it was populated primarily by Hamitic peoples.

V

Vodou: A Haitian spiritual tradition that incorporates elements scholars have traced to Hebrew practices, including ritual purification and ceremonial food prohibitions.

Y

Y-chromosome analysis: Genetic testing that traces paternal lineage, which has identified markers connecting certain African American populations to regions in West Africa with Hebrew influences.

Yahweh: The personal name of God in the Hebrew Bible, often represented by the tetragrammaton YHWH. It is the name by which God revealed Himself to Moses.

Yeshua: The Hebrew name for Jesus. According to historical descriptions cited in the book, he had "black skin" and "scanty curly hair."

Yoruba: A West African ethnic group from southwestern Nigeria and Benin that maintained creation narratives with significant parallels to Genesis accounts and practiced forms of ritual purification similar to the mikveh.

Z

Zilpah: Handmaid of Leah who bore two sons to Jacob: Gad and Asher. She was likely of Hamitic (African) descent.

Zionism: A nationalist movement advocating for the re-establishment of a Jewish homeland in Palestine. The book distinguishes between religious connections to the land and the political movement led primarily by Ashkenazi Jews.

The Obadyah Alliance Recognition of Igbos

The Obadyah Alliance is a Jewish rabbinical court (Bet Din) based in Miami, Florida, comprising rabbis from Sephardic and other Jewish traditions. On January 14, 2022 (12 Shebat 5782 in the Hebrew calendar), the Alliance issued a formal ruling recognizing the Igbo people of Nigeria as descendants of the ancient Israelites. This decision was grounded in historical records, oral traditions, cultural practices, and genetic data suggesting Levantine origins.[1]

The ruling emphasized that the Igbos should be regarded as Israelites in every respect, including acknowledgment of their priestly and Levite lineages. It also recommended that returning Igbos observe traditional practices such as circumcision, recitation of the Shehecheyanu blessing, and participation in the kola nut ceremony, aligning with their ancestral customs.

This recognition holds particular significance for African Americans, many of whom trace their ancestry to West African regions, including Igboland. Given that a substantial number of African Americans have Igbo heritage, this acknowledgment may resonate with those exploring their ancestral roots and cultural identities.

The Obadyah Alliance's ruling contributes to broader discussions on heritage and identity within the African diaspora, offering a framework for individuals seeking to reconnect with their historical and cultural origins.

---

1 Hint Magazine, "Jewish Rabbinical Court Rules Igbos Are Israelites," *Hint Magazine,* January 14, 2022, https://hint-magazine.com/jewish-rabbinical-court-rules-igbos-are-israelites/, accessed April 12, 2025.

Abraham's Family Tree

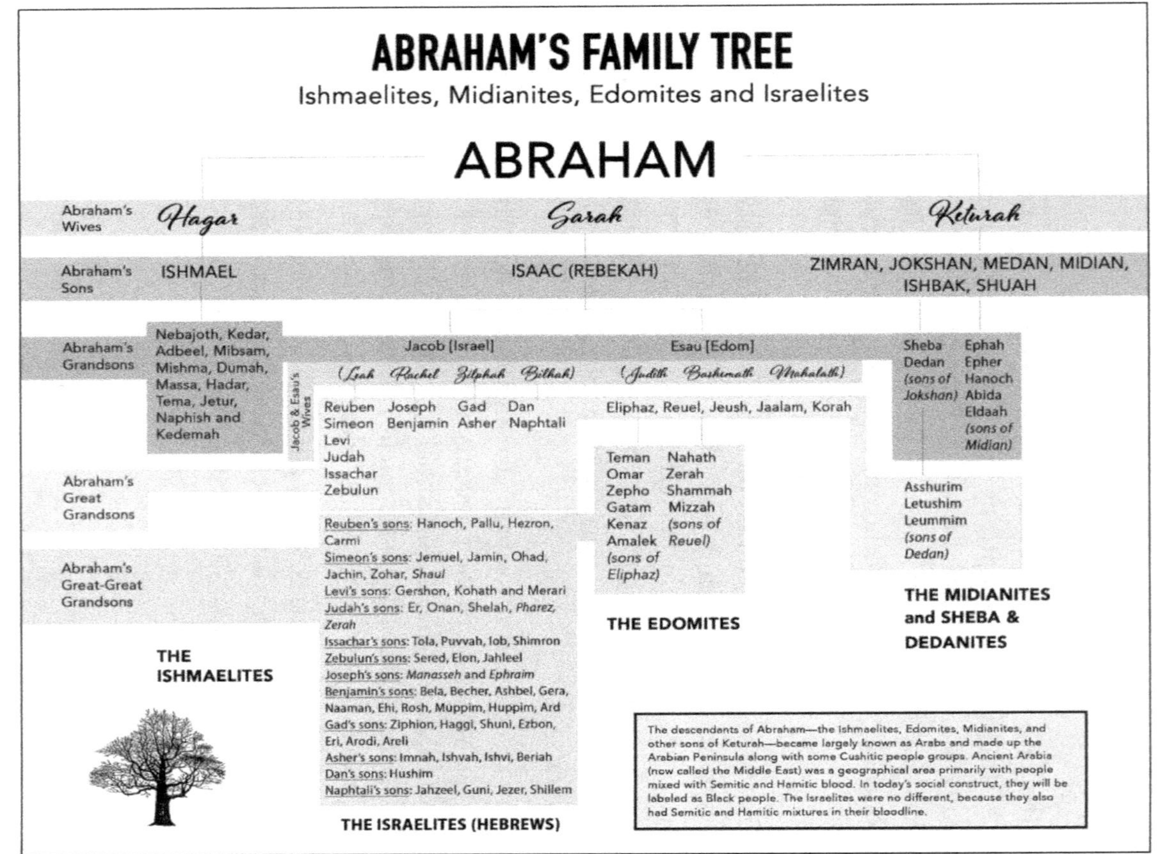

Trans-Saharan Trade Routes

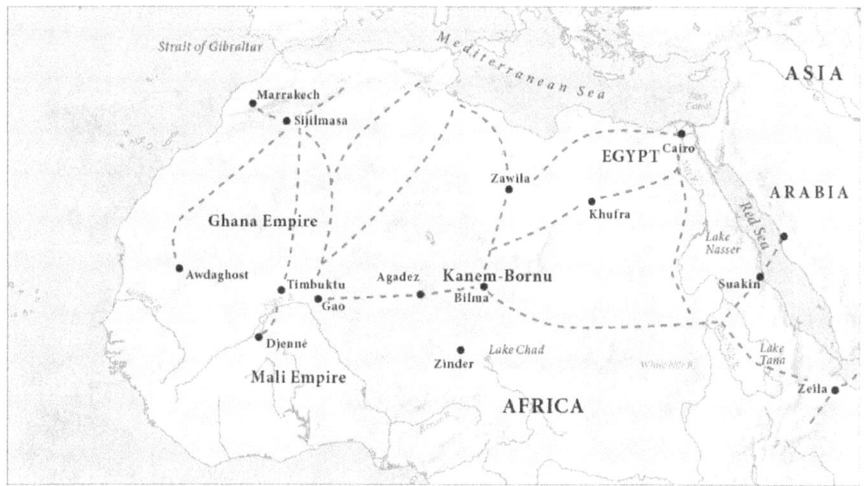

During their various dispersions throughout history, Hebrews likely traveled from Israel to West Africa utilizing established trade networks that connected the Mediterranean world with sub-Saharan Africa. The trans-Saharan trade routes, which reached their peak between the 8th and early 17th centuries CE, served as vital corridors linking North Africa to West African kingdoms. Hebrews would have joined merchant caravans traversing these routes, traveling alongside Berber guides who were essential navigators of the harsh desert terrain. Israel's strategic location on what was known as the "land bridge" positioned it along major trade arteries like the Via Maris along the coastal plain and the International Trunk Road[1], which connected to the trans-Saharan network. These displaced Hebrew communities would have followed established pathways through oasis settlements that provided necessary resupply points for water and provisions. The introduction of camels, which revolutionized desert travel around the 3rd century CE, made regular long-distance journeys across the Sahara increasingly viable[2], enabling Hebrew migrants to reach West African trading centers that eventually developed into powerful kingdoms such as Ghana, Mali, and Songhai.

---

1 https://thebiblefornormalpeople.com/the-geographical-context-of-ancient-israel-part-1-ancient-israels-place-in-the-ancient-near-east/ Accessed May 2, 2025.

2 https://www.vaia.com/en-us/explanations/history/modern-world-history/trans-saharan-trade-route/ Accessed May 2, 2025.

Transatlantic Slave Trade

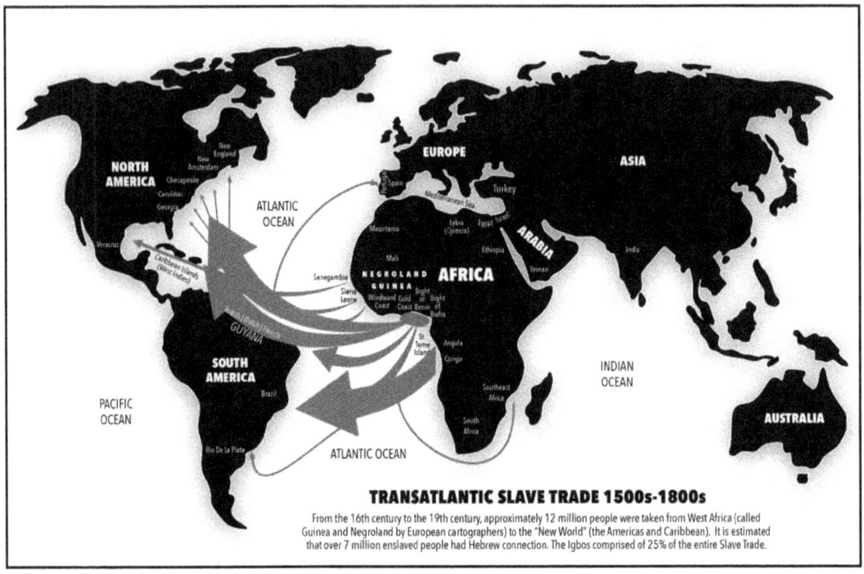

TRANSATLANTIC SLAVE TRADE 1500s-1800s

From the 16th century to the 19th century, approximately 12 million people were taken from West Africa (called Guinea and Negroland by European cartographers) to the "New World" (the Americas and Caribbean). It is estimated that over 7 million enslaved people had Hebrew connection. The Igbos comprised of 25% of the entire Slave Trade.

The Transatlantic Slave Trade, operating from the 16th to 19th centuries, was a commercial system where European powers forcibly transported approximately 12.5 million Africans across the Atlantic Ocean to the Americas, with about 10.7 million surviving the brutal Middle Passage. European traders obtained enslaved people through raids, warfare, and transactions with African intermediaries along the West and Central African coasts. The main ethnic groups captured included the Yoruba, Igbo, Akan (including Ashanti and Fante), Wolof, Mandinka (Mandingo), Fon, Bakongo, and various Bantu-speaking peoples from the Congo basin and Angola. Total with some degree of Hebrew connection: Approximately 7.35-7.75 million people (58-62% of transported Africans).

The trade devastated countless communities across West and Central Africa, disrupting political structures, economies, and cultural development while fueling plantation economies in the Americas that produced sugar, cotton, tobacco, and other commodities for European markets.

Index

A

C

D

E

F

G

H

I

K

L

M

N

Q

R

S

T

U

V

W

X

Y

Z

ABOUT THE AUTHOR

Bishop Antonio M. Palmer is the Senior Pastor of Kingdom Celebration Center and the Presiding Bishop of Kingdom Alliance of Churches International, overseeing a global network of 76 churches. With a ministry rooted in the Gospel since 1993, he planted his first church in Annapolis, Maryland, in 1995 and became a beacon of leadership, service, and transformation.

A passionate advocate for missions, Bishop Palmer leads leadership conferences, plants churches, and provides humanitarian aid to thousands of children in need across the globe. His work includes substantial financial support for orphanages in India and East Africa, demonstrating a steadfast commitment to serving the underserved.

Bishop Palmer, a respected community leader, is celebrated for fostering unity and collaboration among diverse groups. His efforts address critical issues, promote meaningful dialogue, and inspire transformative change. He holds a Bachelor of Divinity, Master's in Pastoral Counseling, and a Doctorate in Divinity. He has been recognized with numerous accolades, including two Governor Citations, two County Executive Citations, Dr. Martin Luther King Jr. Drum Major Award, and the Presidential Lifetime Achievement Award.

As an entrepreneur, Bishop Palmer owns Kingdom Publishing LLC, Antonio Marlin Art, and Kingdom Kare, Inc., a thriving nonprofit organization. He is also the author of seven impactful books:

- Divine Manifestations: Angels and Theophanies in Biblical Studies
- Rooted and Grounded in Love [Anthology]
- Living By the Spirit
- Love Thyself: Empowering Men for Healthy Living
- God's Rest Revealed: A Life Flowing with Milk and Honey
- Building an Effective Prayer Life
- Mark the Perfect Man: How to Find a Model of Maturity
- Revival: God Will Come Where You Are
- Little Kairo Takes on the World (Children's Book)

Dedication

To my ancestors who suffered horrific atrocities and whose voice echoes with resilience through the anals of history for your children to be free and known.

I am because of you.

www.ingramcontent.com/pod-product-compliance
Lightning Source LLC
Chambersburg PA
CBHW070906120626
46546CB00001B/159
9781967006052